The Making of Little Saigon

The Making of Little Saigon

Narratives of Nostalgia, (Dis)enchantments, and Aspirations

Tung X. Bui
Quynh H. Vo

HAMILTON BOOKS
AN IMPRINT OF
ROWMAN & LITTLEFIELD
Lanham • Boulder • New York • London

Published by Hamilton Books
An imprint of The Rowman & Littlefield Publishing Group, Inc.
4501 Forbes Boulevard, Suite 200, Lanham, Maryland 20706
www.rowman.com

86-90 Paul Street, London EC2A 4NE, United Kingdom

Copyright © 2024 by The Rowman & Littlefield Publishing Group, Inc.

All rights reserved. No part of this book may be reproduced in any form or by any electronic or mechanical means, including information storage and retrieval systems, without written permission from the publisher, except by a reviewer who may quote passages in a review.

British Library Cataloguing in Publication Information Available

Library of Congress Cataloging-in-Publication Data

Names: Bui, Tung X., 1953– author. | Vo, Quynh H., author.
Title: The making of little Saigon : narratives of nostalgia, (dis)enchantments, and aspirations / Tung X. Bui, Quynh H. Vo.
Description: Lanham : Hamilton Books, 2024. | Includes bibliographical references and index. | Summary: "The Making of Little Saigon intricately weaves the stories of activists, writers, artists, entrepreneurs, and scholars who shaped Little Saigon in Orange County, California, into a cherished haven for Vietnamese refugees. Each narrative, spanning oceanic crossings to forging a new home, resonates with a history of pain, beauty, disunity, solidarity, failure, and resilience, reimagining community building through storytelling in the US"—Provided by publisher.
Identifiers: LCCN 2024000653 (print) | LCCN 2024000654 (ebook) | ISBN 9780761874287 (paperback) | ISBN 9780761874294 (epub)
Subjects: LCSH: Vietnamese Americans—California—Orange County—History. | Vietnamese Americans—California—Orange County—Social life and customs. | Orange County (Calif.)—Civilization. | Orange County (Calif.)—Social life and customs. | Community life—California—Orange County. | Entrepreneurship—California—Orange County. | Political refugees—Caifornia—Orange County. | Political refugees—Vietnam. | Vietnam War, 1961–1975—Refugees. | Vietnamese Americans—California—Orange County—Biography.
Classification: LCC F868.O6 B85 2024 (print) | LCC F868.O6 (ebook) | DDC 305.8959/22079496—dc23/eng/20240207
LC record available at https://lccn.loc.gov/2024000653
LC ebook record available at https://lccn.loc.gov/2024000654

∞™ The paper used in this publication meets the minimum requirements of American National Standard for Information Sciences—Permanence of Paper for Printed Library Materials, ANSI/NISO Z39.48-1992.

Contents

Acknowledgments

Writing a book about the making of a community requires the collaboration of the people who have contributed to this building effort. The events and stories in this book are reported to the best of my memory, as substantiated by research and the recollections of the interviewees. I deeply admire and respect all of those who shared their stories in this book. I am appreciative of their confidence in me when I approached them for an interview. I am profoundly inspired by their heroic resilience, uncompromising aspirations, and vigilant hopes. Through them, we have imagined ourselves as a hundred selves traveling through time and space in search of a personal connection with Little Saigon. I particularly thank Dr. Nguyễn Mạnh Tiến, Mr. Frank Jao, Ms. Nhã Ca, and many of my siblings—Minh Châu, Phong Thu, Xuân Dương, Xuân Mai, and Bích Huyền—who introduced us to most of the people we interviewed for this book.

I would like to extend my deepest appreciation to my co-author, Dr. Quynh H. Vo, currently on the faculty at the American University in Washington D.C. While she was completing her doctoral studies at the Department of English at the University of Hawai'i, she encouraged me to write a memoir about my life and Little Saigon. I told her that I was not an English major, and my middle school Vietnamese teacher kept telling me that "Thou shalt not talk about thyself." I am grateful to have Quynh H. Vo as my co-author as she did an amazing job in transcribing the interviews I conducted and translating them into revelatory, complex, and at times confrontational narratives for the "Voices of movers and shakers" part of the book that we affectionately call the "character" section. As a business academic, writing this book has been more than a challenge for me. Quynh H. Vo has helped make many passages of the main body more riveting and immersive.

Wendy Toliver and my brother, Xuân Mai, edited a second version of this book with unparalleled persistence. They put their souls and thoughts into every sentence of this long narrative with a dedicated commitment to getting it right. It was gratifying to know that we were not alone in this intimate journey—retracing the making of Little Saigon. With the interviewees' permission, I have preserved the audio recordings as the verbose version of their narratives could not do justice to the vivid and captivating expressions of their voices, nuanced by deep sorrows and daring dreams.

Introduction

In January 2018, I sat down with a group of friends who flew from Little Saigon, Orange County, to the Hilton Waikoloa Village, on the Big Island of Hawai'i. We were all there for the 50th Hawaii International Conference on System Sciences conference that I served as the conference chair. The Hilton Waikoloa Village sits amidst the lava fields of south Kona, surrounded by black rocks and an ocean that varies in shades from light turquoise to deep blue.

While waiting for the keynote speaker, we chatted about everything and anything as Kona winds drifted the fragrance of plumeria and gardenia through the hotel. We reminisced on family, friends, and Little Saigon. Our voices grew joyful as we discussed the people and places we know and the people we once knew who passed away. In passing, the stories became thoughtful, contemplating cherished mutual acquaintances—the stories about retirement and the community's essential members who built the enclave. Many had disengaged from the day-to-day life of Little Saigon. Some have retired. Gratified. Happily and thoroughly deserved. Others passed away of old age.

The Little Saigon community lost poet Phạm Văn Bình, famed for his poem "Chuyện Tình Buồn" ("A Sad Love Story") in July 2018, a few weeks before Monsignor Peter Nguyễn Đức Tiến, the first Catholic priest at the Diocese of Orange and founder of the Center of the Vietnamese Catholic Church in Santa Ana, passed away. Recently, the community felt the profoundly sad loss of another significant community member when noted poet, 77-year-old Du Tử Lê, peacefully went to heaven as he received the last kiss from his beloved granddaughter, Roll, in their Garden Grove residence on October 7, 2019. Lê, an award-winning poet in the 1960s, left a formidable legacy as a Vietnamese American poet. Many American scholars hold him and his body of work in high esteem.

As the world grieves unimaginable losses from Covid-19, the worst pandemic of the century, Little Saigon mourned the passing of two of its well-known and beloved divas and a highly regarded comedian. Lệ Thu, a singer whose golden voice delighted audiences in the 1970s, succumbed to the virus on January 15, 2021, at the Memorial Care Orange Coast Medical Center in Fountain Valley, California. She was seventy-eight. Shortly after her death, the community braced itself for the loss of singer Mai Hương, famous lead vocal for Tiếng Tơ Đồng (Youth Drums), a widely pre-1975 popular band. Mai Hương passed away at seventy-nine, surrounded by her family, greatly lamented by many in Little Saigon and in Vietnam.

Chí Tài, sixty-two, a prominent Vietnamese American musician, comedian, and actor among Vietnamese communities in Vietnam and in the diaspora, suffered a heart attack while working on a show in Vietnam. The community felt the loss deeply, and family members and friends, many from the entertainment world, convened at the nearby Holy Spirit Catholic Church on December 19, 2020, to pay tribute to Chí Tài. The event was broadcast live on YouTube for an audience that paid its respect and grieved in social isolation, while watching on computers, phones, and TVs as many members of the community regaled audiences with stories of the comedian. Chí Tài's body was flown back to Little Saigon, his beloved community.

One by one, many of the twenty thousand Vietnamese refugees who first settled in Orange County, now in their 70s, have withdrawn from active lifestyles and retired to enjoy the community they built. Today, Little Saigon is home to the largest Vietnamese community living in the diaspora in the world. The remarkable people who constructed this vibrant community, homes, and successful businesses have stories that must be written down or forever buried under layers of dust.

We sense their absence, and we feel the sentimental and often wistful longing for loved ones who knew Little Saigon's story intimately because it is their story. The people we've lost built this haven from the ashes of the Vietnam War. When the first generation of refugees gathers, we tell stories.

And this is what we did when we sat around the small table mid-morning outside the conference room doors. The Kona sun warmed us as we spoke of Little Saigon. We reflected on our people's recent passing, and we held silence as each of us remembered. Then, our conversation's tone changed, and we rattled on, shifting to hope and the rising stars, the new entrepreneurs in Little Saigon. Many of these entrepreneurs are the offspring of the first generation who built prestigious companies in Little Saigon. Quickly, like the busy streets of our beloved community, our conversation took a journey to community projects just approved by the city of Westminster and by other neighboring cities.

We invite you to travel through memories and the history of Little Saigon, Orange County, with a few residents who helped create this community. This community has struggled through economic, political, and social upheavals with resilience. As the generation transitions to the next generation, we gather the stories of those who made this community a unique place on earth. The

United States of America, as a nation of immigrants, is invigorated by the energy of newcomers, but the stories of the Little Saigon will remain genuinely unique, an epic evocation of a rapidly vanishing generation.

Memory, like pain, won't last forever. This book pays tribute to all who belong to this community. Stories can reopen wounds, but they also heal through collective voices, empathy, and solidarity. Little Saigon outlived the Republic of Vietnam, which the refugees and residents of Little Saigon left behind (1955–1975). In the last four decades, Little Saigon has made history. Now, standing here and looking into the future, facing the transitional and transformational challenges, the testimonies featured in this memoir and documentary celebrate and sketch the future and aspirations ahead for Vietnamese Americans, who journey on these streets.

We hope you enjoy this journey, through time as a living, nonlinear memory, and history as past and future, as much as we have enjoyed documenting the dynamic voices of Little Saigon.

Welcome with Aloha.

PART I

An Odyssey of Self-Discovery

Chapter 1

Crossings Oceans and Cultures

AN INTIMATE JOURNEY TO BELONGING

I was born prematurely in Haiphong, a prominent seaport town located 75 miles west of Hanoi, during the tumultuous twilight of French colonial rule in Vietnam. The doctors delivered disheartening news to my mother, revealing that I had a life-threatening condition: lactose intolerance. Determined and devoted, my mother stayed awake through the nights, nourishing me with ginseng paste and fruit juice, hoping to fortify my fragile existence. While she fretted over the well-being of her cherished son, the French administration grappled with mounting concerns regarding the surging anti-colonial sentiment sweeping across the nation. This sentiment had taken root within local political parties, appealing to both socialists and Republicans alike. To compound the French's anxieties, the Vietnamese jungle bore witness to deadly guerrilla warfare orchestrated by the Việt Minh, whose intimate knowledge of the treacherous terrain posed a formidable challenge.

Soon after celebrating my first birthday, while under the nurturing embrace of my mother, the French suffered a resounding defeat in the battle of Điện Biên Phủ in May 1954, relinquishing their grip on an arduous eight-year conflict known as the "First Indochina War." Subsequently, negotiations between the warring factions took place in Geneva, Switzerland. Reluctantly, both parties arrived at an agreement to divide the nation along the 17th parallel, assigning the Northern region to the communist-led Vietnam under the governance of Hồ Chí Minh, while a non-communist regime was established in the South.

Apprehensive of the possibility that the Viet Minh would replicate the radical and perilous economic and social reforms witnessed under the Chinese Communist Party in 1949, my parents made the decision to join the massive wave of refugees seeking sanctuary in the South during the 300-day reprieve.

Estimated to be between 600,000 and one million individuals, this exodus was facilitated by the French with invaluable assistance from the U.S. Navy, who provided logistical support for the migration. In August 1954, my mother relinquished ownership of a prosperous bike shop in Haiphong, while my father bid farewell to a flourishing career as an accountant within a French company. Accompanied by hundreds of other displaced families, we gathered our meager possessions and embarked upon the USS Montague, an American Navy cargo ship destined for Saigon. Proudly adorning the deck's summit was a banner proclaiming our voyage as a "Passage to Freedom."

I was too young to recollect and truly grasp the magnitude of the hardships they endured. As I matured and gained a comprehension of the world into which I was born, I seldom heard my mother or any other refugee express grievances about the war and the subsequent exodus. Occasionally, my deeply introspective father, a man of gentle disposition and immense love for his eight children, a scholarly soul fluent in both Vietnamese and French, would utter, "It was immensely difficult. There were moments when I longed for atomic bomb, a means to obliterate all the anguish and suffering." I could never fathom why such thoughts would cross the mind of a man like him, for it was incongruous with his character. Nevertheless, within the voice of this cherished father resided a history of profound pain.

IN THE SHADOWS OF CONFLICT: CHILDHOOD AMIDST WAR AND DEPARTURE

As a child, amidst mealtimes, the conversations that permeated the air revolved predominantly around work and business. Following our flight from home, my father managed to secure a government position in Nha Trang, a charming coastal town nestled in central Vietnam. The prospect of this small town resonated with my mother. She remarked, "And the competition would be less intense compared to Saigon if I were to establish a business here." Business acquaintances from the North, who sought new opportunities in the South, echoed her sentiments. My mother possessed an unparalleled spirit of entrepreneurship, marked by swift and audacious decision-making, complemented by a touch of good fortune. In due course, she replicated the triumphs she had once achieved in Haiphong. Thriving in Nha Trang, she ascended to become one of the foremost distributors of rice and cereals in Central Vietnam. Alongside my second sister, who served as her able assistant, my mother forged a business empire. Her ventures encompassed a construction company specializing in government projects, a robust transportation fleet comprising trucks, a gas station, and a substantial market share in the distribution of rice and cereals spanning from the Mekong Delta to the central highlands. Her remarkable reputation preceded her even to Little Saigon.

During my teenage years, I attended secondary school at the College Français de Nhatrang. By conventional standards, my academic performance left much to be desired. I was a daydreamer, harboring a distaste for rote memorization. Yet, upon reflection, I realize that somehow, the school adequately prepared me for the journey ahead, particularly for my college years. At the age of seventeen, I embarked on a new chapter by leaving Vietnam for Switzerland, where I enrolled in economics and social sciences studies at the University of Fribourg. My mother entrusted me with a mission, setting forth her vision. With a smile, she declared, "When you return from Switzerland, Mom wants you to establish the very first private bank in Vietnam. My bank." She continued, assuring me, "The University of Fribourg is a Catholic institution, so you will be in safe hands there and return home unscathed."

I pursued my studies with unwavering determination and even managed to graduate ahead of schedule. However, the vision my mother had harbored for my future never came to fruition.

While residing in the heart of Europe, I bore witness to the unfolding atrocities of the Vietnam War through the lens of television, as the evening news broadcasted the grim realities. As news anchors and reporters dissected the terms and stipulations of the 1973 Paris Peace Accords between the United States and North Vietnam, I couldn't shake the foreboding sense that they would eventually abandon South Vietnam. Filled with concern, I dialed my mother's number, imploring her to swiftly conclude her business affairs and escape the looming clutches of the escalating war. "I share the same apprehension, my dear. But trust me, I will conduct thorough investigations. Our businesses are thriving. Just grant me a few more months," she assured me.

True to her word, my mother took action. "I reached out to trusted sources in Saigon, and they all assured me that your warnings need not consume us with worry," she explained. In retrospect, I should have persisted in my efforts to persuade her otherwise. However, there was an unwavering trust in her decisions that held sway over me. She embodied the absolute voice of reason in my life. "I will meticulously monitor the situation, my child. Just grant me a little more time. And in the interim, could you perhaps conduct some research on the process of emigrating to Switzerland?" she requested, her words resonating with a mixture of determination and hope.

As the South Vietnamese government, led by President Nguyễn Văn Thiệu, embraced the concept of "Vietnamization" and U.S. troops gradually withdrew from the country, my mother's business continued to flourish. Though she had not disregarded my warning, the demands of day-to-day life persisted, and her business ventures thrived. With a plan to retreat in the coming years, she believed that a semblance of security and normalcy could be maintained amidst a war that had become an accepted backdrop to life for much of the nation. However, events unfolded swiftly, altering the course of our lives.

In August 1974, U.S. President Richard Nixon, a staunch anti-communist, resigned following the eruption of the Watergate scandal. The subsequent Ford administration found itself unable to contend with the Democratic-led Congress, which had resolved to bring an end to the war. The consequences of the poorly conceived Paris Peace Accord soon reverberated throughout Vietnam.

Like the vast majority of the Vietnamese populace, my mother remained oblivious to the shifting political landscape in the United States. Consequently, the impact of these developments caught us off guard. Apart from a select few within close circles of friends, family, and political alliances—particularly those closely aligned with President Nguyễn Văn Thiệu—most individuals were wholly unprepared for the mass exodus that would uproot their lives and force them to abandon their homeland.

My family left behind our beloved country, our cherished home, dear friends, and a substantial fortune tied to significant fixed assets. Had my mother and her "trusted sources" possessed foresight regarding the impending events, they would have chosen to depart prior to the fateful Black April. I have encountered countless similar accounts from fellow refugees, who all recount the element of surprise that characterized that springtime exodus. Only a handful of individuals managed to transfer funds overseas before 1975, while the majority were left to rebuild their lives in foreign lands, forging new paths amidst unfamiliar surroundings.

In light of our family's decision to settle in Switzerland, my journey led me to enroll in a doctoral program in 1974. Before long, I found myself assuming the role of President of the Vietnamese Students Association in Fribourg, as well as serving as an executive member of the Association of Vietnamese Students in Switzerland, a vibrant organization boasting a membership of 800 individuals. Engaging in numerous impassioned discussions with my Swiss and international classmates, I frequently found myself defending the South Vietnamese cause amidst a backdrop of war. While my friends and classmates held staunch opposition to the conflict, with the exception of a few French friends, I remained resolute in my stance.

The news emanating from the frontlines painted a disquieting picture. The rapid victories achieved by the North Vietnamese forces were cause for concern. Ban-Mê-Thuột, a crucial city situated in the Central Highlands and the very heart of my mother's business operations, fell into the hands of the communists at an alarming speed, surpassing all expectations. It was during this period that the North Vietnamese captured not only my mother but also several members of our family, plunging us into a state of profound turmoil and uncertainty.

My mother bore witness to the heartbreaking demise of her thriving businesses, which she had meticulously built over the span of two decades. As the North Vietnamese forces seized control, utilizing her cargo fleet, they swiftly emptied her warehouses, a painstaking process that stretched on for hours. Then, in a cruel twist of fate, they sealed off her facilities, leaving her with nothing. The South Vietnamese government had adopted a strategic retreat, aiming to apply pressure on their ally, the United States, in the hopes of securing assistance. Panic and despair gripped the land.

A youthful North Vietnamese soldier, tasked with monitoring my mother, a perceived "wealthy exploiter," approached her with the chilling news. He informed her that she was slated for execution the following day. Undeterred by the dire circumstances, my mother's resourceful spirit ignited a daring plan for escape. She ingeniously staged a fire, using it as a diversion to slip away from her captors. With the aid of a modest farm tractor, she made her escape, accompanied by my second sister, who was carrying her second child at seven months pregnant, and her family. Together, they embarked on a treacherous journey to reunite with our family in Nha Trang.

Rumors swiftly circulated, painting a grim picture of my mother's fate. Word spread that she, along with a prominent businessman, had met their demise in broad daylight at the hands of their captors in the bustling open market. Deeply mourning her loss and fearing for their own lives, my family made the difficult decision to depart Nha Trang. With heavy hearts and heightened anxiety, they embarked on an arduous journey, covering a distance of 280 miles on foot, motorcycles, and buses, ultimately reaching Saigon.

Upon arriving in Saigon, my mother and a small group of remaining family members discovered that the rest of our loved ones had already departed from Saigon's Bạch Đằng seaport, as the city had surrendered. Filled with a sense of bewilderment and fear, our family grappled with the haunting prospect of losing one another forever. By a stroke of luck, they managed to reunite aboard a cargo ship that transported them to a U.S. Navy freighter. Perhaps fueled by the harrowing experiences endured or driven by the solace of finding temporary safety, my sister unexpectedly went into labor on the Navy freighter. Against all odds, she gave birth to a daughter, whom she lovingly named Mimi. We commemorate Mimi's birthday with unwavering reverence, sending her heartfelt well wishes. However, we seldom speak of Black April. Instead, we choose to celebrate her birth as a beacon of hope amidst the darkness that enveloped our lives.

AN AMERICA BEYOND THE SILVER SCREEN

My family spent weeks in a hastily erected refugee camp at Subic Bay in the Philippines. Afterward, the U.S. government dispatched them to Fort Chaffee in Arkansas. The first encounter with the United States was not the New York City they had seen in movies or the Washington DC they had seen on television, but a hot, dusty, and expansive military compound. My youngest sibling, Quinn, was ten years old at the time and observed, "The U.S. is just like Vietnam. Lots of soldiers, lots of MPs, lots of armored vehicles, lots of bunkers."

Urgently, the refugees' attention turned to finding lost relatives and friends. They rejoiced when they bumped into people they knew while wandering around the camp. However, the search for family often proved futile, leading to tearful moments of worry. In my extended family alone, almost ninety members were reunited in Fort Chaffee's tents.

Eventually, fifteen members of my immediate family landed in Marshfield, Wisconsin, a small town with approximately 15,000 residents. The town was predominantly white, with hardly any Asians, let alone Vietnamese. The four main economic forces in the town were Marshfield Clinic Health System, dairy farms, lumber stores, and a large shoe factory. Downtown Marshfield resembled a typical American city with well-known mainstream department stores such as Sears, JCPenney, K-mart, and Radio Shack, but not much beyond that.

My eldest sister, Minh Châu, a college-educated elementary school teacher, found employment as a teacher's aide in a kindergarten. Her primary duties included cleaning the facilities and taking care of the children. Her husband, Xuân Kế, a graduate in public administration, worked in a shoe factory, hammering nails into shoe heels. In Vietnam, he had been a high-ranking government official managing the budget for city hall. My second eldest sister, Kim Chung, who had been my mother's executive assistant, worked at the clinic as a nursing aide, responsible for changing patients' bed sheets and diapers. Her husband, a mechanical engineer, found a job in a local car repair shop fixing tires. The rest of my siblings returned to school.

In late 1975, I went to the U.S. Embassy in Bern, Switzerland, with my passport from a regime that no longer existed. Holding my passport, I asked for a visa to visit my family in the U.S. It took a while for a visa officer (I presumed) to appear and greet me in the waiting room. The six-foot-tall man hugged me and said, "Son, I am sorry to see what has happened to your country, but I am happy to see that your family is now in the U.S. Would you like me to help with the immigration paperwork for you to join your family?"

Anger surged within me unexpectedly. In my heavy French accent, I firmly replied, "My dad told me that the U.S. abandoned us. No, thank you."

The visa officer stared at me with a perplexed expression. "I'm sorry. I'll get you some special documents to allow you to visit your family. You know where to find me if you change your mind."

I made it a point to visit my family at least twice a year, often meeting their fellow refugee friends. Although I longed for these family reunions to take place in our home in Nha Trang, which we had sadly lost, we instead embarked on journeys across the U.S. in my mother's gas-guzzling six-cylinder Oldsmobile. We traveled to various cities where the U.S. government had relocated other Vietnamese refugees, including New York City, Houston, San Antonio, San Jose, Santa Ana, and Annandale, Virginia. In my mother's eyes, the United States of America only truly existed when she found her people, the people of her native land.

BEST PRACTICES AND LONG HOURS—REVISITING IDEAS OF (NEW) HOMELAND

My mother's initial employment in the United States was as the manager of an Asian food market in the suburb of Washington DC, belonging to a friend of hers from Saigon. "Bác Hân (auntie Hân) wanted me to learn the tricks of the trade. It's a lucrative business, but it requires a significant upfront investment that I don't have," she explained. Subsequently, she spent two weeks in Houston, observing a former business partner from Ban Mê Thuột manage a 7-Eleven franchise. "Uncle Lộc shared valuable insights with Mom to make the convenience store profitable, but the demanding nature of collecting small change is daunting. He works tirelessly seven days a week, and working nights can be quite unsettling," she remarked.

Known affectionately as "Mrs. Greyhound" by those who knew her, my 62-year-old mother embarked on extensive journeys aboard the legendary 45-foot interstate Greyhound buses, actively seeking business prospects within Vietnamese communities.

On a picturesque summer day in 1978, my mother returned home to Marshfield, Wisconsin and called for a family gathering. "This town offers limited prospects for my children and grandchildren's future. I can't simply rely on welfare checks. I refuse to witness my educated sons-in-law toil away their entire lives in a shoe factory, with nails between their teeth, or in a garage, lifting car wheels that weigh more than they do. I know someone who wishes to sell her restaurant in Santa Ana, California. I want to start afresh, build a new life," she declared, unwavering in her resolve.

My father, known for his tendency to play the devil's advocate, voiced his reluctance to embark on yet another daunting journey of rebuilding his life. Having survived two major exoduses that threatened his existence, he, at the age of sixty-six, did not wish to undertake the arduous task for a third time. In Vietnam, there is a mythical tale that recounts the birth of the nation, wherein the Âu Lạc kingdom splits in two—fifty children remaining with the king in the mountains while the other fifty follow their queen mother to the sea. Mirroring this story, two of my sisters and their families accompanied my mother to Santa Ana, while the rest remained with my father in Marshfield, Wisconsin, anxiously awaiting their reunion. Several months later, in 1978, my father joined the family in Orange County, finally bringing them all together.

In the burgeoning community of Little Saigon, my mother embarked on a new venture by opening the Hội Quán Vietnam (Vietnamese Club), the first restaurant of its kind in the area. It swiftly became a beloved gathering place for aspiring entrepreneurs in Little Saigon. In Vietnam, my mother had enjoyed great success and wealth as a prominent businesswoman, always surrounded by influential individuals. However, in her restaurant in Little Saigon, one could find her seated on a red plastic saddle stool, purchased from Chinatown in Los Angeles, diligently chopping fresh vegetables in the kitchen. Despite the contrast, my mother's admirers were not deterred by the sight of an older woman laboring in the kitchen to serve customers who yearned for the flavors of their homeland. Notable figures such as Khánh Ly, the legendary singer, Trần Dũ, the first food supplier to Vietnamese restaurants, and Bùi Thọ Khang, the founder of the first Vietnamese-owned supermarket in Little Saigon, eagerly sought out my mother's presence. They sought her expertise and proposed business ideas and partnerships.

My mother introduced me to a few of her friends who happened to be bankers in Vietnam. "My son has a Ph.D. from Switzerland and is now at NYU. He is talented," she proudly proclaimed. Although she didn't know the specifics of my field of study, she was aware that I had authored a book on business that had been translated into six languages. Whenever I took advantage of United's $99-weekend promotions to fly from NYC to Los Angeles, I would spend my time having breakfasts, lunches, and dinners with many of my mother's acquaintances. During these gatherings, we engaged in discussions about potential business ventures and community matters. Despite my awareness that my true calling was in academia, I played the role of a nonchalant observer and a timid advisor during these meetings. Nonetheless, I willingly shared my insights and assisted my mother's friends in reviewing business contracts and accompanying them on scouting trips to find suitable locations for their ventures.

BEAUTIFUL WEBS WOVEN IN KINSHIP AND COMMUNITY

I am the sixth child in my family and the first boy. It was not uncommon for my parents' generation to have large families. Today, if I look at the kinship or familial relationship chart at the third-cousin level, the Bùi clan in Little Saigon accounts for more than 200 relatives, not counting the next generation's growing population. On level three of my family tree, starting with my parents, siblings, and their spouses, and our children, excluding aunts, uncles, and cousins, we have a broad spectrum of professionals: doctors, dentists, pharmacists, lawyers, engineers, social workers, teachers, FBI agents, and business owners who run a variety of retail businesses such as deli shops and print shops, all located in Orange County. My mother's income from the hard work at the restaurant—from 6 a.m. till 10 p.m., seven days a week—helped fund many of her children and grandchildren's college education. Additionally, she helped many family members start their businesses.

If I extend my familial network to include in-laws and close friends, and in particular, those of my mother, I would need to spend the rest of my life collecting the stories of how each of them has built their life in Little Saigon. And the stories in this book are testimonies of their journeys as refugees in the U.S. Thanks to my family and friends, I quickly established bonds with most of the people I interviewed or cited for this book.

Through the journey of writing this book, I was transported back and forth through time, not just to the history of the making of Little Saigon. I traveled to living testaments of Vietnam's contemporary history, tracing back to the centuries-long Chinese domination of Vietnam, the six-decades-long French colonialism, and the thirty-year-long Vietnam war. Then, I immersed myself in Little Saigon, the largest concentration of Vietnamese refugees in the world. I have come to appreciate the many successful businesses in Little Saigon owned by Vietnamese of Chinese ancestry. My historical perspective has increased, and I now understand the significance of the decorative 17th-century French-style street lights on Bolsa Avenue. And I have come to recognize the community's desire to let the South Vietnamese flag wave proudly in the wind in front of their buildings.

Although I set out to document Little Saigon's origins, inevitably, the interviewees intimately reminisced about their lives in Vietnam and their journey to the U.S. My parents did not tell me much about their experiences. The stories and Vietnamese refugees' personalities in this book gave me an appreciation for my parents. Reflecting on my own life journey, they are to me unparalleled champions in their own way. Their story is in the words and memories of all the stories and vibrant voices in this book.

Chapter 2

Farewell to Vietnam, Embracing Little Saigon

Whenever I find myself in Orange County, a familiar ritual unfolds on a journey to recreate the life of a Saigonese. I make it a point to secure a copy of one of the most beloved daily newspapers, *Người Việt,*[1] *Việt Báo,*[2] or *Viễn Đông.* I seek out the comfort of the food court, Phước Lộc Thọ, the true heart of Little Saigon, where I indulge in a classic Vietnamese breakfast. The aroma of steaming bowls of phở, the rich flavors of Huế beef noodle soup, the enticing seafood rice vermicelli, the delectable mung bean sticky rice, and the delicate rice flour steamed rolls all call out to me. My brother Dương and his wife, Oanh, seasoned connoisseurs of dining out, always recommend these culinary delights in unison. They urge me to visit renowned establishments like Chateau Brodard, Grand Garden, the new Garlic and Chives, Ốc & Lẩu, or a new trend of "progressive" Vietnamese and Southeast Asian cuisine at Nep Cafe or Gem Dining, where the options seem endless, and the abundance of flavors never fails to amaze. Just to name a few. The list of options is endless, as Google and Yelp would make the selection even more daunting.

Amidst this prevailing exuberance, a profound dimension often escapes casual notice—Little Saigon's impact extends well beyond its reputation solely as a culinary and commercial hub.

For those fortunate enough to have lived or visited Vietnam before the end of the Vietnam War, Little Saigon becomes a portal into the cherished lifestyle they once embraced. It stands as a haven reminiscent of the Saigon etched in their memories, where fragments of history are meticulously safeguarded and emotionally conserved.

As I traverse the streets of Little Saigon, a tapestry of personal encounters unfolds, revealing nearly half a century of history. Like whispered echoes from the past, these poignant tales and melodic notes from a South Vietnamese epoch long past gracefully drift through the streets. Each step I take is a journey through time, where memories are brought to life and the past merges seamlessly with the present. Little Saigon becomes to me a conduit for stories long held within, whispering secrets only those who listen can hear.

FLEEING A LAND CALLED HOME—UNWANTED REFUGEES AND NEW IDEALS OF BRAVERY

On the morning of April 30th, 1975, I was struggling to find some sleep in my dormitory. I was terrorized and haunted by images repeatedly shown on TV of dog-tired people fleeing the countryside to the capital of South Vietnam. Like all of my friends at the University, I felt anxious and hopeless. My family in Vietnam had fled their home. There was no home to call. But I did, hundreds of times, hoping someone would pick up the line.

The local radio broke the news, announcing that General Dương Văn Minh, the acting President and last man standing of the American-backed South Vietnamese government, surrendered on South Vietnamese airwaves just moments ago, to the Soviet-backed North Vietnamese.

The first wave of refugees, those closely related to the U.S. military and the South Vietnamese government, began leaving a few days before April 30, 1975, as President Gerald Ford announced to the world on national television that the U.S. had decided to end the war in Vietnam. The "Black April," as they call it.

Tony Lâm, the first elected Vietnamese American council member to the city of Westminster, was among these privileged evacuees. During the war, he worked as a translator for a few U.S. organizations and, subsequently, became one of the contractors for the U.S. Military Assistance Command, Vietnam (MACV). "Many of Little Saigon residents would remember that they were part of the Operation Frequent Wind—the largest boat and airlift of its kind in refugee history, using swarms of giant helicopters and vessels," Lâm told me.

The retreat from Vietnam came at one of the most inopportune moments of American history; the Vietnam War divided the United States. It was an unpopular war, met with protests that surfaced on many of America's college campuses, in celebrity circles, and on the streets. Many disgruntled veterans of the Army of the Republic of Vietnam (ARVN) and U.S. armed forces involved in the war still remember when Jane Fonda went to Hanoi in 1972 to protest the war.[3]

Nevertheless, as the United States deeply mourned the death of 57,692 sons and daughters and held out little hope for those listed as missing in action or prisoners of war, the exodus of Vietnamese accelerated. In the subsequent weeks, the fear of persecution and physical and emotional harm by the victors drove another sixty thousand people to flee their hometowns in small boats, vessels, or by foot to neighboring countries—Thailand, Malaysia, Laos, and China—with the hope of settling in the U.S. or other Western countries. Eventually, from this wave of 140 thousand refugees, more than 132 thousand grew new roots on American soil.

What Tony Lâm poignantly reminded me of the apprehension and unease that engulfed many of his compatriots at a hastily erected refugee camp on the island of Guam, as they pondered whether the United States would embrace them in a land that was not yet their own. With the exception of the privileged elite, who had been exposed to Western culture through education or employment with the U.S military and its allies, the majority of refugees lived in a state of desolation, confronting an uncertain future.

Despite being a nation built by immigrants, early waves of immigrants have historically harbored resentment towards subsequent arrivals who follow in their footsteps.

The prejudices that Vietnamese refugees faced in the spring of 1975 were remarkable. History repeats itself. Once more, as if on a recurring loop, over half of the American populace were unsympathetic to the plight of these refugees,[4] and their journey to find solace in a new land was marred by the shadows of a controversial war they had lost. Many U.S. citizens couldn't even locate Vietnam on a map, yet the mere mention of its name evoked images of an unwanted war and the senseless loss of countless lives. Furthermore, the media frequently referred to the new immigrants as "Indochinese refugees," possibly to avoid using the word Vietnamese in this fraught landscape of American sentiment and politics.

President Gerald Ford's administration sought to help Vietnamese refugees quickly assimilate into mainstream American life, with an intentional scattering of Vietnamese families across the states, preferably to locales with few immigrants from Asia.[5] Furthermore, to alleviate American concerns about lost jobs and tax monies spent on public assistance to refugees, in an economy with a relatively high unemployment rate of 8.3%, the U.S. government dispersed the influx of Vietnamese to reduce the potential economic and social impact on a particular community. Also, politically, the plan to distribute refugees throughout the country strove to avoid similar accumulation, such as with Cuban refugees.[6] Jerry Brown, in his first term as governor of California, attempted to prevent planes transporting Vietnamese refugees to land at Travis Air Force base in Fairfield, arguing that the Golden State already had too many Hispanics and too many on welfare.[7]

Chu Tất Tiến, 81, once an officer in the South Vietnamese Army, now a real estate agent, a political activist, and local TV anchor on SBTN Television, recalled that the government dispersed many of his relatives, friends, and acquaintances across the country to avoid another Miami. During the resettlement process, only immediate family members were allowed to stay together.

Chu Tất Tiến, ended up in New York while the government sent his sister to Orange County, California. Against the dispersion policy, he joined his sister a few months later. "Brother and sister needed each other for emotional, social, and psychological support. Our family size was reduced to two in this foreign land, and we can't be separated," Chu Tất Tiến told me with a hitch in his voice.

RE-IMAGING FIELDS OF STRAWBERRIES AND ORANGES—GLIMPSING THE UNEXPECTED NEW LAND

Among the hundreds of thousands of South Vietnamese ejected into various parts of the world, approximately 20,000 landed at Camp Pendleton, a U.S. Marine Corps military base north of San Diego, California, hastily set up as a refugee camp. Soon after, as Vietnamese deportees were released from the camp, they wrestled with beginning their lives again in a foreign country.

"Orange County, at that time, was not exactly what I imagined about the United States," Quách Nhứt Danh, 85, who opened the first Vietnamese-owned pharmacy, recalled. Indeed, Orange County in 1975 was primarily a farm community with vast lands of strawberries and orange groves and cheap housing. Local authorities struggled to catch up with the economic and industrial might of Los Angeles in its north and the rising high-tech industry and military presence of San Diego in its south. "But, that was all we could afford," Quách Nhứt Danh acknowledged. Looking at me with a delightful smile, he added: "And a major bonus—a climate that is not too different from that back home."

Time and again, I've been privy to the accounts of fellow residents echoing a sentiment similar to that experienced by Quách Nhứt Danh. These dynamics have exerted a magnetic pull on numerous Vietnamese individuals, luring them to Orange County with the promise of reconstructing their lives. Within Orange County, the refugees stationed at Camp Pendleton found precisely what they required most: employment—any form of it—and affordable lodging.

Given their limited or nonexistent English proficiency, absence of accredited professional credentials, and modest financial reserves, the majority of immigrants I've encountered have secured manual labor positions. These include roles as assembly line operators in electronics factories, attendants at gas stations, diligent housekeepers at hotels, and a medley of service-oriented positions at Disneyland. Interestingly, a remarkable parallel emerges: in 1955, Walt Disney conceived his theme park in Anaheim, envisioning a realm of fantasies within a dreamlike domain. Astonishingly, two decades later, his vision seemed to profoundly resonate within the hearts of the newly established community members in Orange County.

In the early years, as I accompanied my mother on visit to her friends, I noticed that many of the inhabitants of Little Saigon had adorned their houses in the traditional Vietnamese style reminiscent of bygone decades, evoking a Vietnam of pre-1975. A 12" x 26" red tear-off daily calendar or a gigantic 25" x 14" monthly household calendar with scenic pictures of Vietnam or floral artwork held a revered place in every living room. The unmistakable aromas of grandmother's fish sauce and shrimp paste permeated the air, serving as poignant reminders of their ancestors and the homeland they left behind. The strains of music that once filled the airwaves, towns, and homes in Vietnam now found their place within the heart of Little Saigon. The attire worn by the vibrant members of the community, including slippers women wore before the war, deviated from the contemporary fashion of Vietnam, yet somehow harmonized with the spirit of this town.

Orange County did not match the expectations of many. It lacked the technology prowess displayed by the US military during war time, the glamor of Hollywood projected on the silver screen, or the capitalism of New York City. Instead, it offered plain, often run-down apartments. Yet, it provided refuge to the new settlers, shielding them from the communists who would never reach their doorsteps. When they are ready, they will speak up their anger. They will voice their anger and defend themselves, and prove that they are not defeated.

SURVIVAL AND ADAPTATION IN HOSTILE LANDSCAPES

My sister, Thanh Hải, and her husband, Thế Bình, were senior business students at the University of Dalat situated in the high plateau of Central Vietnam. Bình's father served as a procurement officer in the Air Force, and his family was airlifted just days before the war came to an end. Upon arriving in Anaheim, his father secured a job as a truck driver. Like many young adult males, Bình held a strong fascination with electronics, and Radio Shack was one of the highlights of his life in the United States.

"My wife was offered an assembly job position at a computer memory manufacturer in Irvine, California." Bình shared. "As for me, I enrolled in a computer repair course at Golden West College." Before long, he found employment servicing computer hardware at local hospitals, astonishing his co-workers and supervisor. While his supervisor, a formally trained computer engineer, followed a meticulous and systematic approach to computer repairs, Bình had an innate ability to swiftly bring these devices back to life.

"I know the specific hardware problems for the many models we service, so I often become the hero of the day," he remarked, a proud smile gracing his face.

Refugees flocked to Orange County, scrambling for a living, accepting any and all odd jobs they could find, and signing up for any and all available vocational courses at nearby community colleges.[8] Golden West College, Orange Coast College, Santa Ana College, Coastline Community College, and other professional schools saw a surge of new immigrants in their classrooms to learn English[9] and acquire professional skills. Young and old, doctors or service people, engineers or artists, the new immigrants considered anything that would help them land a job and bring food to the family table. Women signed up for electronics technician courses, looking for assembly positions at computer factories. Men signed up for auto repair or machine shop programs.[10]

Many found occupational courses based on the professional skills they acquired back home—such as ESL instruction, nursing, and music composition. However, coming from a country with 90 percent of the economy derived from agriculture, forestry, and fishing, one cannot help but note that these Vietnamese immigrants rarely signed up for farming courses.

However, a handful of Vietnamese immigrants found solace in cherished memories of their homeland's rural charm. Among them was Tony Cao, hailing from Santa Ana, who, along with a small circle of friends, embarked on an endeavor to replicate a slice of home. They invested in a farm in Riverside with the intention of cultivating sugar cane, driven by Tony's yearning for the refreshing iced sugar cane drink embellished with a touch of lime—a beloved staple in the South. "I must rake in a fortune to grow sugar canes here," Tony Cao remarked, his laughter brimming with determination. Trained as an engineer and possessing a flair for DIY craftsmanship, Tony embarked on a creative journey. He conceptualized and constructed sugarcane juicers within his own machine shop, spotting a burgeoning business prospect amid the escalating number of Vietnamese eateries and grocery emporiums. The demand for this cherished perennial tropical grass was substantial, and Tony foresaw an influx of friends eager to join him in this enterprising escapade.

Much to his astonishment, he encountered an unexpected challenge: recruiting individuals willing to toil on his farm proved to be an arduous task, even among those without employment. The rugged existence of a farmer in their homeland had left an indelible mark, rendering the prospect unappealing. Only a handful of courageous spirits displayed an inclination to engage in farming within this unfamiliar terrain. Opting for various facets of horticulture, they embraced the nurturing of flowers, fruits, vegetables, and ornamental plants—endeavors intrinsically tied to the cultural tapestry they had transported from their native Vietnam.

Most Vietnamese refugees were determined to seek employment, which was often occupational adaptation. Đinh Truyền was an infantry tanker back home, and in his new homeland, he became a truck driver for a moving company. My sister Minh Châu, a middle-school teacher back home, landed a job at a kindergarten changing diapers. Trọng Minh, an embedded journalist back home, found a job distributing flyers at the South Coast Plaza, Orange County's largest shopping mall. Lộc Nguyễn, a former diplomat, became a legal assistant in a local law office that targeted Vietnamese clientele.

As the American economy grappled with the aftermath of the 1973 oil crisis (oil prices quadrupled due to the OPEC oil embargo)[11] and the subsequent stock market crash (the Dow Jones Industrial Average lost over 45% of its value), the allure of securing a paying job was not lost on many Vietnamese immigrants. Among them was Trần Long, a former fisherman from Rạch Giá in the South-Western part of Vietnam, who found himself grateful for the opportunity to work in the United States.

Life on the assembly line was no walk in the park for Trần Long. Long hours, copious amounts of coffee, and the need to sneak out during breaks for a quick cigarette were part of his daily routine. However, as he reflected on his experiences, he realized that the challenges he faced in this new environment were still less arduous than the struggles of his previous life as a fisherman back home.

The attitudes displayed by my extended family members and their in-laws towards their new jobs in America left me astounded. It was undeniable that their positions and privileges had taken a step down compared to their status before 1975. In their homeland, such circumstances would have been seen as an embarrassment, a subject too sensitive to even mention.

Despite the perceived setbacks, they found solace in the opportunities America provided, even if it meant starting from a lower rung on the ladder. Their perspective shed light on the sacrifices made in pursuit of a better life and the inherent strength that propelled them forward in the face of adversity.

Receiving wages in a challenging economy elevated the self-esteem of these refugees. Some took pride in asserting that Vietnamese workers in computer part manufacturing possessed exceptional manual dexterity. Mary Đỗ of Costa Mesa was 55 when she found her first job as an electronics assembler. Her soldering skills were flawless, allowing her to earn additional income from overtime assignments. Back home, she was a housewife. Her husband retired due to hardships at the reeducation camp, and she was proud to support her family. In addition to her assembly job, while suffering from severe carpal tunnel syndrome that caused uncomfortable tingling and numbness in parts of her right hand, she took on a weekend job as a tailor and alterations specialist. Mary Đỗ was not alone in pursuing additional work; many newcomers did the same. With a smile, she shared with me, "I was just a housewife back home, spending all my time waiting for my husband to come home, and most nights, he got home quite late. Now I have discovered my independence and pride. I can earn money. It's hard work, but it brings me joy."

The initial influx of immigrants into Orange County was warmly embraced by numerous companies within the electronics and service sectors, who found them to be an invaluable workforce. This acknowledgment served as a point of pride for Vietnamese Americans. Nonetheless, a significant portion of these immigrants did not envision their own or their children's futures confined to these roles; instead, they nurtured aspirations of forging their own entrepreneurial paths. This collective yearning gave rise to a remarkable transformation within the community, as a unique Little Saigon economy began to take shape,[12] infused with Vietnamese flair and style.

THE GATHERING PLACE—*RAU MUỐNG* AND GOOD CONVERSATION

If lettuce and sweet corn are commonly found on dining tables across America, the preferred vegetable among Vietnamese immigrants is the legendary *rau muống,* also known as watercress. *Rau muống* proliferates effortlessly, allowing Vietnamese cooks to concoct creative recipes that showcase regional flavors by ingeniously pairing local ingredients such as tofu, mushrooms, or sirloin steak and pork belly.

Fortunately, like many refugees who had extended family, members of my family had enough devoted cooks in the clan to take turns, inviting each other over the weekends or on their days off. The new residents of Orange County gathered at popular and low-cost supermarkets like Albertsons or Stater Bros to grocery shops. They quickly realized that only lettuce and sweet corn lined the produce aisles; they could not find the ingredients they needed for Vietnamese dishes. To find the ingredients, they had to drive 25 miles north on Freeway 5 to Chinatown in Los Angeles. They flocked to these Chinese grocery stores on the block between North Broadway and Alpine Street and filled their car trunks with bags and bags of rice, spices, seasonings, and herbs such as the indispensable five-flavor powder for their favorite recipes. They did not forget sun-dried mushrooms, and there was a variety of them, white or black, straw or shitake, for their famous chicken and bamboo shoot noodle soup. Đức Nguyễn told his friends, "I am going to open a grocery store in Orange County so that you all don't have to carpool all the way up here."

Nguyễn Đức opened the very first Vietnamese grocery store in 1979 on Westminster Avenue, calling it "*Dân Tiếp Vụ*" or the *Store for the People*, a name reminiscent of the food rationing during the war. The store was small. Nhã Ca, a poet and novelist,[13] said, "I had tears of happiness flowing on my dining tables." Nhã Ca added, "Thanks to the store, I was able to offer to my beloved family and friends homestyle stir-fried water spinach with garlic and oyster sauce, or on another day, water spinach sauteed with beef and salted soybeans, without having to carpool to Chinatown in downtown Los Angeles."

Despite its humble size and limited offerings, *Dân Tiếp Vụ* held immense significance for the new settlers. It became their first gathering place, a beacon of hope where they longed to reunite with lost acquaintances. Within its walls, "Missing Person" flyers were posted. It was a place where new settlers found an excuse to socialize with those who shared the same destiny.

It was during one such visit to the grocery store that my sister, Thanh Hải, then 25, encountered her high school classmate, Nguyễn Văn Tiến, from the coastal town Nha Trang in Central Vietnam, 22 miles north of Cam Ranh Bay. Nguyễn Văn Tiến owned a nursery and was a skilled landscape designer. The reunion brought immense joy to my sister, and from that moment on, she became a devoted supporter of the nursery.

To me, *Dân Tiếp Vụ* represented much more than a small ethnic grocery store. It was the genesis of a remarkable community. Within its unassuming walls, the first wave of refugee entrepreneurs emerged, forming dynamic partnerships and seizing new opportunities. Recognizing the needs of their fellow citizens, these aspiring entrepreneurs would gather outside the store, scouting for business ideas, exchanging news, and seeking potential collaborators.

Seeing the upcoming needs of thousands of incoming fellow citizens, would-be entrepreneurs gathered outside the tiny store, scouting for business ideas, exchanging news on who was doing what, looking for business partners. The store was a gathering place where entrepreneurs could find the community networking they needed to succeed.

Eventually, *Dân Tiếp Vụ* became a victim of its own success, unable to handle the overflow of clients, but others saw opportunities from its flame. Sparked by *Dân Tiếp Vụ*'s ingenuity, many new settlers questioned the relevance and benefits of their first jobs in Orange County. Perhaps they did not see a future in pumping gas, deciding instead to open a grocery store. Maybe these new residents quickly got tired of ringing the cash register at a 7-Eleven and decided to open a Phở restaurant. Perhaps some of these new Vietnamese immigrants realized that they were too old to assimilate into mainstream America, choosing instead to rebuild their lives within the safety of the little enclave of Vietnamese familiarity in Little Saigon, Orange County.

While *Dân Tiếp Vụ* was short-lived, it was undoubtedly the first gathering place of the newcomers. It was to them a success story that encouraged friendships, kinships, and ventures into the entrepreneurial world of Vietnamese American Little Saigon. It was certainly an indication to me that many settlers were ready to say goodbye to Vietnam, and hello to their new home.

As I navigate through the bustling expanse of the Little Saigon business district, my purpose is to uncover the "grand openings" of fresh Vietnamese-owned enterprises, explore burgeoning housing developments, and seek out cultural events to partake in. What becomes increasingly evident is how the initial waves of refugees, followed by successive generations of Vietnamese Americans, have not only defied odds but also illuminated the aspirations of the minority of Americans who unwaveringly believed in them.

The community continues to grow, with new Vietnamese-American-owned businesses and manufacturing ventures like Pharma Robinson. Tony Cao shares his pride in the community's ability to offer a diverse range of services. Little Saigon's influence extends beyond Orange County, expanding into neighboring counties.

The year 2021 has seen an unprecedented spike in housing, with appreciation averaging 25% within a mere year. Fewer and fewer are the Vietnamese immigrants who still long for their lost homes in Vietnam. Despite a rocky start, they have eventually built their Little Saigon community. With my customary drive around the community, it becomes apparent to me that Little Saigon is still writing its history through the sounds, sights, smells, and music in the streets.

NOTES

1. "The Vietnamese" in English.
2. *Vietnamese Newspaper* in English. Since December 2019, *Việt Báo* is only available online.
3. In July 1972, famed actress Jane Fonda went to Hanoi to protest a war that she and many of her friends did not understand. A photo of her sitting on an anti-aircraft gun protesting the war was released by the hosts and triggered a controversial debate about the Vietnam War. Claiming her message was misunderstood, she wrote on her website in 2011 that she "would regret to my dying day" the photograph.
4. A Gallup Poll from May 1975 reported that only 36% of Americans welcomed Vietnamese refugees, while 54% opposed, and 12% were undecided (Time, May 19, 1975).
5. The dispersion policy gave rise to Vietnamese communities in Arkansas, New Orleans, Galveston, Oklahoma City, Biloxi, and Kansas City—locations that historically have been least attractive to migrants.
6. Miami, Florida, experienced the largest geographic concentration of Cuban refugees.
7. https://www.sfchronicle.com/nation/article/America-s-long-history-of-shunning-refugees-6639536.php

8. https://oac.cdlib.org/view?docId=hb8g500803&brand=oac4&doc.view=entire_text

9. English as a Second Language (ESL) with basic skills of speaking, reading and writing.

10. Cf. Finnan C.R., Community influences of the occupational adaptation of Vietnamese refugees, Anthropological Quarterly, Vol., 55, No, 3, July 1982, pp. 161–69.

11. OPEC (Organization of Arab Petroleum Exporting Countries).

12. Portes, A. and Back, R., "Latin Journey: Cuban and Mexican Immigrants in the US," University of California Press, Berkeley, 1985.

13. Nhã Ca (1939–) won a literary prize with her famed book *Giải Khăn Sô cho Huế* (1969) telling the horror of the 1968 Tet Offensive in Hue. The translated version, *Mourning Headband for Hue* was published in 2016 by Indiana University Press (translated by and introduced by Olga Dror). Nha Ca has published more than 30 novels.

Chapter 3

Genesis and Pathways

FORGING A NEW COMMUNITY

My mother stood out among the women of her time in Vietnam by owning her own car. It was a source of surprise as she fearlessly drove between cities, navigating challenging road conditions. "I simply enjoyed the wonders of this technology," she would tell me, beaming with pride when she acquired a special Toyota with an automatic transmission.

However, upon settling in the U.S., she preferred to be chauffeured by us. This was a common practice among many settlers of her generation in the late '70s. Often, I would drive her to dinner with her friends, who were all successful business people before 1975. During these outings, I witnessed a variety of cars, mainly older models and station wagons, driven by people my age who were escorting their parents to dining venues. It dawned on me that the car culture had brought a practical mindset to the first generation of Vietnamese Americans, as they embarked on a new life and worked towards building a community. In the act of driving their parents, there was a sense of unity and dedication, an expression of gratitude for their sacrifices and a desire to provide care and support. The car became more than a means of transportation; it symbolized the aspirations and determination of the Vietnamese American community to search and explore a new community far from their homeland. Their ultimate goal was to establish a stable life guided by the popular wisdom encapsulated in the phrase "an cư lạc nghiệp," which means finding a peaceful home that leads to a happy life. With unwavering determination and their cars, my mother and her friends embarked on an intense journey to create a home where they could find tranquility, security, and fulfillment.

THE FAMILY LIVING ROOMS—INNOVATIVE MINDS AND SPIRITS OF THE PAST

A thriving community encompasses essential components such as dining venues, shopping centers, healthcare, and music. These pillars are needed to contribute to the overall well-being and vitality of the community, creating spaces where individuals can connect, seek essential services, and enjoy the enriching experiences of music and entertainment.

In the late seventies, Orange County had only a handful of Vietnamese restaurants, which many new Vietnamese Americans found unsuitable for private and meaningful conversations. As a result, family-style dinner meetings became the norm overnight. Vietnamese refugees showcased their culinary skills, hosting gatherings in their living rooms, where friends and potential business partners would convene.

Neighbors vividly remembered the boisterous laughter and animated conversations that filled the homes of their new Vietnamese neighbors during those early years. Little did they know that these living rooms had transformed into impromptu incubators for burgeoning ideas. Business concepts took shape, partnerships formed, and hastily drafted business plans came to life within the confines of these family spaces.

Tô Văn Lai,[1] the founding president of Thúy Nga Productions and later VietFace TV, arrived in France toward the end of 1976. As a high school instructor at Mekong Data, he taught a range of subjects from Mathematics to French. Nostalgia for his homeland and longing for family led him to gather with friends under the starlit skies of the City of Light. They sang beloved Vietnamese songs and reminisced about life before the war. During these gatherings, Tô Văn Lai produced the first videotapes of Paris by Night, which garnered a positive response from the local Vietnamese community. However, business proved less lucrative than expected. High production costs ate into profits, and the market had its limitations. In light of the massive migration to Orange County, Tô Văn Lai made the decision to fly there and explore this new frontier, driven by a desire for new opportunities and a fresh start.

Anh Bằng, a highly influential music composer and founder of the renowned Dạ Lan (Night Orchid) band (1981–1990) and Asia Entertainment extended an invitation to dinner for Tô Văn Lai. Bằng's contributions to Vietnamese music, including the creation of "tân nhạc Vietnam" and the popularization of the Bolero rhythm, have left an indelible mark.

During their dinner, phone calls constantly interrupted the conversation. Tô Văn Lai recalls, "Orders for music poured in from various parts of the US, Canada, and Europe." Although Paris held its allure and romance, he realized that Little Saigon was the place where he could truly settle and thrive.

Thus, he bid farewell to Paris and embraced Little Saigon as his new home. His productions eventually became one of the most successful Vietnamese enterprises in contemporary entertainment worldwide, even making a glorious entry into communist-controlled Vietnam.

Quách Nhứt Danh told me about a similar experience. Initially arrived in Connecticut, where he interned to obtain his pharmacy license. However, the allure of Little Saigon beckoned to him, just as it had to Tô Văn Lai. Danh boarded a plane to Orange County, immersing himself in countless business dinners and eventually deciding to establish himself in the thriving business center led by the first generation of Vietnamese refugees. Alongside his partners, Frank Jao and Thanh, Danh witnessed the germinal stage of Little Saigon's growth, as it transformed into a deeply-rooted and vibrant community. They shared numerous family dinners, fostering connections and camaraderie, and they became the very first millionaires.

From the intimate gatherings at the settlers' new homes emerged yet another remarkable display of ingenuity. In 1975, when Phạm Đặng Long Cơ[2] arrived in America, he had already completed his coursework to become a physician at the University of Saigon Medical School two years prior. However, the French-based curriculum in Saigon mandated that all physicians submit a doctoral dissertation to hold the title of "Doctor of Medicine." The process entailed finding an advisor within the faculty of medicine, as well as approval and oversight from a committee at the Ministry of Health. The review and approval process was already slow, and the war further complicated matters. As Saigon fell, Phạm Đặng Long Cơ and many other young medical graduates were left without their doctoral degrees, as their research dissertations lay piled high at the Ministry of Health, overshadowed by the pressing concerns of war. Upon arriving in America, Vietnamese physicians were allowed to pursue ECFMG (Educational Commission for Foreign Medical Graduates) certification, a necessary step to undertake residency in American hospitals. However, they faced a crucial requirement: compliance with their alma mater's graduation standards, including approval from the Vietnamese Ministry of Health for their dissertations. With the collapse of the Republic of Vietnam, these doctors in exile had to seek innovative solutions. Dr. Đào Hữu Anh, a former dean of the Saigon Medical Board, reached out to Dr. Ira Singer of the American Medical Association for assistance.[3] Together, they formed a five-member certification board in exile, ensuring that the new doctors could practice in America. In a manner reminiscent of their official roles in Vietnam, yet within the familiar and comforting setting of Dr. Đào Hữu Anh's family living room, he and the committee he assembled certified the yet-to-be-approved theses. This extraordinary act granted Doctor of Medicine degrees to Phạm Đặng Long Cơ and other hopeful doctors. Dr. Đào

Hữu Anh's quick thinking exemplifies the ingenuity often sparked in the intimate conversations around a Vietnamese family dinner table.

I witnessed a range of emotions on the faces of my mother and her friends during these gatherings—excitement, self-doubt, anxiety, and hopefulness. Amidst a bowl of Saigon-style phở or spicy Huế-style beef noodles, there would be peals of laughter. I engaged in discussions about business ideas with my mother's partners, keenly sensing their constant state of perplexity. Yet, even in the midst of uncertainty, I often heard them say, "We have lost everything, almost our own lives. So, we don't have much to lose." It was through their ingenuity and fearless entrepreneurship that I witnessed their resilience and determination in action. In Little Saigon, where dreams were born and realized, where friendships were forged and business thrived, the spirit of Vietnamese refugees shone bright.

LAUGHTER PEALING OVER A FRAGRANT BOWL OF *PHỞ*

I quickly came to realize that the once-typical business discussions held over bowls of phở in living rooms had evolved, finding new settings within churches, temples, and community centers. This shift gave birth to a flourishing web of information exchange within the fabric of Little Saigon. Vietnamese refugees readily exchanged vital business prospects and insights, often prefacing these dialogues with a note of indiscretion: "I possess invaluable insights to share, but let's treat this as confidential. Please, refrain from mentioning my name." Vanessa Hồng Vân, a local journalist and TV reporter for SBTN,[4] recounted to me the origins of Little Saigon's business community and the significant role of whispered information in its growth. She elaborated on stories such as, "This shop owner is considering selling their business, and it might interest you. Here's a contact number for a potential personal business loan."

This lively and unstructured web of knowledge dissemination, predominantly conducted in Vietnamese, stood as the cultural capital of Little Saigon. Much akin to practices in their native land, this network thrived on an ethos of mutual assistance. The act of sharing knowledge emerged as a pivotal pillar for the initial Vietnamese refugees and their successors. Collaboratively, they forged a self-reliant and inclusive community within an unfamiliar terrain that often seemed formidable. With the community's expansion, a proliferation of family-owned businesses naturally ensued.

When I met Kathy Buchoz, the former two-term mayor of the City of Westminster and a real estate agent, she recalled encountering unfamiliar store signs popping up throughout Orange County. "When I stopped by to say hello, I discovered that these were now Vietnamese stores," she shared. During her tenure as mayor, Buchoz garnered recognition from many Vietnamese Americans in Little Saigon, often described as "a Caucasian lady with likely Vietnamese ancestry." Her outspoken support for emerging businesses within the community proved invaluable to the refugees. Unbeknownst to her, she represented the silent majority of mainstream individuals who understood the importance of embracing multiculturalism and fostering a diverse identity in America. In her own way, she directly and indirectly contributed to the vision of a Vietnamese Little Saigon community that welcomes and celebrates a multitude of voices.

Du Miên, the founder of the first newspaper for the Little Saigon community and a long-time admirer of my father, offered insights into the enclave's growth. "New businesses were sprouting everywhere," he explained, pointing to a weathered notebook filled with names. "I recorded the names of new businesses everyday. Grand opening banners and business flyers could be found everywhere, from restaurant cashiers' desks to doctor's offices."

One of my brothers-in-law taught ESL at Orange Coast College in the late 1970's vividly recalled the swift changes and abundant opportunities that characterized the economic, social, and community boom in Little Saigon. He fondly recounted the presence of numerous renowned singers and musicians in his classes, including Elvis Phương, Hoàng Thi Thơ, Anh Bằng, and many others. They gathered not only to learn English but, more importantly, to reconnect and forge business connections, leaving a lasting impression on him.

If these aspiring entrepreneurs, who initially met around dinner tables pealing over a fragrant bowl of phở or in ESL classrooms, couldn't find partners already settled in Orange County, they resorted to making long-distance calls to other Vietnamese communities across the country. Quách Nhứt Danh and Ann Phong, whose stories are featured in our oral history, shared a similar experience. Quách Nhứt Danh, who settled in Connecticut when his family first arrived in the United States, was about to complete his pharmaceutical training and yearned for more from his new life in America. Likewise, Ann Phong, an artist living in New York, sought to find meaning in her fresh start in America. These newly arrived immigrants would spend hours on the phone with acquaintances in Little Saigon, hearing a constant refrain urging them to join the community: "Come here. It's nice and warm. Come here. We can join hands to open a new business. Come here. Many of your friends are asking for you. Come here. Yes, do come here." These words formed a melodic song that resonated within the hearts of Vietnamese refugees across the United States—a song that called out, "Little Saigon is waiting for you."

My own mother has imparted the spirit of entrepreneurship to all of us in our family. When we were sent to Marshfield, Wisconsin in 1975, she embarked on a coast-to-coast Greyhound journey, eventually landing in Santa Ana. Similarly, Quách Nhứt Danh purchased a one-way ticket from Connecticut to Los Angeles, and Ann Phong left behind the bustling streets of New York to board a flight to Los Angeles. Like countless others, both young and old, filled with a mix of hope and apprehension, they converged on Little Saigon—a place that became their beacon of American hope and their new home.

THE ROOTS OF HISTORY BUILD THE FUTURE

The stories of my mother and her friends in search of a new land have deeply inspired me to delve into the roots of Little Saigon's history. As Dân Tiếp Vụ, the first grocery store in Little Saigon, closed its doors only a few months after opening, Vietnamese refugees started to witness the development of their community. Records obtained from the City of Santa Ana and City of Westminster reveal that newly registered business licenses for Vietnamese refugees started sprouting up on First Street in Santa Ana.

However, with the opening of Asian Garden Mall, known as Phước Lộc Thọ, the center of the Vietnamese business community shifted a few blocks westward to Bolsa Ave. Archival photos depict the Mini-Bolsa Mall on Bolsa Ave as a modest one-story building, reminiscent of a bunker. It welcomed the first three Vietnamese businesses in the city of Westminster: Chợ Hoà Bình (Peace Market) owned by Ngô Khương Hân, Restaurant Thành Mỹ (Success Restaurant) owned by Bà Ba (Mrs. Ba), and a Chinese Pharmacy owned by Trúc Sinh. For many, as they admitted to me, their "new" businesses in Little Saigon were a continuation of what they did in Vietnam. Stepping through the doors of these markets, restaurants, and pharmacies, the new owners built a sense of community and opened up new prospects for other Vietnamese refugees.

A few blocks away, on First Street in Santa Ana, visitors could find my family's Hội Quán Vietnam (Vietnamese Club), the first Vietnamese restaurant in Little Saigon, which became a popular spot for Vietnamese workers. Next to the restaurant, newcomers would stop by the well-known Farmers Insurance office, run by Nguyễn Phước, to discuss their insurance needs. Close by, many new Vietnamese American community members would frequent the first local tax office owned by Hồng Song Lưu. Just next door, Saigon Daily, the first Vietnamese newspaper led by renowned reporter Du Miên, printed the latest headline stories for Little Saigon. The Tú Quỳnh bookstore, operated by Ms. Phan Hoàng Yến, welcomed visitors with a wide selection of Vietnamese books, magazines, and other delights. A little further down the Garden Grove pathways, one could find the office of the Boy Scout

Bạch Đằng, where exciting adventures were planned. Finally, at the end of the mall, the humble Trúc Lâm Yến Tử Buddhist temple provided visitors a moment of respite, allowing them to replenish their spirits amidst the soothing scent of incense.

Nostalgia permeates the hearts and minds of every individual in Orange County. Yet, this nostalgia does not limit the community to conventional thinking. Du Miên and Đỗ Ngọc-Yến, part of a generation of trained journalists who benefited from a rare period of free media in Vietnam from 1960–1970, possessed the expertise to establish newspapers in the United States. Du Miên initiated the first weekly newspaper in Little Saigon, Saigon Mới (New Saigon), and soon after, Ngọc-Yến Đỗ released the very first daily newspaper, Người Việt Cali (Vietnamese in California), which was eventually renamed Người Việt (The Vietnamese). Today, Người Việt Daily boasts a print readership of 13,000 and an online readership exceeding 50,000. Furthermore, the Little Saigon Yellow Pages lists businesses that offer a wide range of products and services, making the community almost an autonomous enclave capable of sustaining itself.

By 1979, two years after the initial influx of new businesses, approximately 100 Vietnamese-owned businesses lined Bolsa and Westminster avenues in Westminster, Santa Ana, and Garden Grove. Block after block, new businesses were created, marking the progress of building their own town. The continued migration of Vietnamese refugees from various parts of the United States to Orange County has further contributed to the growth of this vibrant community. "Grand Opening" banners in vibrant yellow and red adorned the streets of Bolsa and Westminster. Many Vietnamese-owned restaurants, gift shops, grocery stores, and businesses emerged as pioneers within the community. The significance of being "first" extends beyond simply indicating the types of businesses—whether it be the first grocery store, pharmacy, or hair salon. To me, the word "first" underscores the ingenuity of Vietnamese refugees and, emotionally, serves as a reminder of their journey—their path to cultivating a community in a new land.

Like my mother, refugees who were unable or chose not to engage in mainstream corporate America found business opportunities within their community. Newcomers required food, lodging, news, and advice to help them navigate life in the United States. They also longed for music and entertainment that would comfort them in this foreign land. These Vietnamese families relied on their new community to offer a sense of normalcy and guidance, from travel agencies for visiting relatives to photoshops for restoring war-torn photographs, flower shops for celebrating and mourning, and jewelry stores for weddings and anniversaries. The visionary first-generation refugees recognized these needs as opportunities for prosperity, all the while remaining connected to Vietnam and embracing their Vietnamese identities.

"In many ways, what is happening in Orange County reminds me of the early years of the 1954 exodus to the South," my father once shared. "Many 'Bắc kỳ 54' (immigrants from the North in 1954) had to rebuild their lives in Saigon. Now, they are dutifully reconstructing their lives once again." Some former government officials, military personnel, and others had to embark on an entirely new path. I recall the countless debates in the media about Nguyễn Cao Kỳ, the once-powerful premier of the South Vietnamese government, purchasing a liquor store in a blue-collar suburban district in Norfolk, Central California, and personally unloading heavy boxes from a delivery truck.

In every corner of Little Saigon, the commercial centers were named after cities in Vietnam, paying homage to the memories of significant landmarks from Saigon's past: Bến Thành Market on Bolsa, Catinat Plaza on Bolsa, Phở 79 on West Hazard, Brodard Chateau on Trask Ave, and Hanoi Corner on Garden Grove Boulevard. These names serve as a reminder of Vietnamese Americans' roots and symbolize the connection to the meaningful landmarks of former Saigon.

"It feels just like doing business back in Vietnam," remarked Nguyễn Trang, a tailor in Midway City. "We converse in Vietnamese everywhere, which makes life easier for me." She smiled, emphasizing that English is not the sole language of commerce. "However, my Vietnamese clients can be quite challenging. They bargain hard, just like they did back home. They have high expectations," Nguyễn Trang paused, meeting my gaze as she winked and smiled. "But they are Vietnamese, and so am I." Her words ring out through Little Saigon, echoing the sentiment, "I am Vietnamese too." The roots of history build the future.

THE MISFORTUNE OF SOME MAKING THE HAPPINESS OF OTHERS[5]

Following the tumultuous years after the fall of Saigon in 1975, Vietnam faced a challenging transition in its economy. The communist party[6] implemented a socialized economy in the South, nationalizing all economic activities and leading to significant difficulties.

The situation was compounded by external factors that added to the country's struggles. President Gerald Ford's decision to disregard the 1973 Paris Peace Agreement, citing "untruthfulness and unfair wartime practices by Vietnam," resulted in a trade embargo imposed by the United States. This embargo prohibited all trade between the United States and Vietnam, including subsidiaries and third parties. Additionally, China, once an unconditional ally, ceased providing subsidies to Vietnam in 1977, while Eastern European countries significantly reduced their financial and commodity support. As subsidies disappeared, prices of essential goods such as rice, sugar, dairy products, clothing, and medicines skyrocketed. Amidst these challenges, Vietnam also faced conflicts with Cambodia and China, along with natural disasters in the Mekong Delta. The war-torn country struggled to adapt to the modus operandi of nationalized cooperatives, further straining its population.

Vietnamese Americans in Little Saigon and across the U.S. anxiously awaited news from their loved ones while witnessing another wave of refugees fleeing the country. Relief came in the form of letters and phone calls, providing solace to those who learned that their relatives had made it to the refugee camps. However, the influx of new migrants presented new concerns and challenges. In the face of adversity, the business community in Little Saigon recognized new opportunities arising from the arrival of these refugees. Entrepreneurs like Quách Nhứt Danh adjusted their businesses to meet the growing needs of the community, supplying essential goods and services. Little Saigon residents also played their part in supporting their friends and family back home, lining up to purchase goods for shipment to Vietnam. Pharmacies, like Quách Nhứt Danh's, became vital hubs for healthcare-related items and essential goods. The community engaged in debates about what to send, often shipping seemingly trivial items out of love and a sense of responsibility.

As the demand for shipping goods to Vietnam and refugee camps increased, specialized stores emerged to cater to this need. Clothing, personal care products, and various other items flew off the shelves. Quách Nhứt Danh, with his pharmacy and FDA export certificate, played a crucial role in supplying necessary medications and antibiotics. Through collective efforts, Little Saigon became a lifeline for those in Vietnam and the refugee camps. The spirit of compassion, resilience, and determination fueled the drive to support loved ones and lay a stronger foundation for the Vietnamese American community, even in the face of adversity.

During this time, Vietnamese Americans in Little Saigon and across the U.S. anxiously awaited news from their loved ones. They worried and longed for words from family and friends. This period also witnessed another wave of what became known as the "Vietnamese boat people," as approximately eight hundred thousand refugees fled the country under extreme conditions. Those who survived the treacherous journey arrived in temporary refugee camps, which offered inhospitable conditions.

Finally, hope arrived through letters and phone calls, providing relief to those who received news that their relatives had made it to the refugee camps in this new wave of refugees. However, the influx of new migrants created additional concerns, as their friends and families needed support.

In response, the Little Saigon business community recognized new opportunities with the arrival of the first and second waves of refugees. Quách

Nhứt Danh's pharmacy opened its doors during this influx, initially serving the healthcare needs of the newcomers. Eventually, he transformed his store into a bazaar, offering a variety of seemingly unrelated goods—fabric, sewing machines and supplies, bicycles, and helmets—to meet the growing community's needs. The troubles back home in Vietnam reshaped the nature of Quách Nhứt Danh's business and that of his business partners. "The misfortune of some becomes the happiness of others," as the 17th-century French philosopher Voltaire said. Quách Nhứt Danh would have agreed, stating, "I told you so." In the late 1970s or early 1980s, many new refugees struggled to make ends meet but wanted to secure additional income sources to help their relatives and friends in Little Saigon. They sought to assist their community in building strong roots while remembering their origins and those they left behind.

Residents of Little Saigon formed long queues to purchase goods for shipment to Vietnam. "Back in 1978, I had long lines of people standing in front of my store every day," recalled Quách Nhứt Danh. "We packed a thousand boxes of medications, healthcare-related items, fabric, and other household goods for our customers to send to Vietnam and refugee camps. It was big business for me, as well as for my friend Mr. Thanh next door, who worked for Air France Cargo. He opened a shipping business called A.F. Cargo—shipping a thousand pounds of merchandise daily." Residents and businesses of Little Saigon carefully considered how to help their friends and family back home. "We spent a considerable amount of time during meals debating what to ship to my sisters in Ban Mê Thuột," shared Nguyễn Lân, who was married to my second sister and is now a retired quality control engineer at a tire manufacturing firm in South Los Angeles. "I thought shipping bottles of liquid shampoos was trivial. The shipping costs were more expensive than the items we bought at K-mart. But out of love and a sense of guilt for leaving them behind, we did it." Like Nguyễn Lân, other residents of Little Saigon bought whatever they could afford, packing standardized shipping boxes with items to send. Soon, specialized stores catering to these needs emerged, fulfilling the demand for sundry goods that Little Saigon residents could easily send to Vietnam or refugee camps. Shirts, pants, shampoo, conditioner, fabric, and dried foods—all items moved quickly from the shelves.

Quách Nhứt Danh had a competitive advantage since everyone seemed to require some form of medication. He noted that antibiotics and flu medicines were particularly popular. However, the United States had strict import-export regulations on certain drugs. Quách Nhứt Danh managed to be the first pharmacy to obtain an export certificate from the Federal Drug and Food Administration (FDA), citing humanitarian reasons.

As I listened to Quách Nhứt Danh's story, memories of numerous phone calls from friends and relatives seeking to raise funds to help the people in

Vietnam flooded back. Even my mother called, emphasizing that assisting those in need had become "the right thing to do" in the Little Saigon community. Groups of first-generation Vietnamese Americans came together to mobilize funds for those in need.

As the network of aid expanded and diversified throughout the community, relatives and friends back home reminded Little Saigon's Vietnamese families that they needed money more than goods. "Don't ship things to us. We can find plenty of imported goods in Bến Thành Market.[7] Many people receive goods from their families living overseas, and they don't know what to do with them, so they try to sell them," recalled Nguyễn Lân, reflecting on the phone calls and letters received from family in Vietnam during that time. "Since then, I have only sent money. My sisters can buy whatever they need, and I did not need to do the guesswork."

Sending money to Vietnam proved to be difficult, as it posed another hurdle to overcome. With the trade embargo in effect until 1994, banks were prohibited from conducting business with Vietnam. Once again, the business community in Little Saigon took the initiative, forming a vast informal and loosely connected network of operators to transfer funds to those in need back in Vietnam.

In June 1978, I ran into Đỗ Hương from Fountain Valley, a few blocks away from my parents' home. She grew concerned about her parents' health while they resided in the humid climate of Pulau Bidong, the Indonesian refugee camp. Seeking help, she visited a parcel delivery service on Brookhurst Avenue. The clerk there directed her to the owner of a jewelry store, where Đỗ Hương was introduced to a young man in his early thirties. This man collected money from his "clients" and personally flew to Pulau Bidong to deliver the funds. Although the fees for this service were exorbitantly high, Đỗ Hương found immense relief when her brother informed her that their parents had received the money she sent. She acknowledged that it was a costly service but one that provided significant relief.

Đỗ Hương's experience reflected the sentiments of many others who were deeply concerned for the well-being of their loved ones in Vietnam. The underground system for these informal fund transfers gradually evolved into a sophisticated process known as "hot transfer."[8] Those in need of sending money would deposit funds with an agent, often a retailer operating a travel agency, grocery store, video store, or jewelry store. The agent would then inform their partner in the recipient's hometown to pick up the remittance. Fees for this service typically ranged from 1% to 10%.

In 1994, Western Union opened its first branch in Vietnam. Established in 1851 as a telegraphic services company, Western Union has become one of the oldest banking institutions specializing in fast money transfers in modern times. It quickly rose to become the largest international money remittance network in Vietnam, with over eight thousand agencies across sixty-three provinces[9] The company formalized the monetary system in Vietnam. However, despite the rise in competition, information transfer networks remain active, with individuals traveling between locations to provide this valuable and necessary service.

Over the years, methods of transferring funds to family and friends across the seas have evolved. Many money transfers are no longer purely driven by necessity but rather by a desire to maintain familial ties during significant family-oriented holidays or occasions such as the Tết holiday, weddings, funerals, and anniversaries. With much of the first generation of Vietnamese American residents in Little Saigon reaching retirement age, many now send money to Vietnam to purchase real estate for vacation or retirement homes. Meanwhile, the community has witnessed a few individuals become the first multi-millionaires.

THE FUTURITY OF TRADITION— SECURITY IN THE NEW LAND

In 1978, there came a pivotal day when Đinh Thế Bình, my brother-in-law and Hải's husband, returned home from work. Just a few weeks into his first job, he approached every member of our extended family, seeking their support. He needed $5,000 for a down payment on a $40,000 home in Anaheim, conveniently located near Disneyland. "Since we're already paying rent anyway, I want to be able to take the children to Disneyland whenever they wish," my brother-in-law declared. His reasoning invoked laughter within me, as the decision to purchase a property next to the famous theme park seemed to defy conventional financial logic. Despite cautionary advice from relatives who deemed it a risky endeavor, my brother-in-law's determination prevailed. He managed to secure a dozen personal loans, with contributions ranging from a few hundred dollars here and there. With the accumulated funds, he successfully closed escrow on a four-bedroom house with a generous yard where his two toddlers could frolic.

As time passed, more Vietnamese immigrants flocked to Orange County, leading to a substantial appreciation in the value of Bình's property. Eventually, he sold the house at a significant profit and relocated to a prestigious neighborhood in Irvine, ensuring his children could attend the University of California at Irvine. Inspired by his success, one by one, our extended family members followed suit. Even his mother, initially the most vocal opponent of her son's "crazy idea," eventually purchased her own home, which now belongs to one of her grandchildren.

Asians, particularly those influenced by Chinese culture, have a strong inclination to invest in real estate. This preference stems from the symbolic representation of wealth in the Chinese word 富, which depicts a person standing on a piece of land. The belief is that real estate, as a tangible asset, holds enduring monetary value and provides consistent profits regardless of the future. The enduring wisdom behind this belief lies in the expectation that the population will continue to grow, leading to appreciation in land value over the long term. Looking at the remarkable appreciation of real estate values in 2021, almost a twenty-fold increase in non-inflation adjusted terms since the refugees first arrived in Orange County, this centuries-old wisdom has once again proven true.

For residents of Little Saigon who had the foresight to invest in land, their acquisitions are seen as strokes of luck and insightful decisions. Quách Nhứt Danh, a highly respected figure in the community, expressed his satisfaction with a radiant smile as he shared, "Using the proceeds from our unexpected success in sending merchandise and medications to Vietnam, we purchased unused land for $2 per square foot. Today in 2018, its value would be around $230 per square foot."

Over the years, the trend of purchasing properties and real estate in Little Saigon has steadily grown. When the American government adopted the strategy of Vietnamization under Nixon's administration, aiming to reduce American involvement in the Vietnam War by transferring military responsibilities to South Vietnam, which ultimately succumbed to North Vietnam, newly naturalized citizens from Vietnam made it their mission to acquire properties in Orange County.

Amid the COVID-19 pandemic persisting throughout 2020 and 2021, the residential housing market in the Little Saigon neighborhood experienced a significant surge, with prices soaring by as much as 10% to 25%. In August 2020, Karen Nguyễn, a real estate agent, faced a setback when her bid to purchase a 1,500 square foot home in Westminster fell through. Her client had offered the seller's asking price, only to be outbid by a Vietnamese family who countered with a final offer that surpassed the listed price by 3%. The Vietnamese refugee community found security and prosperity in Little Saigon through their investments in the local community, their fellow Vietnamese both in the U.S. and back home, and particularly in real estate during a time when Orange County was predominantly covered in strawberry fields and salvage yards in Westminster. Katelyne Nguyễn, the owner of a real estate business catering predominantly to the local Vietnamese community whom I bought a property from, told me, "During the first quarter of 2021, prospective buyers have had to submit bids thousands of dollars above the asking price just for a chance to secure a house in the highly sought-after Little Saigon area."

Frank Jao, comfortably seated in his conference room while discussing the impact of tax breaks under the Trump administration, confidently asserted, "I can confidently say that we have at least half a dozen Vietnamese American billionaires, largely thanks to their investments in real estate." However, he chose not to disclose their names.

Across three generations, the Vietnamese community has left its distinct mark on the cities surrounding Little Saigon. Four of my relatives now reside in Fountain Valley. When my family purchased their first home on Coriender Ave in 1978, the neighborhood was predominantly inhabited by Caucasians. Fast forward to 2023, Vietnamese has become the predominant language spoken among the neighbors, showcasing the profound "Vietnamization" of the area.

NOTES

1. Tô Văn Lai (in Vietnamese)
2. Phạm Long Cơ (in Vietnamese)
3. https://svqy.org/2017/9-2017/gsdaohuuanh/gsdaohuuanh.html__https://chungtoimuontudo2.wordpress.com/2019/03/26/gs-dao-huu-anh-y-khoa-dhd-nhin-lai-60-nam-lich-su-tl-qu-y-gia-march-26-2019/
4. SBTN—Saigon Broadcasting Television Network, with headquarters located in Garden Grove, California, and branches in cities that have a large number of Vietnamese concentration, Washington DC, Boston, Dallas and network offices in Canada and Australia.
5. Voltaire (1694–1778)
6. Ban chấp hành trung ương đảng
7. Ben Thanh market is the iconic shopping arcade in the center of Saigon.
8. "Chuyển tiền tay ba (translation: third-party money transfer).
9. https://www.vir.com.vn/western-union-toasts-its-8000th-agent-in-vietnam-11194.html

Chapter 4

Echoes of Belonging

CREATING REPRESENTATION AND EMOTIONAL TIES

The first time I visited my family in Orange County was in the summer of 1978, just a few months after they migrated from Marshfield, Wisconsin. Legendary for its weather, the Mediterranean-like climate in this southern part of California was comfortably dry and mild, with a cloudless bluer-than-blue sky. But economically, Orange county at that time was just a network of modest towns with rural landscapes separating them. Caring for the socio-economic well-being of my family, I was most interested in the presence of Disneyland and the University of California at Irvine (UCI), and pondered what these two gigantic economic engines of the county do to help secure jobs for the refugee community. While Disneyland appeared to be an increasingly economic force for the neighboring cities, UCI was still at its early development stage. Many newcomers did not speak English. If some did, would they be qualified to seek employment from these organizations?

I told my father that either we have all the adults in the family take vocational training, and work in some of the electronic factories, like my sister Hải, or start a new business . . . again. "I am afraid that many of the refugees in this community are in the same boat," my father replied with his usual candidness. "If this is the case, we would have to rely on ourselves, do what we do best, and rely on each other."

When my mother proposed to open a Vietnamese restaurant to serve the Vietnamese community, my father initially discouraged her, arguing that it would be a tiring business for a woman who would be a sexagenarian in a couple of years. But, he succumbed to the temptation, acknowledging that the family would have no other viable alternatives.

A LITTLE BIT OF SAIGON—THE SIGHTS, SOUNDS, AND FLAVORS THAT BUILT AN IDENTITY

My mother bought the very first Vietnamese restaurant in the soon-to-be Little Saigon, "Hội Quán Vietnam" (Vietnamese Restaurant and Club) from the Mười's brothers. A few months earlier, when they were looking for a venue to open the restaurant, the only location they could afford was in a run-down shopping center on the corner of First Street and Kenton Drive in Santa Ana. The brothers looked for a location with a large parking lot and spacious interior that could comfortably seat 150 diners. Affordability and proximity to Bolsa Ave were the key location selection criteria to open a business. Fortunately, the building cropped up a block away from the Center for Resettlement, which the local government had erected to help newcomers.

Shortly after opening Hội Quán Vietnam, the tiny 1.5-acre 12-unit shopping center flourished with Vietnamese businesses: *Viễn Đông Market*, *P&R Tax and Insurance Services*, *Lập's Photos*, *Thanh Thảo's Tailor*, *Dr. Ngô Trần's Medical Office*, *Gửi quà AF* (Air France Cargo for Sending Gift to Vietnam), and a *Billiard* place. The center looked modest and unremarkable, but it felt just like home. Soon, *Quê Mẹ* (Native Land) bookstore opened, with a section dedicated to the *Trung Tâm Người Việt Quốc Gia* (Center for Vietnamese from the Republic for Vietnam).

My mother's restaurant *de facto* became a reference for Vietnamese-owned businesses. As any economics textbook will state, entrepreneurs create jobs. In February 1979, Nguyễn Long, a former sergeant in the South Vietnamese Army, came to Santa Ana from Baudette, a farming community in northern Minnesota. His friend, Trần Hiệp, told him to leave Minnesota's freezing temperatures and isolation, where there were no Vietnamese-speaking people. "It is too peaceful here. I am so stressed out. I feel like I am under house arrest," Nguyễn Long said. When he arrived on Trần Hiệp's doorstep, he slept on the sofa for four months until he found a mechanic job, working on trucks. The secure job led him to find a room with a family for $100/month, two blocks away from Hội Quán Vietnam restaurant, where he eventually found work as a dishwasher. Most Vietnamese newcomers, particularly those who could not afford a vehicle, preferred to stay close to the community, so the work in the center suited Nguyễn Long. Nguyễn Long and his friends in this first wave of Vietnamese refugees slowly built what is now Little Saigon.

In 1981, five days before the Year of the Rooster, as the community frantically organized the Tết festival, Rosa Kwong, a reporter for the *Orange County Register*, reported on the community's festive mood. Kwong noted the businesses' hectic preparations as they decorated shops and the street stage with flags and fanfare that held deep cultural significance. Kwong wrote that Orange County residents were about to witness a "new scene 'alien' to some business operators in the area" as "Asians make the county home." Her article featured a photo of Quách Nhứt Danh, pharmacist, kneeling on the floor, helping a customer pack a box of goods. Kwong pointed to another more "alien scene": a Vietnamese man selling Asian vegetables on Bolsa's streets. She named her article "Little bit of Saigon."

Du Miên, a journalist and the founder of *New Saigon Weekly*, the first Vietnamese-language newspaper in Orange County, understood the importance of strategic location. His ad-based magazine succeeded because of the growth of the community. "We need a critical mass of Vietnamese businesses and residents concentrated in one geographical area," Du Miên said. He picked up Kwong's article and saw a dream of a thriving Vietnamese American community. Quickly, Du Miên drafted a map of Vietnamese-owned shops and published it in New Saigon Weekly. The map showcased a total of 63 businesses with names reminiscent of the Saigon back home: *Au Printemps*, *His&Her Fashions*, *Kim Phượng Jewelry*, *Vietnam Travel*, *Kinh Đô Barber*, *Vietnam Insurance Center*, and *Tú Quỳnh Music*. The fruition of this dynamic community had begun.

Du Miên's map in the *New Saigon Weekly* sent a hopeful message to his fellow refugees: "American and Vietnamese media have named two shopping centers densely populated by Vietnamese businesses the 'Saigon business districts in the U.S.'" Du Miên, his friends, and many of the new residents Orange County recognized this moment as an opportunity for Vietnamese businesses to grow their presence in the area. "I think the call for Vietnamese refugees to locate their businesses in one area has worked," Du Miên recalled with a smile that indicated deep love for his community. "Just look how Little Saigon is today."

The community did grow, indeed. By 1986, "the little bit of Saigon" expanded to an eight-block business district that traversed the cities of Westminster, Garden Grove, and Santa Ana. Vietnamese-owned businesses populate Edward Street heading East to Bristol and Bolsa and Westminster Avenues, parallel veins of business that pumped with the lifeblood of the community. Du Miên teamed up with a local dentist, Dư Thị Mỹ-Lan and a former instructor to publish the very first business directory of "Little Saigon," including an updated version of the map of "Phố Saigon" (Saigon Shopping Area) that Du Miên printed in 1981. The updated map listed 185 businesses, offering a wide range of products and services that residents would expect to find in a typical town.

And the community continued to grow. Phạm Đặng Long-Cơ, one of the first medical doctors in the community, joined with local leaders to establish the Vietnamese American Chamber of Commerce (VACOC)[1] in 1985. Phụng Minh Tiến volunteered to serve as the first secretary general of the Committee for the Development of Little Saigon.[2] "One of our top items on the agenda was to ask the city councils of the cities where our people did business to allow us to display Vietnamese on the billboards of their businesses," he recalled. There was initial opposition, as some city council members wanted newcomers to assimilate rather than build an "alien" community.

Nevertheless, Du Miên and the community saw new businesses spring up faster than he had hoped. Quách Nhứt Danh, who opened the first pharmacy, using the profits from a shipment of medicines and goods to Vietnam, went on a shopping spree. Du Miên's friends, the first business owners in Little Saigon,[3] continued to build hope and prosperity for their community. They bought land, business and residential properties, at prices that "were too cheap to be true," Quách said. They built new commercial strips, low-cost buildings with functional retail shops and offices. While they intended to build wealth and success, their enterprise also contributed to Little Saigon's development. The timing was also opportune for those who wanted to move out of the "Vietnamese enclave." "Many Caucasian property owners cashed in profit, and moved to other cities," said Kathy Buchoz, a two-term mayor of the City of Westminster.

Eric Jacquet-Lagrèze, a researcher from the University of Paris-Dauphine, came to see me in 1983. I drove him around the new Vietnamese district. "I am impressed by all these shops. But I don't see much of a Vietnamese architectural style," he commented. The number of storefront signs—cheaply made vinyl banners, A-frame metallic signs, or backlit signs—popped up in every corner of the district. My friend Eric was correct. I could not recognize any noted architectural landmarks. The commercial strips were quickly erected by the Vietnamese refugees. Obviously, architecture and aesthetics were not a priority for these business people.

While some council members raised initial concerns about having non-English business names and signs in their cities, they eventually reversed their objections and granted permission to use Vietnamese on business billboards. In 1986, Phụng Minh Tiến founded a committee to lobby to rename the business district "Little Saigon." Thanks to the support of the then council members, in particular, council member Frank Fry Jr., the city of Westminster passed the resolution in 1987, marking the first legislative move to make Little Saigon a reality.

Having lived in Europe for more than a decade, I grew fond of urban architecture. I had no answer to my colleague from Paris. I just offered him a plausible explanation. Like other ethnic communities in the U.S., Vietnamese immigrants started to rebuild their lives and construct communities with low-cost, single-story commercial buildings. Vietnamese immigrant's integration was similar to Indians immigrants' (e.g., Little India on Devon Avenue in Chicago) and other ethnic communities throughout North America: They built typical mid-20th century-urban developments.

As the first generation of entrepreneurs have reached their retirement age, Du Miên, 71, no longer has to worry about creating new businesses in the Vietnamese enclave. Little Saigon began with a mere 63 businesses on the first map that he drew so many years ago, and now the community has more than 15,000 registered businesses. One thing that Du Miên could not have predicted in 1981, was that in less than 40 years, the first three cities—Westminster, Santa Ana and Garden Grove—quickly ran out of vacant land for Vietnamese businesses and residents.

PHƯỚC LỘC THỌ—AN ICONIC STRUCTURE IN CRISIS

I am certain that many of the Little Saigon residents would agree with the comment of my French friend, Eric, on the lack of distinctive Vietnamese architecture of Little Saigon. Due to limited finances, the new citizens of Orange County had to settle for modest commercial strips and mom-and-pop businesses that served their community's needs. "It was the most we could afford. I even had to find an old warehouse to start my business," Tony Cao told me when I visited his machine shop. The commercial developments retained the look and feel of the low-income, unimpressive suburban streetscape seen across America's landscape. However, the Vietnamese Americans identified their business with colorful, uncoordinated store signs in Vietnamese. The sight of a few shoppers wearing the Vietnamese-style bamboo palm-leaf conical hat added to the charm and identity of these businesses. And, for a while, these stores did serve their community's economic and social needs.

But, the entrepreneurial and daring spirit of Frank Jao, in Vietnamese Triệu Phát, a self-proclaimed penniless refugee, quickly redefined the commercial landscape of Little Saigon with the Asian Garden Mall, which became the first iconic structure of the community. In 1987, less than twelve years after Camp Pendleton released the first refugees, the community welcomed the opening of a 150,000-square-foot mall that symbolically marked the location and identity of Little Saigon. A pagoda-style edifice crowns the exterior architecture, and the front garden contains four monumental marble statues imported from China: A Happy Buddha and the gods of Good Luck, Prosperity, and Longevity.

Inspired by the theme-based commercial structures in Las Vegas—*Caesars Palace, The Venetians, New York-New York*, etc.—Frank Jao embraced the "chopstick culture."[4] Chopstick culture derives from a Vietnamese proverb that suggests that one can't break a handful of chopsticks; there's power in solidarity. Frank Jao envisioned an Asian cultural hub in Orange County that showcased Asian cuisines, a shopping arcade on the main floor, and an entire second floor dedicated to jewelry booths. He, thus, named the first and largest two-story mall in the center of the Vietnamese shopping area *Asian Garden mall.*

Frank Jao managed to raise funding with Taiwanese friends and business associates to build Asian Garden Mall, which became the tectonic junction of development in Little Saigon. The mall remains by far the most famous structure of all the Vietnamese shopping centers in Little Saigon. "Every property I introduce to my prospective clients starts with a distance analysis from *Phước Lộc Thọ*," Nguyễn Trí, a real estate agent, admitted. He half-jokingly added, "Phước Lộc Thọ, an alias for the Asian Garden Mall in Little Saigon, is some sort of the *Bến Thành* market in Saigon, Vietnam, the *Le Bon Marché* in Paris, or the *Atrium Shops and Cafes* in Manhattan, New York." Nguyễn Trí's comparison may seem exaggerated, yet, the *Asian Garden Mall* hosts 300 retail businesses.

Compared to other shopping centers in the area, such as the Westminster Mall, Asian Garden Mall is significantly smaller in size and property value. However, for the Vietnamese Americans who fled war, trauma, and loss, many saw it and still see this mall as a symbol that speaks of their presence in the community.

A few locals in Little Saigon voiced their concern when they learned that Frank Jao gave the new iconic structure a generic Asian name, *Asian Garden*. Frank Jao's approach stirred controversy within the community. Vietnamese refugee leaders within the Little Saigon community, led by Phùng Minh Tiến, protested Jao's move, arguing that their community was Vietnamese and only Vietnamese. Jao suggests that these remarks were identity politics in the new society; perhaps they were growing pains as the community struggled to name its identity. "It is just a silly thing to claim that I am too Chinese. Yes, my grandparents did emigrate to Vietnam from China. I was Chinese-Vietnamese. But, today, I am an American and an American businessman," Frank Jao said.

Like many of the earlier controversies, the debates were intense, widely broadcasted on local Vietnamese media, but they were short lived. With the ongoing expansion of the Little Saigon business district, *Phước Lộc Thọ* remains the central gathering place for local Vietnamese residents and visitors alike. Katherine Jao, Frank's wife and partner, proudly introduced herself as the "Chief Happiness Officer" at the 2019 Tết Celebration. "Phước Lộc Thọ? It's the rendezvous spot. It's the Little Saigon Friday night market. It's the Tết New Year. It's the enchanting flower festival. It's the cultural heart of the community," she said, looking at me earnestly. "So, please, encourage people to simply enjoy it."

REPRESENTATIONAL BELONGING

The success of the Bridgecreek Group, led by Frank Jao, has undoubtedly inspired many others to follow in his footsteps. Influential businessmen like Quách Nhứt Danh, Trần Dũ, and Đặng-Phạm Long-Cơ have either acquired established centers or embarked on developing new ones.

The rise in popularity of Asian Garden Mall and 99 Market has changed the perception of community leaders who were previously skeptical about refugees' ability to finance their business ventures. Early Little Saigon entrepreneurs, including Frank Jao, still recall the initial rejections they faced when applying for loans from banks. However, as the success of Vietnamese refugee entrepreneurs became evident, these banks, including major national institutions such as Bank of America and Wells Fargo, began to actively support and invest in the Vietnamese business community.

The community has witnessed a wave of construction-related businesses emerging. Property owners and commercial tenants have taken proactive steps to remodel both the interiors and exteriors of their buildings, showcasing a strong desire to express their cultural identity. Each time I return to Little Saigon, I can't help but exclaim, "Wow!"

The remodeling of outdated structures and the construction of new commercial buildings have transformed the business and social dynamics of Little Saigon. Although the architectural designs have been somewhat timid, they have contributed to the ongoing gentrification efforts, turning Bolsa Avenue into a vibrant public space. To borrow Nguyễn Trí's metaphor, Little Saigon is akin to the "Carrousel du Louvre of the Vietnamese community in Orange County." The growth and success of Little Saigon have fueled the aspirations of business leaders to elevate the community to new heights.

"We will have larger and bigger supermarkets. We will have larger and bigger shopping centers. We will have bigger and larger restaurants," predicted Nguyễn Phụng Tiến, one of the founding members of the Vietnamese American Chamber of Commerce of Orange County, now 81 years old. My old friend Nguyễn Văn Trắc from San Jose regularly drives to Santa Ana to visit his sister. He marvels at the continuous development he witnesses in Little Saigon. "Every time I come here, I see new developments. It feels like Little Saigon is experiencing a second wave of urban transformation," he remarked with awe.

CHINESE VIETNAMESE IN LITTLE SAIGON—THE SIGNS OF HISTORY AND FUTURE

After four decades of active community engagement, Trần Dũ, 81 years old and a long-time business partner of my mother, remains widely known as one of the first and most dependable food distributors for Vietnamese restaurants. However, like many businesses in 2020, the pandemic dealt a severe blow to his revenue. "I've lost about 70% of my income as restaurants have significantly reduced their orders these days," he lamented. Nevertheless, he continues to go to his shop every day, finding joy and purpose in his work. "Work keeps me healthy, and I am grateful for my health. I believe that we will eventually return to normal life," he optimistically stated.

My sister, Minh Châu, is well acquainted with Trần Dũ. Trần Dũ, an orphan of Chinese descent who grew up in the city of Sóc Trăng in the Mekong Delta, named his business Delta Foods Warehouse as a tribute to his roots. Prior to 1975, he was a successful entrepreneur in Vietnam, owning various restaurants and coffee bars in Saigon. Even then, he had an entrepreneurial spirit. "I observed grocery shoppers at Dân Tiếp Vụ and asked them what items they couldn't find. Then, I would seek out suppliers, either directly from farms owned by other ethnic immigrants or from Asian food wholesalers in Los Angeles," Trần Dũ shared. Even at the age of 81, he continues to display impressive entrepreneurial skills. When he established his business in Little Saigon, he reconnected with trusted business partners from Vietnam before his departure in 1975. Soon, he owned multiple supermarkets and eventually became the first Vietnamese refugee to own a food distribution company that services over one hundred Vietnamese restaurants.

Reflecting on his life, it can be argued that Frank Jao's success is undeniably influenced, at least in part, by his Chinese ancestry. Born to a Chinese father and a Vietnamese mother, Jao has effectively leveraged his Chinese connections. While most Vietnamese refugees sought to raise capital within the Vietnamese community through personal or family savings, "hui" practices of money lending and borrowing, and conventional loans, Jao managed to secure funding through a Taiwanese investment network. With a global perspective of what Little Saigon could become, he reached out extensively to attract investments to the community.

Another noteworthy entrepreneur of Chinese Vietnamese heritage is David Trần, the creator of Sriracha sauce, who fluently speaks both Cantonese and Vietnamese at home. Alongside numerous Vietnamese entrepreneurs of Chinese origin, these individuals have been widely recognized by the local business community as pivotal contributors to the economic development and community growth of Little Saigon.

Before 1975, Chinese Vietnamese made up a small percentage, just over five percent, of the South Vietnamese population. However, they held a significant share, more than seventy percent, of the nation's commerce. The majority of Chinese Vietnamese hailed from southern provinces in China such as Guizhou, Chaozhou, Fuzhou, Guangxi, Guangdong, and Hainan, which were located east of Haiphong in North Vietnam. When Saigon fell, many Chinese Vietnamese, as descendants of migrants, were among the first to flee Vietnam, which explains their prominent presence in Little Saigon.

The prominence of Chinese Vietnamese in Vietnam's commerce can be traced back to the period of Chinese rule over Vietnam from 111 BC to AD 939 when Vietnam regained its independence. Chinese migrants to Vietnam included colonizers such as administrators, landlords, and farmers, as well as political refugees seeking to escape upheaval in different parts of the Chinese Empire. Over the centuries, Vietnam served as a safe haven for Chinese refugees fleeing political turbulence, with a steady migration of Chinese refugees arriving by the 18th century. These migrants, with their astute business skills and industrious farming practices, assisted Vietnamese emperors, particularly during the reigns of Kings Minh Mạng and Gia Long, in expanding their territorial control over the Mekong Delta region in exchange for political protection and economic privileges.

Trần Thành, a local oncologist and the brother of my brother Dương's wife, has parents who originated from Guizhou and migrated to North Vietnam in the late 1940s. Known among his business partners as "Uncle Tứ," Trần Tứ was fluent in Guizhousese, Vietnamese, French, and English, reflecting the complexities of his relationship with Vietnam. During the French colonial era, which lasted from 1887 to 1954, the presence of Chinese Vietnamese in the country's economy grew rapidly with the approval of the French authorities. As a political strategy to exert control over the rebellious Vietnamese population, the French forged an agreement with China that encouraged Chinese immigration to Vietnam and allowed the Chinese to collaborate with France in managing key sectors of the economy. Initially, this partnership revolved around rice production and trade, later expanding to mining, selected industries, real estate, and money lending.[5]

As the Chinese population increased during the French colonial period,[6] assimilation through intermarriage became more common. Generation after generation, Chinese Vietnamese developed their own distinct identities. They emerged as a new Sino-Vietnamese ruling class, forming a transnational community within the larger society, distinct from their ancestral traditions and culture in the North but not fully assimilated into Vietnamese nationalism. Tứ's family, descendants of Guizhou emigrants, belonged to the first wave of refugees arriving in Orange County. Subsequent generations no longer speak Chinese and they proudly consider themselves "100% Vietnamese." Like their great-grandparents, I trust that they carry within them the entrepreneurial spirit and business acumen that contributed to the growth of Little Saigon.

To me, *Dân Tiếp Vụ* holds a special place in local history as the first grocery store in this enclave. However, it was the Chinese Vietnamese who introduced the community to the concept of a full-service supermarket with *Nam Hoa*, followed by chain stores like *Thuận Phát*, which eventually expanded to twelve locations. These enterprising individuals secured funding from local Chinese American investors and obtained loans from Chinese banks in the area. Chinese Vietnamese business owners established connections with well-established food supply chains and collaborated with multi-million dollar import-export wholesalers based in Los Angeles. Trần Dũ, for example, developed a network of trusted creditors and partners to support his operations. My mother was one of Trần Dũ's longstanding business partners, and she often spoke highly of him, saying, "He is a businessman I trust."

I would argue that, unlike others, Frank Jao took a more institutional approach, seeking substantial funding for his ventures. Recognizing the growth potential of the community, Jao established a commercial real estate development business in 1978. His first project involved building a small shopping center in Westminster for a Hong Kong investor, which proved to be highly lucrative. Jao recognized the importance of building networks with Chinese investors within the Vietnamese enclave. In an interview with the Orange County Register, Jao mentioned that he had cultivated a network of "mostly Asian investors," including notable figures such as Usman Admadjala, an Indonesian tycoon of Chinese origin, and Roger Chen, the Taiwanese-born founder of the 99 Ranch Market grocery chain.[7]

THE PASSIONS OF A PEOPLE—ENVISIONING LITTLE SAIGON

Bùi Thọ Khang leaves me a lasting impression as a quintessential Vietnamese entrepreneur. Unlike the Chinese Vietnamese who sought business networks within Chinese communities, Vietnamese refugees like him relied on their fellow Vietnamese. With a bachelor's degree in Management Information Systems from California State University Fullerton and a programming certificate from the Control Data Institute, Bùi Thọ Khang began his career servicing computers at local supermarkets. Recognizing the operational inefficiencies in these stores, he took the initiative to establish his own company, Universal Computers, in 1988. Bùi Thọ Khang's business idea was to develop scanners for local supermarkets, enhancing checkout efficiency and inventory management. His idea proved successful, leading to a flood of orders and the flourishing of his business.

Late at night, Bùi Thọ Khang tirelessly wrote code for enthusiastic Chinese supermarket owners serving the Vietnamese community. It was during this time that he and his partner, Huỳnh Thọ, made the decision to open their own supermarket, driven by the desire to run a more cost-effective store and better cater to the specific culinary needs of their compatriots. This marked the beginning of their journey as entrepreneurs in the supermarket industry. Bùi Thọ Khang eventually became the CEO of Dalat supermarket. Today, alongside his business partner Huỳnh Thọ, he owns seven supermarkets: *Á Đông, Saigon, Dalat*, and three *Green Farms* markets located in Garden Grove, Gardena, and El Monte.

As a business scholar, I couldn't help but inquire about his competitive strategy. Bùi Thọ Khang emphasized the importance of labeling products in Vietnamese whenever possible and expressed his mission to provide employment opportunities for community members. He was determined to prevent his people from relying on financial assistance and welfare, envisioning a self-sufficient and prosperous community.

While Vietnamese restaurants in Little Saigon typically consist of family-style businesses with a limited number of tables, Chinese restaurants are known for their capacity to host weddings and banquets. Chinese restaurants such as *Seafood Cove* and *Seafood Paradise* have emerged throughout Little Saigon, capturing a significant share of the banquet business. It wasn't until 1987 that *Grand Garden* opened its doors on Bolsa Avenue, providing a Vietnamese venue and becoming a local landmark. Mr. Trần Cung, the owner, described the interior design of his restaurant as a departure from the vibrant and busy decor typical of Chinese restaurants, incorporating a touch of French romanticism. Since its establishment, Grand Garden has become a sought-after venue for Vietnamese political and cultural events.

Chinese Vietnamese community members had the option to leave Little Saigon, but individuals like Trần Dũ and Frank Jao chose to stay and contribute to building a vibrant society, creating a sense of home, and forging new identities in their new country. Chinese Vietnamese individuals are essential pillars of the community, making significant economic, social, and political contributions to Little Saigon. The relationship between the Vietnamese and Chinese Vietnamese has always existed in various modes of reciprocity and solidarity. Cultural exchanges spanning generations and crossing borders between southern Chinese provinces have shaped a complex love-hate relationship. For a moment, a smile creeps across my face. In my lectures, I often discuss the concept of "coopetition"—the intricate blend of cooperation and competition. Little Saigon serves as an exemplary case, demonstrating that coopetition, where cooperation and competition go hand in hand, allows this diverse enclave to grow steadily and harmoniously.

THE LIGHTS OF A CITY—AWAKENING TO IMMIGRANT POLITICS

In 1992, Tony Quang Lâm made history as the first Vietnamese refugee to be elected as a city council member in Westminster, marking a significant milestone for the new immigrant community. His election garnered national attention, serving as a symbol of Little Saigon's growing political influence in local elections and as a model for other Vietnamese communities across the nation. However, with this pride came great responsibility.

Despite being a part-time elected official, Tony Lâm dedicated an extensive amount of time to the development of Little Saigon. His schedule was filled with meetings with community leaders, business associations, fraternity gatherings, and various cultural and religious activities as he actively worked for the betterment of his community. "The Little Saigon community activists expected me to serve the community well," Tony Lâm reflected from the comfort of his home. While he had the desire to serve his community, he soon realized the political realities that come with being a public official in a diverse, multicultural city.

As Tony Lâm worked towards officially recognizing Little Saigon as a distinct geographical entity, he encountered several legal and logistical challenges that were previously unknown to him as a private citizen. He shared with me the difficulties he faced in garnering sufficient political support for the resolution to recognize the enclave, as well as budget allocation and traffic concerns raised by non-Vietnamese council members. "I tried to convince the city council that beautifying Bolsa Avenue would be a valuable investment for the city," Tony Lâm recounted. "However, I was told that the tax income generated by merchants in Little Saigon was not substantial enough to allocate funds for significant public projects. It was challenging to confront this reality." Nonetheless, Tony Lâm successfully negotiated funding for his beautification projects. "I wanted residents and visitors to remember the street lights in Saigon, so we worked hard to find black antique French street lights. They are now a unique feature in Orange County."

Throughout his tenure, Tony Lâm faced countless issues and challenges, including the Trần Trường incident and the intricate process of securing "Little Saigon" freeway signs. These ethnic politics and Tony Lâm's eventful years as a councilman are further explored in Chapter 14. Despite the turbulence, Tony Lâm deserves credit for encouraging residents to actively participate in public office and pursue positions of leadership within their community.

THE 13 FREEWAY SIGNS—VISUALIZING A NEW COMMUNITY

Every time I take the 405 freeway to reach Little Saigon, the sight of the "Little Saigon" sign fills me with a deep sense of belonging and pride. Looking back, June 17, 1988 was a momentous occasion and a day etched in the memory of many Little Saigon residents. After years of persistent lobbying by community leaders through various governmental channels, California Governor George Deukmejian officially recognized the community. The governor, along with numerous local officials and dignitaries, gathered at *Phước Lộc Thọ* mall to inaugurate Little Saigon as an economic and cultural hub, unveiling the new freeway exit signs that guided motorists to the largest Vietnamese community outside of Vietnam.

On the center stage, a freshly made banner caught everyone's attention. It boldly proclaimed, "LITTLE SAIGON'S INAUGURATION: A HISTORICAL DAY FOR THE VIETNAMESE COMMUNITY." The red letters against a vibrant yellow background matched the four South Vietnamese flags fluttering alongside the lone American flag atop a 142" x 42" freeway sign.

Though no banner displayed beautifully inscribed Vietnamese characters, elegantly dressed women, including Miss Vietnamese 1988, stood on stage and assisted the governor in unveiling the sign that read "LITTLE SAIGON, NEXT EXIT."

It was an official declaration. The California State Transportation Department erected 13 signs along the exit ramps of Interstate 405 and State Route 22, the main thoroughfares leading to the cities of Orange County. For the Vietnamese community of Little Saigon, it was a historic day. As Thuy Vo Dang, librarian and archivist at the Orange County and Southeast Asia Archive in UC Irvine, argues in her dissertation on the local community, these signs symbolize a profound sense of belonging.

As Governor George Deukmejian unveiled the sign, jubilant refugees joined in chants of pride. However, the journey to reach this destination was filled with obstacles, cracks, and bumps. Upon reviewing the behind-the-scenes stories, I couldn't help but think that the dramatic quest for the sign would make for a captivating Hollywood movie.

The first obstacle in naming the community was officially selecting the name "Little Saigon." In my interviews, it remains unclear who exactly coined this name for the community of over 300,000 Vietnamese-origin residents. It may have resonated with those who carried the history of the country they left behind. Many Vietnamese Americans may have drawn inspiration from their visits to "Little Tokyo" in Los Angeles. They were likely aware of the existence of "Little Italy" in Manhattan, New York City, immortalized by the Oscar-winning movie "The Godfather," which had captivated them before their departure from Vietnam in 1975. Perhaps someone believes that the name held the memories and cultural roots of their Saigon in Vietnam. I previously mentioned Du Mien's news article following Lisa Kwong's report on a "Little Bit of Saigon."

The search for identity in Little Saigon is an ongoing journey. With the growing presence of Vietnamese American officials at various levels of government, the community exercises its creativity in incorporating Vietnamese street names into the enclave. In 2015, Mayor Trí Tà of Westminster proudly unveiled a street sign with the name "Saigon," symbolizing the community's pride and connection to its heritage. In 2017, on the anniversary of the fall of Saigon, Mayor Trí Tà and Deputy Mayor Tyler Diep joined community leaders to celebrate Vietnamese King Trần Hưng Đạo by designating Bolsa Avenue as an alternate name. These projects are part of an ongoing effort to interweave Vietnamese representations and identity into the fabric of the locale, serving as a vivid tribute to the Vietnamese refugees who arrived in the country in 1975. Through these acts of renaming, the community strives to shape a sense of place that reflects their own experiences and aspirations.

NOTES

1. https://vacoc.org. In 2018, the chamber reported it had more than 1,000 active members, arguably about 6 to 8% of the registered businesses owners of Vietnamese ancestry https://vietbao.com/a276674/phong-thuong-mai-viet-my-vacoc-to-chuc-tiec-ra-mat-hoi-dong-dieu-hanh-2018-2019-va-trao-giai-thuong
2. Members of the committee include Van Van Nguyen and Duy Trung Dao.
3. Frank Jao, Quách Danh, Dr. Cơ Phạm, Thanh Nguyễn
4. https://www.ocregister.com/2015/04/30/frank-jaos-story-from-refugee-to-business-mogul/
5. The French aided the Chinese; Chinese migrants were subject to a variety of heavy taxes and special fees, in return for preferential trade and industry status.
6. From 138,284 Chinese migrants in 1908 to 607,045 in 1953. Amer R. French Policies towards the Chinese in Vietnam: A study of migration and colonial responses, Recherches en sciences humaines sur l'Asie du Sud-Est, 2010, Vol 16, pp. 57–80. https://journals.openedition.org/moussons/192
7. https://www.ocregister.com/2015/04/30/frank-jaos-story-from-refugee-to-business-mogul/

Chapter 5

Enchanting Nostalgia

A DANCE WITH THE PAST

Most immigrants navigate between two cultures—the culture attached and inherited from the home country left behind and the host country's culture that requires assimilation, adaptation, and adoption. For me, having lived and worked in three continents, professionally galloping from many parts of the United States, Europe, and Asia, I straddle these cultures, sometimes feeling that I belong to each uniquely. At times, however, I sense that I am a spiritless bystander, watching from the sidelines as each country performs its particular ways of being, inherently.

My American colleagues sympathetically tease me that my eloquent emails have the flair of French diplomacy. On the other side of the Atlantic, my European friends contend that my administrative style, at times, is too simplistic and at times realistic but rude. "Just like Americans," they say. The third side of my identity is too sweet and mellow, "just like Asians," they say, smiling with warm friendship. But when I worked in Hong Kong, people asked me, "Why do you look Chinese but don't speak the language?"

The one thing that most friends and colleagues seem to agree upon is food and good company. When they invite me out to dinner, they say, "Let's go to a Vietnamese restaurant. We trust you to order. And we know you can answer our questions about Vietnam as well." Perhaps, this is where my identity is—woven into the deep roots of Vietnamese food and language.

Even as of today, I'm never truly home. These disparate and conflicting cultural habits and identities permit me to view a sense of myself as a "self" dynamically. However, often, I am a divided "self" that doesn't have a permanent location to call home. Wherever I am, I am mindful of the culture, and I am thankful. But I long for the other cultures when I am away from a particular country– the people in the U.S., the eloquent beauty of the Old Continent, and the frenetic change of the Far East.

When I shuffled between the two Saigon's—the original, now renamed Ho Chi Minh City, and Little Saigon—this sentiment of longing for each culture filled me with a wistfulness for the past and a life that no longer exists. As a globe-trotter and someone who lives in the margins of identity, I intimately comprehend the intricacies of defining or calling one place home. Yet, the Little Saigon community has performed this act of self-determination and self-defining since landing in the U.S. and looking for safety in the definition of "new" home. The people of Little Saigon construct home and identity between cultures in their daily lives with the customs and traditions they brought from Vietnam and from the experiences of war and healing trauma.

BLOSSOMS IN THE WIND—THE FIRST *TẾT* FESTIVAL IN EXILE

Whenever possible, I made it a custom to visit my parents and siblings in Orange County for the Tết Festival, or the Lunar New Year. The festival was a time to visit friends and relatives, and many community organizers like to feel the community's pulse during the festivities. For the Vietnamese, Tết is the most important national holiday. It is the time for family reunions and celebration.

Over the years, Tết events in Little Saigon have grown, with longer parades, more flower markets—with a variety of ornamental plants such as peach blossom, the apricot tree, and the kumquat tree—more gifts and treats to buy at local markets, and of course, more restaurants in which to taste culinary delights.

I drove to a machine shop in the industrial zone of Santa Ana early on a Sunday morning in 2019 to track down Nguyễn Ngọc Cang. Local organizers credit him for making the first Tết festival in Little Saigon a reality. Nguyễn Ngọc Cang works as an engineer in a machine shop owned by his classmate Tony Tài Cao. The two of them graduated with mechanical engineering degrees from California Polytechnic State University at Pomona.

Sitting in the cold and a bit dusty design room of the machine shop that Tony Cao founded in 1986, we chatted about his career and Little Saigon. "But my passion is in music," Nguyễn Ngọc Cang said, when I asked about his work. Nguyễn Ngọc Cang spoke with a soft voice, adding, "Sorry I am just recovering from a cold. But if you wish to know about all the social events in the community, just ask me. I was the guy who organized the very first Tết Festival in 1977. It was quite a learning experience. So anytime, any association that wants to set up a public event, I am there to help them."

Nguyễn Ngọc Cang dresses casually, like most Vietnamese Americans living in Little Saigon. And like many Vietnamese Americans, he zips around town in a Toyota Camry, sipping on "café sữa đá" (Vietnamese iced coffee). Like many in the community, he has two jobs. He shuttles back and forth between Tony Cao's American Machine Shop—a business that designs and builds metal and polymers parts and products—and his small music studio. Nguyễn Ngọc Cang teaches piano and violin to children of Vietnamese ancestry. But to seasoned event organizers of Little Saigon, Nguyễn Ngọc Cang is known as an unsung hero. Over the last forty years, he has lent a hand organizing Tết, Middle Autumn Festival, and the annual "Black April" event commemorating the fall of Saigon.

"I did not know how complicated it was to organize a large-scale public event. Every step required a city permit . . . I had to drive from one office to another, the City Hall, the Police Department, the Fire Department . . . you name it." Nguyễn Ngọc Cang recalled he received a citation for failing to seek a permit to set up the stage and its complex audio-video systems. Then, he received another citation for forgetting to inform the local police about the massive public gathering. Citation after citation, ending with another fine for setting up food booths without a permit. Nevertheless, Nguyễn Ngọc Cang make magic happen, and to the delight of the residents, the festival lit up Little Saigon in glory. The community calls him the fixer; Nguyễn Ngọc Cang knows the ins and outs of meeting government compliances.

"Now, I know the tricks of the trade," Nguyễn Ngọc Cang said, nodding with a timid smile.

Over the years, Nguyễn Ngọc Cang continues to organize the Tết Festivals in Little Saigon that now attract more than 100,000 guests annually—the largest Tết event in the world outside of Vietnam. Tết in Little Saigon is a celebration of its half a million inhabitants. It is not as grandiose as the Rose Parade in Pasadena and not as majestic as the Macy's Thanksgiving Day Parade in New York City. Still, Nguyễn Ngọc Cang has helped create an event into an annual week-long tradition with live entertainment, a showcase of regional foods, spectacular fireworks show, and entertainers, playing music popular before 1975. It has become an annual inter-city festival that attracts visitors from near and far.

Forty-seven years after the first Tết in Little Saigon, Nguyễn Ngọc Cang and local leaders have slowly handed the tasks of preserving the festival to the next generation. This is another succession issue, I promptly figured out. We all age, and help is eventually needed. In recent years, the Vietnamese Student Associations (UVSA) Union in Southern California, a collaboration of eleven local universities, has been the principal organizing entity for the annual event. The administrations of the colleges UVSA members attend only recognize the official flag of the Socialist Republic of Vietnam. However,

UVSA honors the spirit and souls of Little Saigon by displaying the "yellow flag with three red bands" of the Saigon government.

Cloe Nguyễn, a student at California State at Long Beach, participated in the Tết parade. She and nineteen teammates carried a gigantic 20 x 40 foot long South Vietnamese flag. "I am only nineteen, and I have never been to Vietnam. This is the flag that my grandparents hang at home. They seem happy here, but they are somehow homesick, and the flag soothes them," Cloe Nguyễn told us. I heard compassion in her voice, and I saw her face glow as she talked about her family. "I want to honor their lives and the past that they narrate to me. The flag means everything to them."

After our conversation, Nguyễn Ngọc Cang walked with me to the parking lot. "Students come and go. They work hard and are devoted to preserving our culture and identity. But when it comes to organizing big events, they don't have the experience that I have. So, I am here, still doing the same thing," he said, smiling. Cang opened the door and stepped into his white Toyota Camry. He waved as he turned his car in the direction of his studio. I watched his car disappear down the street, and I felt for an instant as if I was again back in Switzerland as a student.

In Switzerland, I also had to organize the Tết event. Like Nguyễn Ngọc Cang, I had no experience. I had to learn the ABCs of organizing a big event by trial and error. I enjoyed the experience, but unlike Cang, I didn't devote 40 plus years to the Tết festival. I did it because with my compatriots, I wanted to showcase our identity through arts and culture to our Swiss friends. But, life goes on for students, once they graduate. Community members like Nguyễn Ngọc Cang are unsung heroes who define the soul of Little Saigon.

THE LOTUS BLOOMS FLAGRANTLY—CULTURAL HISTORY AND KING HÙNG'S DAY

April 21, 2018. It was my birthday, and I was pleased that it fell on a Saturday. I considered inviting my siblings out for a party on another beautiful day in California. Instead, I followed the suggestion of my cousin, Bùi Văn Luyện, and visited the King Hùng shrine on Bolsa Ave in Westminster. The atmosphere was vibrant and bustling as hundreds of residents had gathered to commemorate the king's 4,897th anniversary according to the Vietnamese lunar calendar. The surroundings were adorned with exquisite lotus flower bouquets, colorful festival flags, and a splendid array of traditional long silk tunics, reminiscent of royal celebrations.

The Vietnamese people claim to be the "Con rồng, cháu tiên" (children of dragons and grandchildren of goddesses). According to the creation myth, taught globally, the Vietnamese first came to the world through Âu Cơ. Âu

Cơ was a beautiful and immortal fairy living in the mountains. She was the daughter of Emperor Ai, who married Lord Lạc Long Quân, the son of the dragon goddess Thanh Long, who ruled both the sky and the ocean.

Âu Cơ gave birth to a sac of 100 eggs, which hatched into 100 boys. Lạc eventually claimed that he and Âu Cơ were incompatible, like fire and water. He was a descendant of the Dragon, and she was a Fairy. Each took half of the children. Âu Cơ took fifty of her children to the mountainous north, and Lạc led fifty to the south sea. The oldest, eventually, succeeded his father and ruled the land as the Hùng King.

As I joined the procession of flowers, silks, and flags, I reached the shrine and paused to take in the sight of the densely packed crowd. It was a remarkable gathering with representation from numerous local businesses, political affiliations, and religious associations, all coming together to celebrate the occasion. The presence of Vietnamese American elected officials was prominent, a reflection of a cultural practice they had brought from their homeland. It reminded me of a past experience at the University of Đà-Nẵng in Central Vietnam back in 2005. During my visit, I attended the wedding of the son of the library's vice director, who was graciously hosting me. I recall feeling hungry as the delicious food grew cold while the local officials delivered lengthy speeches. Apart from the Vietnamese American Student Association and a vibrant group of teenagers from the King Hùng folklore dance troupe, the majority of attendees were senior citizens, similar to the scene at the vice director's son's wedding lunch.

Elders approached the shrine, solemnly placing on the altar a personal royal "linh vị" (a wood plate with Vietnamese-Chinese scripts honoring the dead) and pots of soil from the sacred land of Phú Thọ where King Hùng had reigned. The drumbeats, candles, and burning incense announced the beginning of the traditional rituals. In their prayers, those around me, in this sacred moment, offered gratitude to the king who had founded Vietnam.

Next to the central altar of King Hùng, photos of five generals of the South Vietnamese Army that lost their lives during the fall of Saigon were arranged on the lower section of the shrines' dome ("chính điện"). After the ritual, one local leader after another came to the podium, telling success stories of Vietnamese overseas. They thanked King Hùng for uniting the nation of *Việts*. I thought it was an ideal narrative of rescue. In front of the altar, invited speakers expressed a sense of humility and pride. Then, as I expected, the speeches turned political. The speakers addressed the challenges facing the people of Vietnam at home and abroad. And, under the roof of King Hùng's shrine, they collectively and unanimously pledge unity. I heard the word "unity" again and again. "We need to unite so that we can rescue the land that we lost," the voices cried out.

Three young adults stood to my left, positioned near the podium. One of them, the president of a Student Association, gracefully walked towards the stage. She expressed her gratitude to the senior leaders for their tireless efforts in preserving their rich cultural heritage. I was genuinely impressed. Her command of the Vietnamese language and her profound understanding of Vietnamese traditions exceeded my expectations. It was a bit disconcerting for me, having left Vietnam for Switzerland when I was seventeen. This young student was likely born in the United States, yet her connection to her Vietnamese roots was undeniable. I couldn't help but smile when another nearby student remarked, "We are the children of dragons and the grandchildren of goddesses, forever separated. How can we ever find our way back to each other?"

Indeed, it is the power of the rescue narrative that will likely ensure the continuity of this cherished cultural ritual.

During the lunch banquet that followed the ceremony, the organizers eagerly discussed their plans to raise funds for the purchase of Regent West, a recently closed restaurant in Santa Ana, with the intention of constructing a new shrine. The atmosphere at the King Hùng ceremony transcended the past and reinforced the deep sense of belonging for its people. It was evident that the community found solace and a strong connection to their history and identity through such meaningful traditions.

Leaving the event, I carried a profound sense of fulfillment. Although I had learned about the story of King Hùng during my elementary school days in Nha Trang, the war had restricted large gatherings, unless approved by the government and heavily guarded by the military. Thus, I had never witnessed the grandeur of this ceremony until that memorable day. The night was still young, and I had the opportunity to enjoy a bowl of *phở* with my cousin, who is twelve years my senior. I yearned to delve into the activities and experiences of Vietnamese refugees in Little Saigon. While my question about the community's romanticized nostalgia remained unanswered, it was a birthday celebration that will forever hold a special place in my heart.

KEEP THE LIBRARY RUNNING

To prepare for my fifth trip to Orange County for this book, I reached out to Du Miên, one of the esteemed community journalists, requesting an interview. My sister, Phong Thu, had urged me to speak with him, stating, "If you want to know the history of Little Saigon, talk to Mr. Du Miên. He knew our dad and often refers to him as 'a comrade or something.'" While my sister and I are unsure of the exact nature of their camaraderie, I was eager to learn more. After promptly receiving a response from Du Miên, an invitation was extended to meet during the ongoing celebration of the 20th anniversary of the "Thư Viện Việt Nam" (Vietnamese Library). The address was provided, and we agreed to speak further upon my arrival. I felt flattered by his words of respect for my father, but I did not inquire about their connection. The email agenda indicated that he was one of the library's founders.

I made a stop at 10872 Westminster Avenue in Westminster. A striking, cherry-red street sign bearing the words "Thư Viện Việt Nam" (Vietnamese Library) caught my attention from a distance. A gathering of over 200 individuals had convened in the conference room. Du Miên, donning a theatrical pink suit, commanded the center stage at the podium. "The library's collection comprises cherished books and artifacts generously donated by our residents," he announced. "We established this library as a sanctuary for some of the most valuable publications from South Vietnam." With over 2,000 books spanning various subjects, the library also housed a captivating assortment of artifacts, including a collection of currency, stamps from the Republic of Vietnam, and traditional Vietnamese musical instruments.

Most of the founders, all seemingly in their seventies, were in attendance, while Du Miên acknowledged the passing of a few members. He appealed to a handful of younger individuals, likely in their mid-thirties, stating, "We need you to be prepared to assume leadership roles in the library." Raising his walking cane, Du Miên added, "We must safeguard the pride of our community, which is at risk of being overshadowed by dark forces." While I did not fully grasp the meaning behind "dark forces," I surmised that the center faced challenges such as limited donations and insufficient volunteers to sustain library operations, and there may be concerns about the perceived value of the collected books in the future.

Thư Viện Vietnam, which opened in 1998 in the heart of Little Saigon, was founded by members of the 1.0 generation who recognized the importance of preserving their national heritage as they approached retirement age. They established the library with the goal of gathering books published before 1975, aiming to maintain a strong sense of identity in their new homeland. "We have to collect the remaining copies of books that the enemies burned at home," one of the founding members passionately expressed.

For any ethnic community, the preservation of culture naturally connects transnationally to the homeland. At the library, the trauma of the 1975 exodus was vividly omnipresent among the attendees. In the reading area, I overheard conversations that hinted at the fact that many Vietnamese Americans had not found closure regarding the "loss of their homeland."

"I had a two-hectare farm with numerous fruit trees in Vĩnh Long, in Vietnam's Mekong Delta. Now it's in the hands of some 'bộ-đội' (North Vietnamese army soldiers)," a man in his seventies shared with his friends. It was clear that this wasn't the first time he had recounted this story. Although more than forty years had passed, reconciling with the current government back home remained a taboo topic. Speaker after speaker, the founding members of the library emphasized the importance of unity in promoting Vietnamese language and culture in Little Saigon and supporting their compatriots in Vietnam.

I had anticipated that societal racism and cultural oppression would be key concerns at the meeting. However, to my surprise, I didn't overhear anyone expressing worries about life in the U.S. Given my personal experience of the difficulties of assimilating into a new culture, it struck me that this group seemed unconcerned about American culture. What excited and bothered them the most was the opportunity to share their existence with the world.

They were thrilled to learn that I was writing about their experiences in English, intending to share them with a wider audience. A few attendees approached me as the meeting concluded, offering me spring rolls and shrimp salad and sharing their contact information. "If you would like to know more about what we do, we have a gathering at my house. We will discuss our book collection drive," they kindly invited me. As a college professor and a fellow bookworm, I deeply admired their love for reading. Seeing these elders holding onto the books that had shaped their upbringing, I felt a strong sense of solidarity and fellowship.

During the lunch break, an elderly gentleman in his early eighties, dressed in a meticulously pressed army uniform, led me to a brown oak bookcase. He opened the glass door and carefully retrieved a book titled Việt Nam Văn Học Sử Yếu (History of Vietnamese Literature) written by Dương Quảng Hàm and published in 1968. "I brought this book with me when I left Vietnam. It's an incredible piece of academic work, but I believe the communists must have destroyed most copies. The back cover indicates that the U.S. Agency funded its publication for International Development," he explained, examining the book closely. Instantly, I recognized the book.

My father had sent me a copy when I was a student in Switzerland. In his letter, he wrote, "Son, take the time to read this book. Don't forget your Vietnamese heritage."

Considering the circumstances of the people gathered at the event, many of whom were among the first to leave Vietnam, I realized that books were precious possessions, even though their weight and limited carrying capacity posed challenges. Looking around the library, I pondered the intrinsic value of this collection of 2,000 books. Du Miên and his fellow founders believed they were invaluable. As a student more concerned about exams than the history of the Vietnamese language, perhaps I had not fully grasped their significance. But now, I did.

I firmly shook the hand of the gentleman standing before me and turned around, holding the book close to my chest. "When I return home, I must finish reading this book," I resolved. My father had passed away, and I would never have the chance to express my deep appreciation for his thoughtful gesture. But he took the time to send me the book when I was a student, which means the world to me. And now, the Vietnamese Library has a copy of the book, allowing me to borrow it and read the words my father lovingly urged me to explore all those years ago. Placing an envelope in the wood donation box, I quietly whispered to Trí Tà, the mayor of Westminster, and a few Vietnamese American elected officials standing nearby, trying to capture their attention. "Perhaps we should consider donating this collection to a public library or a college library that would take good care of them," I suggested. Trí Tà smiled at me but maintained an air of perplexity.

A year and a half later, Du Miên and eleven of his library colleagues flew to Hawai'i for a summer vacation they had planned, but which was postponed for a year due to the COVID-19 pandemic. When I informed Du Miên that copies of books published before 1975 could now be found in several bookstores in District 1 of Saigon, Vietnam, I noticed the same perplexed expression in his eyes. "I've heard that Quán Sách Mùa Thu (Autumn Bookstore) now has thousands of books printed before 1975, some dating back even before the war. They are now being legally sold as collectibles."

THE SOULS OF EXILES—COUNTRY AND HEARTS LEFT BEHIND

Du Miên and his fellow visionaries hold a clear purpose for their Vietnamese Library: to collect and preserve publications that the authorities would rather be forgotten. However, Little Saigon possesses another significant asset. Many writers who managed to escape from Vietnam have chosen Little Saigon as their literary capital.

Growing up as a high school student in Nha Trang, a charming coastal town in Central Vietnam, my exposure to Vietnamese literature was limited to the few courses required for the national exam. Most of the assigned readings were from classical authors associated with tumultuous times involving the Chinese, the Xiêm, and internal conflicts. These writers included Nguyễn Du (1766–1820), Nguyễn Công Trứ (1778–1858), and Cao Bá Quát (1809–1855). Additionally, in my courses, I had the opportunity to read works by other esteemed novelists who had grown up under French colonial rule and experienced transnational cultural influences, such as Khái Hưng (1896–1947), Nhất Linh (1906–1963), Hàn Mặc Tử (1912–1940), and several other celebrated writers and poets.

However, it wasn't until I visited Little Saigon that I had the chance to meet many of these celebrated authors in person. I had the privilege of meeting Zen

Master Thích Nhất Hạnh (1926–2022), Nhật Tiến (1936–2020), Du Tử Lê (1924–2019), Bùi Bảo Trúc, Trần Dạ Từ, Nhã Ca, and a host of other writers who have embraced Little Saigon as a haven for intellectual and literary freedom. Lê Đình Điểu and other notable figures, including Lê Văn Khoa and Phạm Phú Minh, respected journalists, writers, composers, and artists before 1975, established the Vietnamese American Arts & Letters Association (VAALA) in 1991. Their goal was to create an artistic and cultural space for the refugee community, and their activities initially revolved around organizing film festivals, art exhibitions, performances, community art classes, and book launch events.

Over the years, novelists, poets, and historians have held book launches and readings at venues such as Việt Báo, Người Việt, Radio VNCR, and restaurant banquet halls. VAALA provides a grassroots alternative to these events. Whenever I visit the community, I make it a point to stop by Tú Quỳnh bookstore, the first bookstore in the community, which was opened in 1979 by Đỗ Ngọc Yến and his wife. The store, though small and with sagging bookshelves, is filled with an assortment of books and audio/video materials that are lovingly curated.

I find myself grabbing new releases by various authors from the bookstore, and my study at home has now transformed into a smaller version of the Tú Quỳnh library. The list of authors on my shelves continues to grow, and the variety of topics, particularly memoirs recounting the journeys after 1975, fills my quiet reading hours with contemplation on life. Some retired military officers and government officials have written their versions of the history of the war, and I approach these works with thoughtful consideration. At times, I turn to the handful of fictional stories that line my study, finding solace in the world of imagination.

However, in my view, the true literary brilliance lies with a select few authors who established their reputations in their homeland, Vietnam. This dynamic literary circle is small, comprising only half a dozen authors whom I deeply admire: Nhật Tiến, Du Tử Lê, Nhã Ca, Trần Dạ Từ, Lê Tất Điều, Đỗ Quy Toàn, Trần Mộng Tú, and Bùi Bích Hà. They eloquently write about life in exile with profound insights and nuanced complexity, capturing the essence of those who fled their homeland.

Nhật Tiến, who passed away in his Irvine home in 2020, was one of the boat people who established a new home in Orange County in 1980 at the age of forty-four. He continued to write, reflecting on the lives of Vietnamese in exile. In 2018, I had the opportunity to meet him at an event commemorating the anniversary of beloved musician Trịnh Công Sơn's passing. I praised his work and inquired about his efforts to uphold the quality of Vietnamese literature. He simply nodded and said, "Thank you."

Du Tử Lê, who arrived in California in 1975, was an award-winning poet and novelist during the war. Renowned for his children's books, Lê gained fame for his love poems, many of which were turned into songs. Du Tử Lê's poetry explores themes of love and loss, hope and despair, passion and detachment, and reunion and separation—all familiar to soldiers on the frontlines longing for the safe return of their loved ones ("Anh tiền tuyến em hậu phương"). The poems-turned-songs by Du Tử Lê ignite my interest, with lines such as:

> Don't ever ask me why
> we become lovers
> my lips turn hot
> my arms get cold
> my body trembles
> my legs become shaky
> and why and why.

Du Tử Lê's poems reflect a love for the land he left behind, a nation with southern heritage. In 1977, he witnessed "boat people," as they were labeled, heading into a deadly ocean, and he longed for the day he could return to Saigon. His poems imagine death and the ocean as a current that can bring him back to his motherland:

> When I die, take me to the sea
> An exile like me doesn't even have a grave
> Being buried in a strange soil, my bones can't decompose
> My soul can't go home again
> When I die, take me to the sea
> Where the water flows me away
> To the other shore where my homeland stays
> And the green bamboo range forever sways. (Du Tử Lê, 1977)

Yet, when I last met Du Tử Lê, Nhã Ca, and Trần Dạ Từ just a few weeks before Lê passed away, I found him serene and gentle. No more mustaches. No cigarette in his hand. A tender smile of a person who had seen it all. If I had not known his work, I would never have guessed that the person with whom I spoke was once intense and passionate, and a beloved figure in the literary world who employed artistic talent to speak for the souls of the people living in exile. With his passing, I was struck by another bit of sad news. A victim of COVID-19, the widow of the late Đỗ Ngọc Yến permanently closed their historical bookstore on December 31, 2020.

ETERNAL MEMORIES OF A LOVE LONG LOST—REMEMBERING HOME

Nhã Ca called me, reminding me of the then-upcoming 2019 Writing On America Awards and the Teen Writing Awards which took place in August. "We are celebrating our 20th anniversary of the program. We count on your presence," Nhã Ca said. How could I miss an event that I treasure? I first met Nhã Ca in 2004 when a mutual friend approached me to support her project "Bé Việt Văn Việt" (Vietnamese Youth writing literary work in Vietnamese). To pass the homeland culture to the next generation, they have created an annual essay contest to encourage the subsequent generations of Vietnamese Americans to speak and write in Vietnamese. I eagerly and happily volunteered to be one of her sponsors, editing a book that showcased forty-seven short essays and poems written by American children of Vietnamese descent.

I was dazzled by one of the essays:

"Many of my Vietnamese Americans have Americanized names—David Hoàng, John Nguyễn, Nathan Lê, [. . .] Just me, my name is 'Lê Trần Việt Nam.' I asked my parents (why they gave me that name) . . . 'Dad and Mom gave you a name, so that you will always remember that you are Vietnamese.' I then understood. I have a Korean friend because his parents are Koreans. My parents are Vietnamese, so I am Vietnamese too. My name is Viet Nam." Indeed, the winner of the essay contest was, Viet Nam, a 10-year old student.

Nhã Ca and Trần Dạ Từ gave their precious time to preserve the Vietnamese language in Little Saigon. They founded Việt Báo (Vietnamese Newspaper) in 1992, the second-largest daily newspaper in Vietnamese in the U.S., hoping to provide news to those who can't read in English. In addition to the annual contest on "Bé Việt viết Văn Việt," one of the most popular columns in their daily newspaper is the "Người Việt Viết về Nước Mỹ" ("Vietnamese writing on America"), which they launched in 2000. "We have had about 7,000 articles in the last 20 years," claimed Trần Dạ Từ.

Most writers are ordinary everyday Vietnamese refugees. They jot down thoughts and feelings about their daily lives in the new land. To many in Little Saigon, it is "FaceBook" for the Vietnamese community, by the people, and for the people here. To me, this column is the pulse of a community in exile. Their writing is often as eloquent as famous authors. Most of the time, the essays by everyday Vietnamese Americans exhibit raw emotions with candid displays of sincere consciousness. From the sorrow of being rejected by the children who don't understand the culture, to the joy of a mother attending her adopted daughter's graduation, their personal stories are poignant, touching the hearts of thousands of readers.

"These stories came from lonely souls written for lonely souls," Trần Dạ Từ said. "It has the highest number of readers, far more than any other column, even the breaking news of the day." In my academic career, I have helped order thousands of books for my institutions. I have also helped build libraries in Vietnam and populate them with books in the early 2000s. But my biggest fear was that reading was on a steady decline. Why do we acquire books that will just collect dust? Nhã Ca and Trần Dạ Từ might have found the magic formula. At the time of this writing, their 7,000-plus essays had been read online more than 98 million times on VietBao.com.

THE ETIQUETTE WITHIN LANGUAGE—MANNERS FIRST, LITERATURE NEXT

Just a few miles away from the Vietnam Library, the Hồng Bàng Vietnamese Language Center (Trung Tâm Việt Ngữ Hồng Bàng) held its classes at Jordan Intermediate School in Garden Grove. I felt a sense of pride knowing that my sister, Bùi Phong Thu, a senior clinical lab specialist at a private hospital in Huntington Beach, was serving her third three-year term as the head of the Hồng Bàng Center. In Vietnamese history, Hồng Bàng is a mythical giant bird associated with the creation of Vietnam. The school was founded in 1993 and stands as one of the longest-running non-profit Sunday schools dedicated to teaching the Vietnamese language. Prior to the outbreak of COVID-19, the school experienced peak enrollment with over 800 students and more than 80 volunteer instructors.

The school operates as a philanthropic organization, with organizers and teachers offering their services on a pro bono basis. The center rents the school premises on weekends to provide a range of Vietnamese language courses primarily targeting students in grades K–7. Huỳnh Thị Ngọc, the co-founder of the school, provided some context. "Most of our students are children of Vietnamese refugees, but we do have a few adults as well. Some adults enroll to learn Vietnamese because their spouses are Vietnamese," shared Huỳnh Thị Ngọc. She continued, "Our faculty consists of dedicated volunteers. Some are parents of the students they send to the center, and many of them hold college degrees from their home country. During the week, I work in medical emergency care, and taking care of the children on weekends brings me solace." I could see the pride in her eyes as she spoke. "We also have some young teachers who were once students here themselves."

The activities of the Hồng Bàng Center intrigued me. Living halfway across the Pacific Ocean from my family, I often call my sister Thu and other relatives to stay connected to our home, culture, and family. However, our conversations are frequently interrupted. "Sorry, brother, I need to take this call," my sister would say, briefly hanging up before calling back to explain. "That was a parent of one of our students. She asked if the center could offer a discount if she enrolled another child," she would say.

Through these interrupted phone calls, I've come to learn more about the challenges my sister faces. She often begins with stories of persuading someone to join their team of instructors, or dealing with situations where parents want to send their kids to the school but the children themselves are reluctant. On other occasions, it's the opposite scenario, where parents trust the center completely, while some scrutinize every aspect of their teachings. The school plays an essential and vital role in the community.

As an educator and department chair myself, I encounter my own set of daily challenges at work, including curriculum design, teaching assignments, faculty shortages, and student grievances. However, I am grateful that I do not face the same issues as my sister. "Every Sunday, just before we beat the drum to signal the start of classes, I have to ensure that all the instructors are present. We do have last-minute no-shows, which means I either have to quickly find a substitute or, if no one is available, step into the classroom and teach the class myself." It comes as no surprise that my other sister, Hải, two years younger than Thu, is at the top of the substitute teacher list.

The level of Vietnamese proficiency varies considerably. Some middle-schooler children speak pretty fluently. But they tend to switch to English when the students are by themselves. "Yes, we do the best we can. Some come here regularly. Some others don't. Some have families who speak English at home. Some don't. We are just happy that they speak Vietnamese, any level of Vietnamese," my sister said, nodding. "And the parents and students certainly appreciated the efforts of the founders and teachers at Hồng Bàng. They organize an annual 'Teachers' appreciation day.'"

My sister's comment reminded me of an interview with Trọng Minh, the author of a book series titled, *The Pride of Vietnamese Americans*. With this book, he wanted me to send a message to the readers: "Please do not miss family dinners at home. And make sure you speak Vietnamese." His resonated well a saying by Bùi Văn Bảo, an authority in writing textbooks before 1975, which is widely disseminated by the local media in Little Saigon:

> Chỉ sợ đàn con quên Việt ngữ
> Đừng lo lũ trẻ kém Anh văn

(Translation: We only fear our children forgetting Vietnamese/Don't worry, they will excel in English [in the U.S.])

Teaching Vietnamese at Hồng Bàng and other language centers across the U.S. is a reflection of the exile experience. One day, my sister Hải and another teacher engaged in a heated debate with a parent who disagreed with the spelling methods used at Hồng Bàng, specifically the whole-word-reading method and the look-and-say approach. The debate spread within the community, and a few parents raised concerns to the school board, stating, "We cannot allow your instructors to use the spelling methods adopted by the communists!"

Some older students, who watch Vietnamese movies or talk shows on YouTube, find themselves grappling with linguistic dilemmas. They question, "Why do we say 'sân bay' for airport in Vietnam, but are taught 'phi trường' at Hồng Bàng?" or "Why are there two Vietnamese words for 'government'? 'Nhà nước' in Vietnam and 'chính phủ' here at Hồng Bàng?"

"I simply tell the kids that there are two Vietnamese languages. One is the Vietnamese language we used in South Vietnam before 1975, which we refer to here as 'the freedom language'—the language spoken by your grandparents and parents. The other language is the language currently used in Vietnam. After 1975, the communists changed the grammar, vocabulary, semantics, spelling, and pronunciation," Hải explained.

I pondered how much the second generation in Little Saigon cares about the distinction between the "freedom language" and the "communist language." Most of them only speak Vietnamese with their parents and grandparents at home, so they are more familiar with the language as it existed before 1975. As a pragmatist, I shared my thoughts with my sister Hải, saying, "I understand it's a dilemma, but I do hear people in Little Saigon using vocabulary from Vietnam."

"I know. Language serves the purpose of communication. However, as a school, we must handle these sensitive issues," she replied.

To lighten the mood, I injected a bit of humor, saying, "Remember Mr. Trọng Minh, the author who glorified the Vietnamese American community? He advised, 'Just cook a great home dinner and speak Vietnamese.'" I added, "I speak French and Swiss-French. Over the years, without even noticing, I automatically switch to the local language. When I'm in France, I speak French. When I'm in Switzerland, I speak Swiss-French."

Language is indeed a complex and evolving aspect of cultural identity, and the Vietnamese community in Little Saigon continues to navigate the challenges of preserving their linguistic heritage while struggling to embrace changes and variations that arise over time and across different regions.

My thoughts returned to the Vietnamese refugees in Little Saigon, and I reflected on their dedication to promoting the "freedom" language as a means of preserving their history and identity. While sitting in silence with my sister, a fifteen-year-old boy approached her with a respectful gesture. He held his arms around his belly ("khoanh tay" in Vietnamese) and bowed his head as he greeted her. "Teacher, I seek your permission to go home," he said. I was impressed by his display of etiquette, something I hadn't witnessed in a long time.

My sister noticed me observing the interaction and explained, "We don't just teach Vietnamese as a language. We also impart Vietnamese history, tradition, and culture. We follow the educational philosophy of 'Tiên học lễ, hậu học văn' or 'students should learn proper manners or etiquette first before studying literature.'" She pointed to the slogan imprinted on the stand of the school hand drum.

I smiled at my sister and bid her farewell, mimicking the student's words and actions. As I got into my car, I took a moment to pay one last tribute to the teachers at Hồng Bàng at Jordan Intermediate. Memories flooded back to the day my father took me to kindergarten in Nha Trang, my childhood town in Central Vietnam. I recalled how the principal had patiently knelt down, guided my hands together, and taught me the art of bowing.

MUSIC BEATS AS A RHYTHM FOR THE COMMUNITY

In the fall of 1970, I carefully packed my luggage as I prepared to leave Vietnam for Switzerland to pursue my college education. Air France informed me that my baggage could only weigh 20 kilograms, presenting a challenge for a seventeen-year-old embarking on student life in a foreign land. In light of the advice from an acquaintance of my mother, who warned of Switzerland's high expenses, I packed as much as I could. Amongst the textbooks, triple-knitted sweaters, custom-made shoes, and extra-strength Tiger ointment, I managed to squeeze in half a dozen reel-to-reel audio tapes recorded by Jo Marcel, a rising singer and producer in pre-1975 Vietnam.

Like many of my classmates, I would spend hours upon hours playing and replaying these tapes without realizing that I was unwittingly embodying Daniel Levitin's later discovery. Levitin, a neuroscientist, argued that "music predates the emergence of language itself, and whenever humans come together for any reason, music is there." While strumming the songs from my homeland on an old guitar I purchased from a flea market in Fribourg, a classmate named Trần Quang, who was taking a political science course with me, suggested that I replace the original lyrics with concepts from our lectures to aid in our memorization of the abstract content.

If indeed music is a "sonic language," then the songs I had brought with me to my dorm room served as a reflection of Vietnam's recent history. This musical mirror encompassed the romanticism brought by French colonialism, the songs known as "Nhạc Tiền Chiến" (referring to songs written before the Vietnam War), and the compositions by South Vietnamese songwriters during the war. Notably, artists such as Trịnh Công Sơn, Phạm Duy, Ngô Thụy Miên,

Lê Uyên Phương, Anh Bằng, Lam Phương, and Trần Thiện Thanh captured the anxieties and hopes of millions of souls during that tumultuous period. In my generation, adults possessed vinyl records or tapes of renowned singers like Khánh Ly, Lệ Thu, Jo Marcel, and more.

Except for a few notable exceptions, such as Trịnh Công Sơn, most of the pioneering figures in the entertainment industry from the South eventually found themselves reunited in Orange County.

When my family moved to California in 1978, several well-known individuals from the music world approached us, requesting to use our restaurant as a venue for their performances. However, at the age of 69, my mother had decided to retire, so we had to decline the opportunity to host these musical giants from Vietnam.

Many people I knew made copies of their tapes and shared them with family members and friends. The sound quality was often poor, and the cassette tape labels were reproduced with blurry photos and text. Subsequent copies became increasingly difficult to hear. Nevertheless, the music from pre-1975 was everywhere, playing in family rooms, cars, restaurants, and shops. Those who couldn't find bootleg copies flocked to Tú Quỳnh bookstore to purchase their favorite tapes, which had slightly better sound quality as they were reproduced by professional audio engineers.

First-generation Vietnamese, including many from my extended family, bought multiple recordings of each album. They would say, "I can't get used to Western music. This is the music I grew up with. I want to be transported back to Saigon before 1975. Listening to these tapes soothes my soul when I miss home terribly. I always turn on my cassette player in the car on my way home. Vietnamese songs recharge me after a draining day at work."

"My brother Mai expressed his longing for new singers of his generation, saying, 'I don't have anything else to listen to now. I wish someone would offer something new.'" Mai came to the U.S. when he was eighteen and was part of a student band at Kansas State. His wish came true when a family band called Mây Bốn Phương (Clouds from the Four Corners of the Earth) relocated from Kansas to Orange County in 1978. The family released an album titled Tứ Ca Chuyện Tình Buồn (Quartet of Sad Love Stories), which became an instant hit in the exile community. The producer carefully selected the most beloved love songs, evoking memories of the rainy season in Saigon, such as "Tháng sáu trời mưa" (The Rain in June) and "Nắng thủy tinh" (Crystal Sunshine). These songs lyrically reminded Little Saigon of the joys and sorrows of love, as well as the tropical climate of their homeland.

The young, unknown singers of Mây Bốn Phương didn't possess the golden voices of established divas, but their album was proudly made in Little Saigon. "I knew them back in Kansas when they were entertaining local refugees there. This is amazing. Now we have our own band, our own music from our motherland, our own production, and the world, including Vietnam, will come to know of our existence," exclaimed Mai. Mây Bốn Phương became a source of pride for the burgeoning community.

Despite my mother's decision not to convert her restaurant into a nightclub, others in the community saw the opportunity. As a growing number of artists from various parts of the country and the world migrated to Orange County, the renowned musician Anh Bằng opened another music center in 1983. He changed the center's name a few times until it eventually became Trung Tâm Asia (Asia Entertainment Inc.). Asia Entertainment produced music and organized the first show at Caesar Palace in Las Vegas, collaborating with celebrities, making it one of the two largest Vietnamese music centers in the world, outside Vietnam.

I firmly believe that Vietnamese music has permeated every aspect of the refugees' lives. It is present at weddings, anniversaries, Sunday schools, church masses, and temple services. If my mother were still alive, I would invite her to join me for dinner at Phi Khanh's Bleu Restaurant & Dancing. I would express my gratitude for her accompanying me to Maxim's nightclub in Saigon on the eve of my departure to Switzerland in 1970. It was the first time we had ever been to a nightclub together, and it remains the only time we were alone as mother and son in such a setting.

I often imagine listening to music from Little Saigon with my mother. I put on a record, and the melodies fill the room, evoking memories of Saigon before 1975.

Chapter 6

Exiled Identities in Motion

A SYMPHONY OF JOURNEYS

Food carries with it a rich tapestry of history, language, identity, and a deep connection to the land. It is through the flavors and aromas of Vietnamese cuisine that I often introduce my non-Vietnamese friends to the vibrant culture of Little Saigon. For me, food becomes a loving gateway to history, family, and heritage. I cherish these moments of culinary exploration and the bonds formed over food in Little Saigon.

I had the pleasure of hosting my colleague Eric Jacquet-Lagreze and his family at my parents' home in Fountain Valley, Orange County. While we initially connected at New York University for a research project, I couldn't resist sharing the vibrant Vietnamese community of Orange County with them and allowing them to experience its rich food culture. As we delved into discussions about Vietnamese identity in the diaspora, Eric, with his astute French intellect and deep love for the country, posed a thought-provoking question: How do Vietnamese in America differ from those in France? Having encountered many Vietnamese in the diaspora community in Paris, Eric always seeks to view the world through various lenses of knowledge.

It's worth noting that France has a longer history of Vietnamese immigrants than the United States. Over 50% of the 400,000 Vietnamese living in France reside in Districts 13, 18, and 19, as well as around L'Ile de France. In 1975, France welcomed approximately 42,000 Vietnamese refugees, but even before that, a wave of around 30,000 Vietnamese immigrants had arrived in the 1950s at the end of the French war.

"We have a few researchers from Vietnam, and they are quite talented," Eric shared. "I used to go out for lunch with them at a couple of restaurants near the campus. I absolutely love Vietnamese cuisine. I imagine Vietnamese food in Little Saigon must be truly 'authentic,'" Eric exclaimed, his eyes filled with excitement. He reminded me that nothing brings people closer than good food.

As we gathered around my parents' beautifully polished dining table in Little Saigon, the fragrant aromas of fresh herbs, fish, chicken, beef, and flavorful broths filled the room. The late-day sun bathed the scene in shades of orange and gold, casting a warm glow upon us. I couldn't help but feel a surge of pride. Eric and my friends deftly wielded their chopsticks, dipping the grilled and meticulously prepared meats into *nước chấm*, a sauce made from fish sauce, finely minced garlic, vibrant chili peppers, and tangy lime juice. They savored the dishes that my parents had lovingly prepared, dishes that had nourished me as a young child in Vietnam and now, here in Little Saigon. This food, an integral part of my national identity, was undeniable, resilient, and evoked a sense of peace. It intertwined with the flavors, fragrances, and joyful laughter that filled the room. We shared not only a meal but also the history of who we are as Vietnamese in Little Saigon, California.

FOOD STORIES—FROM HỘI QUÁN VIETNAM TO THE SILK NOODLE

To the pride of her parents, Victoria, my daughter, graduated with a triple major in political science, psychology, and English from the University of Hawai'i at Mānoa. After graduation, she flew to Orange County to meet with members of our extended family living in Orange County and reconnect with high school classmates studying at California State University in Fullerton and UC Irvine. "You are in town? We need you to introduce us to Vietnamese food," Victoria's friends insisted.

For anyone seeking an introduction to Vietnamese food outside Vietnam and Vietnamese living across the world in the diaspora, craving tastes of home, Little Saigon is a mecca of flavors, dishes, and gastronomic artistry. Little Saigon streets fill with the aromas of Vietnam—hundreds of restaurants, bakeries, and cafés line Bolsa Avenue, and the abundant variety of regional food makes my mouth water even in memory.

I gave Victoria a crash course on different types of *phở*. Northern-style *phở* tastes of salt and beef flavored with rich ginger that warms the body. Southern-style, sweet and overflowing with anise, lingers on the tongue. Northern-style *phở,* its herbs (onion, coriander, green onion, basil) come chopped, mixed, and placed on top of the *phở* before serving. Southern-style arrives at the table steaming with the herbs on the side so that diners can mix them to their delight.

Phở has become the national food, a national identity, and a symbol of friendship for the Vietnamese. Treating a guest to an authentic bowl of *phở* to the Vietnamese in Vietnam or in the diaspora acts as a form of diplomacy at its best. In 2000, Bill Clinton, the first American President to visit Vietnam after the war, conducted an official visit to Vietnam. During the visit, the President who had lifted the trade embargo in 1994, which caused substantial economic damage, said to the millions of Vietnamese who warmly greeted him: "The history we leave behind is painful and hard. We must not forget it but we must not be controlled by it." Many Vietnamese used this moment to heal the trauma left behind from the war. Healing is a reciprocal act.

During his visit, President Clinton took his then-young daughter Chelsea to enjoy a bowl of phở at Phở 2000, situated next to Saigon's iconic Bến Thành Market. It has often crossed my mind why Clinton's advisors didn't choose a phở restaurant in Hanoi, where the beloved dish originated.

According to my research, the first version of phở emerged in North Vietnam in the mid-1880s. Influenced by Chinese immigrants who had a penchant for cooking noodle soups with an assortment of ingredients such as meat, seafood, vegetables, herbs, and flavorful broths, the Vietnamese developed their unique rendition. As the story goes, the introduction of fresh red meat by the French prompted the Vietnamese to incorporate it into their phở.

From its humble beginnings, the Vietnamese perfected their own local version of "pot-au-feu" by utilizing rice noodles, beef broth, and indigenous spices, including anise. Food critics argue that phở is lighter and less greasy compared to the noodle soups commonly found in colder northern climates.

The mass migration of around half a million North Vietnamese, myself included, to the South in 1954, following the country's division orchestrated by the French, further influenced the evolution of phở recipes. The South adapted the dish, incorporating ingredients readily available from the bountiful agricultural lands, such as bean sprouts, fresh basil, saw herbs, green chilies, and lime. It has become customary to enhance the flavors with hoisin sauce and Sriracha.

The first phở establishments in Little Saigon warmly welcomed Vietnamese refugees and new residents alike. Named after renowned restaurants from their homeland, particularly those in Saigon—*Phở Hoà, Phở Tầu Bay, Phở 79*—these eateries evoked a sense of home for many refugees through their familiar spices, flavors, and ambiance. The dining areas were reminiscent of small, family-owned restaurants found in bustling business districts in pre-1975 Vietnam, featuring rows of affordable square or rectangular tables adorned with vibrant checkered vinyl tablecloths. Bamboo chopsticks and plastic soup spoon holders graced the tables.

While the initial restaurants in Little Saigon recreated the atmosphere of their Vietnamese counterparts, there was a significant difference in the conceptualization of the beloved dish. The typical bowl of phở served in Little Saigon was twice the size of those found back home in Vietnam. Nonetheless, the atmosphere remained vibrant and joyful in both corners of the world. The distinct flavors of phở's signature ingredients—star anise and ginger—greeted guests like cherished memories.

During an evening in Little Saigon with my friends, Eric and his wife Christine, we sat in the corner of Hội Quán Vietnam. To our right, a Vietnamese couple caught Christine's attention as they meticulously wiped their chopsticks with a paper napkin. The couple didn't pause their diligent, almost ritualistic cleaning, even after receiving a cup of hot tea from the server. Curious, Christine asked, holding her own set of chopsticks, "Why are they wiping the chopsticks? They seem clean to me."

I was caught off guard by the question. Indeed, the chopsticks appeared clean to me as well. My best explanation was that perhaps the Vietnamese have carried this tradition from their homeland. It could be a hygienic practice, even if it's no longer necessary.

Over forty years since the opening of the first restaurant in Little Saigon, run by my family, phở establishments have evolved beyond being exclusive gathering places for Vietnamese locals. New restaurants have emerged in shopping areas across Orange County's thirty-four cities, offering modern settings and employing bilingual serving staff to cater to a diverse clientele. This new vision for phở restaurants serves as a charm offensive, captivating a broader audience and introducing them to the delights of phở. Vietnamese restaurateurs have expanded their horizons over the years, showcasing gourmet Vietnamese cuisine in prime locations like LSXO on the Pacific Coast Highway in Huntington Beach, or with "progressive" cuisine at Gem Dining in Fountain Valley.

Second-generation Vietnamese chefs have boldly ventured into Vietnamese fusion cuisine, combining food with cocktail services. The enduring charm of Vietnamese phở takes on various forms in Little Saigon, adding a touch of sophistication to reflect this transnational influence. Restaurants with names that appeal to millennials, such as Phở Lovers,' Garlic and Chives, Silk Noodle on Beach Blvd in Huntington Beach, The Decadence in Hermosa Beach, and The District by Hannah An on West 3rd in Beverly Grove, grace the streets. Little Sister in Manhattan Beach, led by Chef Tin Vuong, and ROL RollHandRoll in Huntington Beach, helmed by Chef Viet Nguyen, were ranked 2nd and 7th respectively by critic Brad A. Johnson as the best new restaurants in Orange County in 2021.

Once, when deciding where to dine, my daughter Victoria grabbed her oversized Samsung phone and, with her eyes fixed on the screen, scrolled through numerous pages. She exclaimed, "Dad, there are so many restaurants! Which one should we go to?" Yelp listed 2,805 Vietnamese restaurants in Orange County, with Little Saigon claiming the lion's share of 1,079. These restaurants not only showcase culinary expertise but also embody the history and culture of a country that experienced fear and war just half a century ago.

As phở reaffirms and reshapes the identity of Vietnamese refugees, replacing the narratives of a "bloody war" and "boat people" in the minds of many Americans, T-shirts featuring various phở designs have become popular attire among teenagers and young adults. COVID-19, in its eagerness to reshape our world and the way we live, has unintentionally contributed to this fashion trend. Websites like Redbubble.com offer a collection of masks adorned with phở symbols designed by artists such as Van Huynh, thesaurus, WorldPrintTees, Desiree Nguyen, Adamriz, and others.

Observing people passing by with phở-patterned face masks, I contemplate life and identity. I wonder about the popularity of these masks. They are undoubtedly delightful and reflect the passions of the wearers. However, I can't help but chuckle at the thought. Perhaps I wouldn't personally wear a phở face mask—I wouldn't want people staring at me and instantly thinking about food.

During my friends' visit to Little Saigon, we embarked on a culinary exploration, immersing ourselves in the tastes, textures, and artistic presentation of Vietnamese food. As we perused the menus, preparing for discussions on the history of Northern-style versus Southern-style phở, the server approached our table. Christine decided on a Tofu phở, while Eric opted for a seafood phở. I couldn't help but smile, realizing that our quest for authentic Vietnamese cuisine had taken a detour. Tofu and seafood variations are adaptations, reflecting culinary trends of the 21st century. As for myself, I simply requested a bowl of phở with beef broth, excluding the meat but including cooked vegetables.

The restaurant offered numerous options to cater to our unconventional group of phở enthusiasts, straying from the realm of traditional cuisine. However, this departure may serve as an affirmation of the evolving authenticity for Vietnamese in exile. Regardless of the chosen phở rendition from the menu, phở has undeniably emerged as a charming emblem for refugees, flourishing within the vibrant Vietnamese communities across the diaspora.

CÀ-PHÊ SỮA ĐÁ TO-GO—AFTERNOON TEA AT MORNING LAVENDER

"It is the soil that gives our coffee its delicious taste," my mother used to say as she took me on a tour of her coffee farm just outside the city of Ban Mê Thuột in the central plateau. Before our departure for America, my mother exclusively cultivated Robusta beans. In the mid-19th century, the French, in collaboration with Catholic missionaries in Hà Nam, attempted to grow arabica, a variety originating from Ethiopia. They believed arabica offered a wider range of flavors, from sweet and soft to sharp and tangy. Hawaii's Kona coffee, which I blend with my Vietnamese coffee each morning at home, shares a similar spectrum of flavors.

Arabica coffee is also appreciated for its delicate fragrance. However, the French growers and Catholic missionaries failed to achieve the desired quality, cost, and taste through their collaboration. Subsequently, they experimented with liberica and robusta beans from Congo. It took nearly forty years for the French to realize that robusta coffee plants were best suited for the Vietnamese environment.

"I loved the Robusta plants. They are resilient against diseases and pests and easy to cultivate," my mother would often say. "You should try some freshly roasted coffee at the demonstration booth. Ban Mê Thuột coffee is renowned for its sugary flavor and low acidity." As a teenager, I was too young to appreciate coffee fully, but at my mother's urging, I consumed two large cups of iced coffee. While I don't recall the precise flavor, her words echo in my mind.

Similar to phở, which was adapted from the French "pot of feu" and Chinese noodle soup, the Vietnamese created their own version of coffee—strong and thick like espresso. Initially, most Asians found the taste of coffee bitter upon their first encounter. The Vietnamese shared this sentiment, likening the flavor to Chinese medicine. Yet, as with any precious ingredient, coffee should not be wasted, and local farmers began brewing coffee in small hand-made metal cups that fit over a *phin*, a Vietnamese coffee filter.

The *phin* is designed to hold three tablespoons of ground coffee and boiling water, allowing the grounds to brew slowly. "The secret to the best coffee is to pour just enough hot water to moisten the coffee powder. Wait for a minute or two, allowing the coffee grains to expand. Then pour hot water to brew the coffee. It is a slow dripping process, but it yields the most flavor and caffeine," the demonstrator at my mother's farm once explained to me, as if sharing a secret and granting me a privileged understanding of coffee. "To balance the strong taste of the coffee, mix it with an equal amount of condensed milk. Look at the resulting brownish color to determine if you've achieved the right balance. If you prefer a cold drink, add the coffee to a glass of crushed ice."

Whenever I order a cup of *cà-phê sữa đá* in a Vietnamese restaurant in Little Saigon, I always inquire about the coffee's origin, reminiscing about my mother's farm and the words of the farm worker. This memory, akin to the taste of Vietnamese coffee, holds a special place in my heart. In 2020, Vietnam exported approximately 12 million kilograms of coffee to the U.S., making it the second-largest coffee market for Vietnam after Germany and ahead of Italy, two major coffee markets.

Yet, even for beloved coffee beans, Vietnamese-grown coffee cannot avoid the realm of exile politics. When I visited Bùi Thọ Khang, the owner of seven Vietnamese supermarkets, at his home, I playfully brought up a question I had seen circulating on social media. "A few people on Facebook have claimed that Vietnamese coffee is impure and improperly processed," I said.

Bùi Thọ Khang proudly pointed to the jar beside his coffee maker. "Look, I sell coffee that is made in Vietnam and approved by our FDA (Food and Drug Administration). I personally use it every day. If some people choose not to drink it due to political reasons or stories they've read on social media, it's their decision," he asserted. The topic struck a sensitive chord for Bùi Thọ Khang and many others who continue to navigate the complexities of politics and Vietnamese identity long after the war.

Cà phê sữa, whether served hot or as a refreshing iced beverage, has become a beloved daily drink for many Vietnamese and those introduced to it in Vietnamese restaurants and cafes. Similar to phở, the original Vietnamese coffee recipe—thick espresso coffee with a generous amount of condensed milk—has evolved into creative variations crafted by second-generation entrepreneurs. At 7-Leaves and Tea, customers enjoy a lighter version of iced coffee created by the Nguyễn brothers. In Tustin, just a short distance from Westminster, Jason and Kim Lê offer colonial-era morning and afternoon tea and coffee service at the Morning Lavender restaurant. Although the owners of Morning Lavender appear youthful, they have brought back a sense of romanticism reminiscent of French-style coffee shops. It seems that a love for romance never truly fades away.

BÁNH MÌ (VIETNAMESE SANDWICH)

When I arrived in Monterey for my first job in California, I developed a tradition of driving north to San Jose to visit relatives, friends, and savor Vietnamese cuisine. On my way back, I always made a stop at Lee's Sandwiches to grab a couple of bánh mì sandwiches, the epitome of Vietnamese-style sandwiches. This small shop near San Jose State University started as a food truck extension. In 1980, Lê Văn Chiêu and his father, Lê Văn Ba, operated the food truck while he attended English classes. A bánh mì sandwich only cost ninety-nine cents back in 1986. It was a taste of home—a delightful combination of savory meats, orange and white crunchy homemade pickles, all lovingly tucked into a French baguette—at an unbeatable price intentionally set by Chiêu's parents to "help the poor students have a decent meal."

While phở has become the culinary symbol of the Vietnamese worldwide, I would argue that bánh mì carries a deeper and more complex notion of identity among refugees. In less than a decade since 1975, bánh mì has become a staple in American cities with thriving Vietnamese communities and has gained global fame. Its recognition is such that the Oxford Dictionary included a definition for the sandwich in 2011. The entry describes it as "(in Vietnamese cuisine) a sandwich consisting of a baguette (traditionally baked with both rice and wheat flour) filled with a variety of ingredients, typically including meat, pickled vegetables, and chili peppers." Other dictionaries, like Merriam-Webster, followed suit by adding similar descriptions for this Vietnamese culinary creation.

The origin of *bánh mì* is a subject of debate among historians. However, Bánh Mì Ba Lẹ, established by Mr. Võ Văn Lê in 1982 on Bolsa Avenue, Westminster, is believed to be the first bánh mì restaurant in Little Saigon (although historians debate this claim). Võ Văn Lê initially opened his first restaurant in San Jose, proudly showcasing the iconic Eiffel Tower logo as a symbol of Vietnamese cuisine. His aim was to bring the same flavors to the enclave of Little Saigon. Võ Văn Lê, hailing from humble origins in the Mekong Delta countryside, migrated to Saigon during the colonial era. With his imaginative fusion of Vietnamese and French cuisines, he aspired to create affordable versions of French food for the local population. Võ Văn Lê crafted recipes using French baguettes and paté, incorporating local ingredients to fulfill his culinary dreams. Over the years, he brought his love for bánh mì to California and other states in the U.S., including Hawai'i, alongside his partner Lâm Quốc Thanh.

Bánh mì has become the quintessential meal for busy working individuals and students. It is served in food stalls along bustling streets, from food trucks to nearby schools, and in cozy hole-in-the-wall cafés, eagerly satisfying customers' senses. For budget-conscious diners, a simple spoonful of sweetened milk can accompany bánh mì, or it can be dipped in a bowl of milk coffee. For those with more refined palates, bánh mì comes alive with an array of flavors when filled with various delicacies like paté, grilled chicken, beef, Vietnamese-style ham, or char siu pork. To enhance the taste, fried eggs, tangy pickled vegetables, cucumber, coriander, cilantro leaves and stems, mayonnaise, Maggi seasoning sauce, and chili paste are added, taking taste buds on a culinary journey.

Similar to phở and Vietnamese coffee, the recipe for the famous bánh mì reflects the Franco-Chinese-Vietnamese fusion. During the French colonization of Vietnam (1887–1954), the colonizers introduced livestock and crops to the country. Wheat was needed for bread, cows for meat and milk, and coffee for their beverages. However, the Vietnamese had limited access to wheat until the end of World War I when it was imported from Germany. This prompted the exploration of recipes for their own version of the baguette.

In 2001, leveraging their decade-long experience of selling bánh mì from a fleet of approximately 500 food trucks, Lê Văn Chiêu and his eldest son, Minh, opened a franchise with a Subway-style fast-food concept but centered around Vietnamese coffee and bánh mì. Like Ba Le, Lee's Sandwiches has over sixty locations across the U.S. As bánh mì gained recognition beyond Vietnamese communities, Little Saigon's takeout options expanded with establishments such as Bánh Mì Saigon, Mr. Baguette, Bánh Mì Cali, Tân Hoàng Hương, and the list goes on.

During a flight to Honolulu with Alaska Airlines, I had a delightful realization—I no longer needed to seek out Vietnamese fast-food restaurants to enjoy bánh mì. Since 2015, the airline has included bánh mì on its menu. This is a testament to the entrepreneurial ingenuity of Vietnamese refugees, who have played a significant role in elevating bánh mì from its humble origins to achieve global recognition. From establishments like Bale Sandwich, Lee's Sandwiches, Bánh Mì Saigon, Tân Hoàng Hương, and others in Little Saigon and neighboring cities, the legacy of these resourceful individuals has allowed bánh mì to transcend its local roots and become a beloved culinary delight embraced by people worldwide.

TREAT YOURSELF: DEMOCRATIZING THE SELF-CARE INDUSTRY

Ten years ago, I received an application for our Executive MBA program, where I serve as the program director. The applicant was a Vietnamese American and the president of a Florida-based company specializing in luxury pedicure chairs and desks for nail salons. His position as a leader in this growing industry and his desire to improve the supply chain and expand his business intrigued me. I saw the potential for him to provide equipment to numerous Vietnamese-owned nail salons across the United States. During the interview, I expressed my enthusiasm and assured him that our curriculum would equip him with the knowledge needed to address these challenges.

As I wandered the streets of Little Saigon, I couldn't resist looking through the windows of nail salons to see if any of them used the equipment sold by my student. Most of the time, I didn't recognize the brand, but I was always intrigued by the ingenuity behind these businesses. The nail salon industry seemed to be an attractive option for many Vietnamese refugees, and the pay and compensation for manicurists appeared to be quite promising.

However, it was not until I had a conversation with Tâm Nguyễn Jr., the president of Advance Beauty College, and his father, that I truly grasped the magnitude of this business. He revealed that nail salons, with approximately 50,000 locations in operation, make up a staggering $6 billion industry in the U.S. According to Nails Magazine in 2012, a significant proportion of licensed manicurists in California (80%) and nationwide (45%) were Vietnamese. This percentage was even higher in California and Texas, the two states with the most significant concentrations of Vietnamese refugees.

When I interviewed Tâm Nguyễn Sr., the founder of Advance Beauty College in Garden Grove, he shared the inspiring story of creating a vocational school that offered manicuring programs with classes available in Vietnamese and affordable tuition. Intrigued by the origins of the Vietnamese nail business, I asked about its inception within the refugee community. Tâm Nguyễn Jr. informed me that Nathalie Kay "Tippi" Hedren, an award-winning actress known for her roles in movies directed by Alfred Hitchcock and Charlie Chaplin, played a crucial role in shaping this vocation for the refugees. "Tippi is the godmother of the Vietnamese-American nail industry," Tâm Nguyễn Jr. proudly stated.

Following the fall of Saigon, Hedren, then 46, served as an international relief coordinator. When Vietnamese women at the refugee Camp Hope near Sacramento complimented her on her long, polished nails, Hedren recognized the potential for them to pursue careers as manicurists. She brought her own manicurist, Dusty, to Camp Hope, where she taught twenty Vietnamese women refugees the art of manicuring, introducing them to cutting-edge techniques such as silk nail wrapping. After these initial students graduated, Hedren used her connections in Hollywood to secure them jobs in Southern California. This opportunity did not go unnoticed by Lê Thuận and Tâm Nguyễn Sr., a stressed-out hairdresser and a bored accountant, both former military officers in South Vietnam. They saw the potential for growth in this industry and promptly opened a cosmetology school that offered classes in Vietnamese.

"Hedren's act of kindness had far-reaching consequences," Tâm Nguyễn Jr. said with admiration. "She intended to help a few Vietnamese women find decent jobs doing nails for the privileged class in Beverly Hills, but she ended up contributing to the establishment of a multi-billion dollar industry, creating thousands of jobs for Vietnamese in America. In return, we now make nail art affordable for millions of Americans."

During our conversation, I raised concerns about the potential hazards of chemical exposure in nail salons to both Tâm Nguyễn Sr. and Jr. They acknowledged the risks related to daily exposure to chemicals and mentioned that they have friends working in the industry focused on research and development to reduce harmful substances that may affect workers' health. While the State Department of Health has strict codes for workplaces, the high turnover rate among nail workers remains a concerning issue to me.

Recently, I talked to a Vietnamese student who applied to an undergraduate mathematics program at an UC campus for Fall 2021. Her application essay touched my heart as he shared his journey as a manicurist working to pay for his education. "I love mathematics," the aspiring student wrote, "and when I use my brushes to paint nails, I think of these art forms in terms of mathematical functions."

I am constantly amazed by the skills, grace, and determination of the Vietnamese people, and it is evident that the transformative and uplifting impact of Tippi Hedren's serendipitous charity work and Tâm Nguyễn's successful Advance Beauty College have left a profound mark on the lives of the countless individuals in Little Saigon, as well as throughout the nation.

RISING IN THE FLAMES OF EXILE IDENTITY

When Kathy Lâm, a friend from Hawaii who shares my vision about social engagement, called me to discuss her "Our1World" philanthropic work, I brought up the Little Saigon memoir. "You might want to talk to my dad. He's retired and has decided to leave politics, but he can give you quite a bit of insight," she said.

"I did talk to him. He played an important role in shaping the exile identity of the Vietnamese community in Orange County," I replied.

In 1992, Tony Quang Lâm, Kathy's father, was elected by popular ballot as a councilman to the City of Westminster. In the grand scheme of things, it was just a mundane local community election. After all, there are 39,044 general-purpose local governments in the U.S. Nevertheless, the news that the first Vietnamese refugee had been elected to a political office made local and national headlines. The New York Times marked Lâm's rise to the political scene as a milestone for Vietnamese presence in the country.

In hindsight, it's evident that Tony Lâm ran the election with a winning strategy. He focused on issues that concerned most residents—not just Vietnamese refugees—of the city of Westminster, such as fighting rampant crime and economic revitalization through fiscal policy. Only one-third of the votes Lâm received came from Vietnamese American voters. He needed additional non-Vietnamese votes to win the council seat, and he received them.

Tony Lâm's victory signaled new life and new opportunities for many Vietnamese refugees. As the refugees settled into their everyday routines in their new land, they learned that it was essential to have an official voice in local politics. In 1981, my mother applied for a permit to sell alcohol for her Vietnamese restaurant in Santa Ana. The city council rejected her application, citing location insecurity and a lack of public safety. My mother claimed that no one explained these issues, and she could not find anyone who could speak on her behalf to the city administration. My mother would have indeed voted for Tony Lâm if she had still been alive when he ran for office.

Before winning the election, Tony Lâm actively participated in the Little Saigon community. Known mainly as the first vice president of the Vietnamese Chamber of Commerce in Orange County, he worked tirelessly to better his community. As an elected official sitting on the City Council, Vietnamese residents expected Tony Lâm to serve the community. He did. He attended most community events and meetings.

He worked diligently to secure city funding to beautify Little Saigon by installing French colonial-style street lights on Bolsa Avenue. He said, "They looked like they belonged in some old quarter of Saigon." Furthermore, Tony Lâm fought to secure freeway signs for Little Saigon.

Nonetheless, Tony Lâm always reminded himself that his duty was to serve the interests of the entire population of Westminster, not solely the Vietnamese community. During his three-term tenure, he found himself torn between his role as a councilman of an American city and his status as a political refugee fleeing a communist regime. To many local first-generation community leaders, he was not serving the Vietnamese enough. The unrest continued: "He supported the Chinese," "He was a 'communist sympathizer' because he refused to join in the demonstrations against a video store owner who displayed a poster of Ho Chi Minh and a communist flag," and so on.

As I interviewed him in his quaint Westminster home, I sensed bitterness in Tony Lâm's eyes. He was recovering from knee surgery, and the dynamics of exile politics had visibly worn him down. Six years after his decision not to seek re-election for his council seat, I saw the rhetorical narrative of rescue haunting him, still. I felt a bit uneasy, asking questions that made him relive memories of war, the early years in Little Saigon, and politics.

"Do you regret having run for city office?" I asked him gently.

It took him a while to answer. "I was pleased to be the first Vietnamese elected official in the U.S. But, I am even more pleased now that many others [Vietnamese Americans] have entered the political arena," he said.

The 2018 elections marked another significant milestone in the political journey of Vietnamese Americans in Little Saigon. It was an unprecedented moment with twenty-four candidates of Vietnamese descent running for various offices in Orange County, an event fondly referred to as the "Nguyen wave" by the Los Angeles Times. Among these candidates, thirteen shared the popular last name "Nguyen" from Vietnam.

During the intense election campaigns, I was invited by Chu Tất Tiến, a TV anchor for the Vietnamese-language cable TV station SBTN (Saigon Broadcasting Television Network) in Garden Grove, to join his weekly talk show. During our conversation, Tiến asked about the ongoing trade war between China and the U.S. and urged me to share my thoughts on the upcoming election. He often emphasized the phrase "Vietnamese vote for Vietnamese" (Người Việt bỏ phiếu cho người Việt) to his audience. At that moment, I couldn't help but recall what Tony Lâm had said just weeks earlier: "I was the first elected official. I hope to see more exile political engagements." Lâm's hope had materialized, as Vietnamese refugees took part in the mid-election, running for various positions such as California State Senate, Assembly, mayor, sheriff, school boards, and water and sanitation districts. Tony Lâm's early efforts had indeed sowed the seeds of political involvement twenty-five years ago, and now the Vietnamese community was making its presence felt in mainstream politics through the power of their ballots.

CONTENTIOUS COLOR LINES—THE FIRE AND DAMNATION RHETORIC OF 2020

History will undoubtedly remember the unprecedented circumstances surrounding the 2020 presidential election in the United States. As the Vietnamese community in Little Saigon continued to grow, the quest for exile identity found its way into the forefront of the U.S. Presidential election agenda. Due to the pandemic, I closely monitored the political developments in the enclave through my laptops and phones, witnessing politics invade numerous American households like never before. Even my extended family in Little Saigon felt the ripple effects of polarization from the political landscape.

While the presidential debate revolved around pressing national issues such as the COVID-19 pandemic, economic recovery, diversity, inclusion, immigration, and trade wars, the Vietnamese refugees in Little Saigon viewed the election through a distinctive lens. Unlike Asian Americans of other origins, such as Chinese, Indian, Japanese, Korean, and Filipino, most first-generation Vietnamese refugees tended to align with the Republican party. Their perspective was influenced by memories of the Republic of Vietnam, the country they left behind. History also reminded them that President Gerald Ford, a Republican, had made efforts to rescue South Vietnam in the months leading up to April 1975. However, the Democratic-led Congress ultimately terminated the Vietnam War, leaving many Vietnamese refugees facing the aftermath.

Some members of my extended family expressed their intention to vote for Trump out of fear that "the Chinese will invade us soon if Biden wins." While I wanted to engage in nuanced discussions, I sensed the rising tension during our casual conversations. Seeking to bring peace to our family, which had already endured enough trauma and hardship, I would often change the topic to something light like the weather in California. The election permeated our homes, conversations, and lives, and I found myself patiently listening as fear echoed in their voices. "The communists will take over Little Saigon," they repeated. I yearned to offer different perspectives beyond the rhetoric promoted by political pundits and specific media sources, but I chose to steer our discussions back to less contentious subjects, like the weather.

On the other hand, the younger members of my family passionately advocated for change, fueled by the urgency and idealism of youth. "We don't need Trump. He made his points. Life should move on," they argued.

The 2020 elections brought forth six Vietnamese American politicians, all Democrats, who secured victories at national and state levels. Their names, Stephanie Murphy-Dang, Bee Nguyễn, Trâm T. Nguyễn, Rochelle Nguyễn, Thái Mỹ Linh, and Hubert Võ, spoke volumes about the growing presence and shifting dynamics of our Vietnamese American community in America.

In California, 35 Vietnamese Americans ran for various offices, 28 in Orange County and 7 in Santa Clara County, with many competing for the same positions. The high level of participation in Orange County, reaching 87% of the eligible voting population, led to 12 candidates of Vietnamese origins securing victories. Notably, Janet Nguyễn, a Republican and former state senator, narrowly won the state assembly against Vietnamese refugee Diedre Nguyễn, a Democrat. Additionally, Andrew Đỗ, a Republican, was re-elected as the First District Supervisor for Orange County. These numbers showcased the growing engagement of Vietnamese Americans in the political arena and the changing tides of our community.

As I delved into the election results, I couldn't help but contemplate the increasing number of Vietnamese politicians aligning with the blue party, and my thoughts turned to Tony Quang Lâm and his perspective on the recent City of Westminster election. Back in 1992, he stood as the lone star caught between the high expectations of his fellow refugees and American compatriots. Now, twenty-eight years later, after a decade of service, four out of the five top elected officials in the city are Vietnamese refugees: Trí Tà as mayor, Charlie Nguyễn as vice-mayor, and Tài Đỗ and Kimberly Hồ. Unlike the challenging landscape Tony Lâm faced, these newly elected officials don't have to worry about in-fighting within the Vietnamese American community. They enjoy the support of their followers who recognize the importance of representing everyone's interests.

Reflecting on Little Saigon mirrors my own journey as a Vietnamese refugee leading a fortuitous nomadic lifestyle. I have spent three-quarters of my life outside my homeland. While I integrated relatively well into this new world like many refugees arriving in the U.S. after 1975, those who know me still consider me more Vietnamese than American, with Vietnamese heritage shaping my identity. Phở, bánh mì, cà-phê sữa đá—these foods define me, and they carry the rich history and culture of my heritage. Yet, the years living outside Vietnam have also influenced my identity, causing changes in my preferences. I no longer opt for the "original" or "authentic" phở, fully flavored with steamy animal fat. Instead, I choose lean meat or vegan options. My bánh mì orders now include "easy on paté and no butter, please," a departure from the extra paté and French butter I once enjoyed. Even my coffee has evolved, with me now requesting "just a tiny bit of condensed milk, less than half a teaspoon, please," for a lighter, more adjusted taste.

Yet, amidst these changes, there's one identity that remains steadfastly associated with Vietnamese refugees—the nail salon business. As I shared an evening with long-known friends in Little Saigon, the conversation naturally gravitated towards Vietnamese refugees known for their nail salons. It's an enduring part of our community's identity. Someone remarked, "The 'Nguyens' are now taking on local and national politics." As the conversation continued, and the California sunset enveloped us with comfort and ease, I realized that regardless of the diverse professions Vietnamese refugees now occupy or the new trends in our culinary heritage, the stories and histories of Vietnamese Americans continue to flourish. As a community of refugees, we endure and thrive in our new homeland, creating a tapestry of experiences that enriches the fabric of America.

Chapter 7

Sweet Dreams and Bitter Realities

Every Sunday morning, until his passing in 1987, my dad would call me at 9 a.m. California time to catch up. Our conversations would begin with the latest happenings in Little Saigon: news about new grandbabies, delicacies in the shops, and updates on my siblings' activities. Whenever something was "breaking news" to my father, he would pick up the phone and call me, regardless of the day or time. His notion of breaking news might have been similar to our regular Sunday chats, but I cherished every moment of these calls. To him, daily life in Little Saigon was worth sharing with me, and those memories remain dear to me.

Over the years, some of my father's "breaking-news-of-grave-concerns" conversations involved people I've interviewed for this book. Somehow, he knew that one day, I would find the everyday lives and people of Little Saigon worth sharing with the world. Throughout this project, I've received a wide range of reactions from people—some empathetic, others indifferent, and a few relentless. Nevertheless, everyone I've spoken to about this vibrant community of Vietnamese refugees and their descendants has had a definitive opinion.

My mother was a practical businesswoman, focused on our family and businesses, while my father, on the other hand, enjoyed intellectual discussions. He viewed life and our community through the lenses of a scholar, always seeking to understand the "root causes" and origins of various issues. He encouraged me to adopt this mindset, and we bonded over our shared interests. Though I sometimes met his expectations with my investigative curiosity, my scholarly perspective sometimes left him with unanswered questions. Nevertheless, our relationship flourished as we dared each other to explore the world with our minds, even when it meant facing both sweet dreams and bitter realities.

ALIENS WITHIN THEIR OWN UNIVERSE

In 1978, our family's restaurant, the first in Little Saigon, was situated in a nondescript building in a bustling yet low-income area of Santa Ana. At that time, the Vietnamese community was still in its early stages, and most of our patrons, drawn in by the enticing aroma of herbs and broth, were fellow Vietnamese. Occasionally, Vietnamese customers would bring their friends or colleagues from work to experience our restaurant. Our clientele grew primarily through word-of-mouth, and perhaps the alluring scents of our dishes helped attract curious passersby.

As our business expanded, I urged my mother to reach out to "non-Vietnamese" patrons, emphasizing that we were now in the United States. With Thanksgiving approaching, I proposed an idea to attract new customers. "You don't have to do anything; I'll handle this," I assured her. I designed a flier in English promoting our Vietnamese cuisine, offering a 25% "Welcome" coupon. Together with my father, we made 500 copies at Kinkos and set out on a sunny Saturday to place the fliers on shoppers' car windshields in various shopping centers around Westminster.

Over the weekend, the 500 promotional fliers had caught the attention of just one woman. She introduced herself as a nurse who had been stationed in Danang in the 70s. She shared that she had driven past our restaurant many times but had been unsure if she would be welcomed. She was a pleasant woman in her mid-forties, but there was a hint of hesitation in her demeanor. After enjoying our phở, she expressed her gratitude, saying, "It reminded me of my time in Vietnam. I don't remember exactly how it tasted back then, but yours was good."

Unfortunately, she never returned. Despite our efforts to extend our reach, it seemed that one flier was not enough to overcome the barriers that existed at the time. We are aliens within our own universe. Nonetheless, I look back on that experience as a reminder of the challenges and opportunities we faced as pioneers of Vietnamese cuisine in the U.S. We continued to serve our community with dedication, hoping that one day, more people from diverse backgrounds would feel welcome at our restaurant.

Diễm Châu had a similar experience. Her 300-square-foot hair salon in Midway City, just a few blocks from Phước Lộc Thọ mall on Bolsa Ave, was where she had been caring for and cutting my hair for years. Diễm Châu's skilled hands moved swiftly and accurately, effortlessly trimming each strand without needing any instructions from me. She always managed to fit me into her busy schedule, even on short notice.

"How's your business going? Are you getting a lot of new customers?" I would inquire during my haircut, a question I asked on every visit. "No, mostly regulars. I do have a few Latinos and a couple of Caucasians who come regularly, but it's challenging to attract new non-Vietnamese customers. It seems they're hesitant to step into the store," Diễm Châu replied with a hint of disappointment.

Speaking about the lives of immigrants, I must mention Trọng Minh. A former news reporter attached to South Vietnamese military units before 1975, he encountered a similar fear and prejudice during a weekend trip to Las Vegas in 1989. The encounter left Trọng Minh feeling overwhelmed with anxiety, as he faced preconceptions and verbal attacks. Although Las Vegas is often portrayed as a fantasy land of fun, this encounter reminded him that biases against Vietnamese refugees still lingered.

A hurtful incident occurred at a casino dining table, where a tall white man stared at Trọng Minh and his companions and uttered, "VC, you have no business here, just go home." The derogatory term VC, referring to the Việt Cộng, amplified the traumas of war and the struggles faced by Vietnamese refugees after the war, many of whom found themselves without a home. Humiliated, Trọng Minh lost his appetite and retreated to his hotel room. Restless and unable to sleep, he decided to leave early and drove 270 miles back to his apartment in Santa Ana without stopping.

That incident sparked a deep commitment in Trọng Minh to correct biases against Vietnamese refugees. For thirty years until he ran out of personal resources, he dedicated his journalism career to this mission, publishing five bilingual volumes of The Pride of Vietnamese American in 1998. These volumes celebrated the successes and achievements of Vietnamese Americans and individuals around the world with Vietnamese ancestry.

Among the inspiring biographies featured in The Pride of Vietnamese featured Việt Đinh, who played a significant role in crafting the Patriot Act while serving as the Assistant Attorney General (2001–2003) under President George W. Bush. Another notable figure was Dương Nguyệt Ánh, recognized for her achievements in developing advanced weapons systems for the military, earning several prestigious awards, and delighting many veterans of Little Saigon.

Trọng Minh's biographies gave a powerful voice to the accomplishments of Vietnamese Americans and Vietnamese in the diaspora. In one of our conversations, he expressed his hope that people wouldn't view them as "aliens." Vietnamese in the U.S. and abroad have made remarkable contributions to various fields, enriching the communities they are a part of. They are more than the history of a tragic war. Fear of the unknown often creates barriers in our community.

Trọng Minh pointed out, "I can cite numerous scientific studies that show new migrants contribute significantly to the wealth of this nation." His disillusionment, decades after the Las Vegas incident, remained as deep as ever. As I smiled at him, I could see tears welling up in his eyes once again.

RESISTANCE AND MISUNDERSTANDING— PASSIONATE VOICES CALL OUT FOR EQUITY

A year after my mother's restaurant opened in Santa Ana, she called me seeking help with yet another issue that had plagued her business. While the restaurant was a favorite among Vietnamese and their co-workers for breakfast and lunch, and families gathered there in the evenings for phở and other Vietnamese delicacies, she faced a roadblock with the City Council's rejection of her application to serve alcohol. The council cited concerns about public safety incidents related to the restaurant's location, even though these issues had occurred before her establishment opened. Frustrated, my mother felt that her Vietnamese ancestry played a role in the denial, especially when she witnessed another non-Vietnamese restaurant owner receiving an alcohol license just moments before her application was rejected.

During this conversation, my father remained quiet, offering his insight when he finally spoke. He gently suggested that the denial might be a blessing in disguise, as my mother had never been a fan of alcohol, and it spared them from dealing with potential issues related to intoxicated patrons. My father's soft-spoken words often carried profound wisdom.

Frank Jao, a successful real estate developer, shared similar experiences of what he perceived as blatant discrimination in the early 1980s. While helping Chinese clients apply for construction permits and build commercial centers, he encountered a troubling incident when a city official advised him to hire a white person to increase his chances of getting a project done. Jao faced numerous challenges in a country that touted freedom and the American dream but often made it difficult for immigrants like him.

When I asked Frank Jao about other struggles Vietnamese refugees faced while creating Little Saigon in its early years, he recommended speaking to Kathy Buchoz, the former mayor of the City of Westminster, who spent a significant amount of her official time assisting Vietnamese entrepreneurs in opening businesses.

I reached out to Kathy Buchoz and, among the many memorable stories she shared, one stood out in my mind. As the first female elected mayor of the City of Westminster, she had seen and experienced enough to fill a book. She recounted an incident from a council meeting in 1981 when she was handed a petition, signed by 105 residents, requesting the City Council to stop granting business licenses to Vietnamese immigrants.

Thirty-five years later, sitting in her real estate office in Huntington Beach, Buchoz still expressed anger about the incident. She remembered looking the man in the eyes and firmly stating that the matter would be put in the trash bin. The council backed its mayor, and the discriminatory petition was dismissed.

While my father's thoughtful analysis of the liquor license issue didn't entirely convince my mother, he acknowledged that discrimination was a pervasive issue throughout history. He sought my counsel, and I could attest to having witnessed discrimination in various workplace settings around the world.

Humanity has grappled with racism, jealousy, protectionism, and selfishness for ages, and these systemic issues have often been used to benefit the few at the expense of others. Such resistance against newcomers, as seen in the case of Vietnamese refugees, can be traced back to the historical fallout of an unwanted war. Some non-Vietnamese residents may have viewed the refugees as an invasion of their way of life, assuming the refugees would eventually return to their homeland. The complexities of these issues are indeed multifaceted and deeply rooted in history.

Nonetheless, a minority of the population in the U.S. holds extreme views like Thomas Linton Metzger's. While reflecting on Trọng Minh's Las Vegas incident, I understood the complex reactions of Vietnamese refugees to discrimination. Over the years, they have faced various forms of racism, hindering their settlement efforts in the new land. However, some local government officials have acknowledged the contributions of newcomers to the community, signaling a start towards positive change.

During a visit with my eldest sister, her son Thiện Nguyễn and his wife, Vân, shared stories about their uncle, David Trần, the founder of Huy Fong Food. Despite his success with the famed Sriracha chili sauce, David Trần encountered disappointments and challenges, such as the public nuisance lawsuit filed against Huy Fong Co. due to the pepper odor from the factory. Trần expressed frustration with the unfriendliness towards business people in the U.S., but eventually, the situation was resolved through negotiations.

Discussing Vietnamese refugee resistance movements with Michael Võ, the mayor of Fountain Valley, he emphasized the importance of understanding rules and regulations at different levels of governance. He mentioned that communication and dialogue between people could have mitigated resistance caused by perceived changes in their daily lives due to the influx of refugees.

I brought the issue of Vietnamese refugees receiving city citations to Andrew Đỗ, the Orange County supervisor. "I know, speaking as a lawyer, there is work to be done. My concern is some of the local leaders are themselves not exercising their responsibilities. There is a great deal of complacency. I am working hard to change that," he said.

"How?" I asked, pressing him to continue.

"Just clean things up," he said, smiling.

"Things will change. The first generation of community activists will soon leave the scene with their cultural baggage, personal agendas, and strengths and weaknesses. Things will change, don't you think?"

"Yes, we have a few leaders who are young and brilliant. But those who are corrupt are still around, and they will be around for some time," Andrew Đỗ responded as a politician and lawyer. His statement was equivocal. Nevertheless, judging the compassionate tone of his voice, I felt that he knew how to deal with discrimination, from both sides, in his role as the Chairman of the Orange County Board of Supervisors.

REDLINING NEW IMMIGRANTS—JAO'S FORTUNE IS MORE THAN LUCK

A while back, one of my students showed me a recording of an interview with Frank Jao on a local cable TV show in Orange County. This interview provided a glimpse into Frank Jao's struggles and achievements. Jao shared the challenges he faced while applying for a loan at Bank of America to build a commercial center. Unfortunately, the bank rejected his application without any explanation. Undeterred, Jao showed remarkable resourcefulness by securing loans from friends and investors in Taiwan and Malaysia to create the Asian Garden Mall and the Asian Village, two significant centers in Little Saigon.

Some might consider Frank Jao fortunate, but I argue that his fearlessness and relentless entrepreneurial drive allowed him to seek alternative funding sources. In contrast, others who faced similar loan rejections found it difficult to obtain financing. Nguyen Cang, the owner of several coffee shops, had to work overtime as an electrician to improve his credit scores before relying on his savings to finance his projects.

When the first refugees arrived in Orange County, they realized that self-employment was a viable path to lift themselves out of poverty due to language barriers and lack of professional credentials. However, with little money, possessions, and non-existent credit scores, accessing financing became a paramount challenge. Tony Cao, who owned a machine shop in Santa Clara, highlighted that new business owners, especially refugees, faced difficulties due to limited financial resources upon arrival, unlike other ethnic immigrants who could access funding from their home countries.

My sister, Hải, tired of working in an electronic assembly line, had dreams of opening a family-owned business with her husband. They opened a video rental store in the late 1980s after months of market exploration and navigating the challenge of securing a business loan. Despite their excitement and effort, the business did not thrive, and they eventually had to close the store at a significant loss due to high interest rates on their loans. Sadly, many others faced similar struggles, unable to keep their businesses afloat.

Years later, the video rental business boomed nationwide, and Blockbuster successfully opened a store in the same location my sister's store once occupied. Reflecting on their experience, my brother-in-law expressed that with a supportive and patient banker, they might have been able to weather the initial challenges and keep the store until business turned around.

These stories shed light on the difficulties faced by Vietnamese refugees and other aspiring business owners in accessing financial resources, which played a significant role in shaping their entrepreneurial journeys.

Years ago, before 1975, when I was studying economics in Switzerland, my mother had a vision: "We need to have our own bank." Had she heeded my advice and left Vietnam after the 1973 Paris Accord, we might have had the resources to establish a Vietnamese-owned bank, catering to the financing needs of the Little Saigon community. During the community's early stages, U.S. banks faced cultural and language barriers while attempting to engage with refugees. An ethnic bank owned by local Vietnamese would have gained a competitive advantage in reducing investment risks.

Finally, my excitement peaked when I witnessed the opening of the First Vietnamese American Bank (FVAB) on Westminster Avenue in May 2005. With over $11 million in capital, the bank's president, Nguyễn T. Hiếu, promised personalized assistance to Vietnamese business owners and sought to tap into the $8 billion annual cash remittances and trade between Vietnamese Americans and their connections in Vietnam. However, FVAB's success was short-lived, as it faced financial trouble and eventually had to be acquired by another bank.

Undeterred, the establishment of Saigon National Bank on Brookhurst Ave in Westminster brought renewed hope. Owned by Nguyễn D. Kiêm, a successful businessman, and run by experienced banker John J. Kennedy, the bank aimed to understand and support the community's economic growth. Despite receiving a $1.5 million investment from the U.S. Treasury Department during the mortgage collapse in 2008, the bank faced a devastating setback. In 2015, the U.S. Department of Justice indicted sixteen bank officers, including its president and CEO, Tu Chau "Bill" Lu, for alleged involvement in a criminal organization, trafficking drugs, and money laundering.

The subsequent ownership change and rebranding as California International Bank N.A in Rosemead, with a new office in Westminster, signaled a challenging future for local banking in Little Saigon.

The dream of a Vietnamese-owned bank has yet to materialize, as political refugees lack partnership opportunities typically available to ethnic banks backed by investors from their homeland. Furthermore, fears of protests and boycotts in the politically charged environment further complicate the establishment of such banks. Major U.S. banks have stepped in to address the community's banking needs, with Bank of America, Wells Fargo, and others employing Vietnamese-speaking staff in their Little Saigon branches.

Observing the abundance of lender ads on Vietnamese media, it became evident that more than 15,000 businesses in Little Saigon had banking needs that could not be ignored. Major U.S. banks like Bank of America, Wells Fargo, and others finally recognized this demand and enlisted numerous Vietnamese-speaking employees for their branches in the area.

The disappointments of the First Vietnamese American Bank and the legal troubles faced by Saigon National Bank shattered the hope of having a Vietnamese-owned bank in Little Saigon. Du Miên, a prominent community organizer, owner, and operator of local Vietnamese newspapers, and founder of the first Vietnamese library in Little Saigon, expressed his preference for a bank he can trust, even if it's a big American bank. For hopeful entrepreneurs in Little Saigon unable to meet the requirements of large banks, alternatives like Cathay Bank and HanMi Bank from China and Korea, respectively, along with other third-party lenders, are open for business.

Admittedly, conventional banking institutions have provided limited loan options at best. As a result, the remarkable growth in business development and property ownership by Little Saigon residents and investors reveals the rise of informal community funding networks and local Vietnamese loan brokers, bridging the gap.

Reflecting on the situation, I mentioned to my finance scholar colleague the need for a study on the return of investment of the Vietnamese business community in Little Saigon. The high costs incurred by many local businesses to finance their ventures suggest that numerous refugee businesses may face challenges and fail. Those who succeed do so through hard work and perseverance.

During a meeting with my sister and her husband after they had to let go of their dream business, I hesitated to ask the typical questions of "How are you?" My sister sensed my unease and reassured me, reminding me of their resilience after surviving the trials of 1975. She confidently stated, "Bro, it's just a hiccup. It's disappointing, but it's not the end of the world. We've been through worse."

FORGETTING A COMMUNITY'S SHAME—EARLY-MORNING RAIDS AND COFFEE DON'T MIX

"I must have Vietnamese blood in my body," Kathy Buchoz bragged proudly. Suddenly, she held her breath, clenched her hands, and looked exalted. I'd just asked her the question I ask all my interviewees. "Can you share with me an event that you remember most?"

On the night of February 16, 1984, the Little Saigon community was jolted by a shocking event that unfolded on local and national televisions—the "Southeast Asian Project" raid. Twenty-four Vietnamese physicians, pharmacists, and other related personnel in Orange County, along with a few from other counties were arrested for fraudulently collecting Medi-Cal cards, charging the government for prescribed drugs and medical services they hadn't provided.

Shops in Little Saigon were deserted. My sister, Kim Chung, said that the family restaurant, which was a few miles away from the epicenter of the crisis "was empty like Temple Bà Đanh." My sister referred to the myth of Temple Bà Đanh, in Vietnam. It was said that the temple located in the jungle was haunted, and no visitor would want to stop by. My mother's eyes fixated on the local TV news stations. She scanned the local Vietnamese newspapers, but they didn't provide much information. Like many other families living in Little Saigon, all the members of my family debated the event. Even school-aged children talked about the "event" because "the Vietnamese made news on mainstream TVs," they said. It was a massive panic.

We knew a few of the arrested fraudsters well. For many, if not all, a new life in Little Saigon was the beginning of a long-lasting epic. Against all odds, they had come to Little Saigon impoverished and unemployed, and these Vietnamese refugees overcame loss and hardship, securing their qualifications to practice medicine. Vietnamese immigrants lined up to see Vietnamese doctors. They were heroes to the community.

The media coverage of the raids was not just a blow to those involved but also to the image of the entire community. It challenged the perception that Vietnamese immigrants were hardworking contributors to society. One of my sister-in-laws worked as an auditor for the Department of Defense. She said, "It's so sad. I am taking a day off." The incident taught us that the land of opportunity is not lawless, and individual misconduct can have far-reaching consequences for the entire community. The humiliation and embarrassment affected the entire community, not just those arrested or under investigation.

The fallout from the event led to heated discussions within my extended family and their friends. "The system here is fundamentally based on trust, and we broke it," someone said. "It is sad, but I don't know if they get the message," another added. "I wonder if the system wants to shame us," a friend said. "Let's move out from Little Saigon," a scared voice answered. "Everyone will forget about this soon," a sister reassured. "Oh, I don't think so. It will be in history," a brother said. "Don't stereotype a few bad apples," he said. "A dead fly spoiled the whole bowl of soup," they responded. "Yes, but there are other fraudsters, too—car insurance. Food stamps. And others," someone answered, and the conversation grew quiet. Judging by the general anger that escalated across my family and their friends, the calamity challenged the community's aspiration of a proud renaissance. Even as a bystander, the incident experience was psychologically grueling to me. Little Saigon faced a test of its resilience and aspiration for a proud renaissance.

After his arrival to the U.S., my father conducted an almost reclusive life. He socialized with the extended family and a close circle of friends but otherwise remained removed from community life. He followed the community from afar as a bystander. I noticed he was visibly disturbed by this particular catastrophe. I had an earful from my father, an extraordinarily rare earful. Although he knew that I was a bystander, too, he talked to me about the event. "Sadly enough, it will likely happen again, regardless of the ethnicity of the perpetrators. In particular, in a diverse community with continual arrivals of new immigrants, and some with low self-control will commit crimes if given the opportunity. Hopefully, it will not be as widespread. Hopefully, it will be caught and heavily penalized. Hopefully, the next generation will learn the lessons of their elders."

I was not sure I fully understood what he meant, but I listened as he spoke.

"These criminal acts are like ugly-looking and sharp-edged rocks lying in the river. They will occasionally divert the water flow now and then, here and there. They will eventually be used by the critics to undercut the integrity of the community. But the torrent will not stop," he said.

"We do have a system of checks and balances in our society, and we do teach business ethics in business schools," I replied.

Afterwards, my father asked my sister to help him find a new internist. "Find me an American doctor," he said. He meant a physician outside Little Saigon. I was saddened that he no longer trusted the doctors in our community. However, his search for a new doctor proved a little too late. My father passed away shortly after the event.

A WOUND BEST LEFT ALONE— COLORS WAVING IN THE WIND

Like most crises, the highly agitated raid against the medical fraudsters faded away in residents' minds. Little Saigon experiences a relatively quiet time, although it's essential to emphasize the term "relative." The local media continued to be filled with endless debates, controversies, and conflicts as community leaders often struggled to find common ground. Even if they agreed on certain issues, there were always disagreements lurking in the background. Nevertheless, life in Little Saigon moved forward, with a steady stream of immigrants, new stores, and vibrant cultural and community events that continued to shape and grow the neighborhood.

After my father's passing, I deeply missed his phone calls and the wisdom he shared. In the spring of 1999, as the residents excitedly prepared for the 23rd Xuân Tha Hương (Spring festival away from home), the atmosphere seemed lively. Stores were busy taking orders for the upcoming Tết holiday, and local restaurants were gearing up for Tết parties hosted by hundreds of local business associations, political groups, and fraternities, welcoming thousands of Vietnamese overseas visitors. All appeared to be going well for the community.

However, the wound in the community was unexpectedly reopened by Trần Trường, a 37-year old owner of HiTek TV and VCR video store in the heart of Little Saigon. A tenant of three years at the first all-Vietnamese shopping plaza in Little Saigon, Trần Trường hang a portrait of the late Hồ Chí Minh and draped an official Vietnam flag known as "the communist flag" to locals in his shop. The flag was clearly visible, through the window of his store. Almost immediately, hundreds of protestors, many with the South Vietnamese flag wrapped around their bodies, showed up to protest.

Protesters filled the square, calling for the removal of the Vietnamese flag and the portrait of Hồ Chí Minh. I had booked my ticket to visit the enclave and planned to take two large empty suitcases to buy traditional and symbolic food for the Tết New Year, but my sister called. She suggested that I postpone the trip.

Protests disrupted traffic and normal business operations at the center. Little Saigon was on national news again. *Time magazine* called Trần Trường "(t)he man who brought back Hồ Chí Minh." *The Washington Post* reported on "days of rage in Little Saigon." And the *New York Times* attempted to diagnose the cause: "Passions of the Vietnam war are revived in Little Saigon. How much and how far could the refugees preserve their anti-communist identity under the auspices of the American constitution?"

Westminster Mayor Frank Fry Jr. and councilman Tony Lâm remained neutral. Their hands-off stance, a compromise, functioned as a form of respect for the freedom of speech, protected by the First Amendment of the U.S. Constitution. However, both vented in private that it was a "stupid thing for Trần Trường to do." Local police cordoned one part of the parking lot to make room for the protesters, and they ensured that the entrance to the center was accessible.

Years later, Tony Lâm reflected on his highly consequential decision, "Well, I did struggle on this issue, but I followed the advice of the city legal staff." In the serenity of his own home, the retired city councilman and businessman looked at me pensively, with a hint of nostalgia, or perhaps regret. He acknowledged that he sorely underestimated the reactions of his countrymen. "I was caught between my position and council members' alignment with the broad interpretation of the First Amendment, which sees Trần Trường's display of the North Vietnamese flag and the poster of Hồ Chí Minh as freedom of speech."

The conversation quieted briefly, caught in memories, we both knew well the complexities of the past.

Tony Lâm nodded, and then his voice raised, "I also knew that the protestors out there, they understood that Trần Trường could do what he chose to do, but not here. To them, it was the right of the landlord to evict an unwanted business. I chose to be neutral, and my fellow residents accused me of betrayal, and I sustained tremendous collateral damage."

I perceived his anger from his trembling voice and puckered face, but I didn't respond. I waited for him to recall the event again.

Some 400 demonstrators had camped out in front of the store, protesting and chanting, "Down with communism!" Quách Nhứt Danh, the landlord, served a 30-day notice of eviction to Trần Trường, citing nuisance to the center and public safety. Neighboring businesses petitioned Quách. They requested that he resolve the issue quickly because the protests hurt 90% of their business. Quách sought an injunction to enter the store and remove the controversial items. However, a local judge ordered Trần to take down the two items. However, the Los Angeles Chapter of the American Civil Liberty Union saw the case as a violation of Trần Trường's right to free speech, and Trần appealed and won.

The court decision opened a quarter-of-a-century-old wound for the community. For three consecutive months, peaking on March 6, 1999, an estimated 15,000 demonstrators gathered in front of Trần Trường's store. The crowd increased in size but also in its nature, becoming peaceful. In January, three months earlier, when the story had first broke out, protesters simulated machine-gun fire from loudspeakers, chanted loudly, and issued threats. The court's argument protecting Trần's freedom of speech changed the residents' approach. Trần Trường said that Ho Chi Minh brought peace to the country. He wanted to "open a dialogue," and the crowd responded with shrines of incense, candles, and flowers in front of two mock coffins representing American and Vietnamese victims of war.

Merchants from across the streets brought Vietnamese-style sandwiches and soy milk to feed protestors. The message to Trần Trường was subtle and equally enigmatic: "We respect your freedom of speech, but don't abuse the First Amendment. Don't use it as an excuse to cause dissent in this community."

Nobody knows for sure whether or not Trần Trường took the message to heart. Nobody knows what motivated him, initially. "Trần Trường might not know himself. I still don't know why he did not have a clean record to start with," Quách Nhứt Danh, the center's owner, said. "Two years ago, before this silly incident, he spent twenty days in jail for hitting his wife, claiming that it was not illegal to do it in Vietnam."

During my research on Trần Trường, I discovered that he was involved in selling pirated videos and CDs. When I mentioned this to Quách during our interview, he expressed regret, saying, "I should have thoroughly reviewed his lease application." Trần Trường claimed to be proud of being an American and non-communist, yet he seemed to revel in the attention from media requests and even boasted about displaying the portrait of a communist leader as a conversation starter about Vietnam. However, his actions left a lasting negative impression, and as a result, he will always be unwelcome in Little Saigon.

The wounds caused by the events of 1975 are deep and complex, and Trần Trường's provocative actions only added to the pain. Twenty years later, he is nowhere to be found in Little Saigon, while the community continues to heal and seek peace. Chu Tất Tiến, a staunch anti-communist who endured seven years in a reeducation camp, criticized Trần Trường's actions, calling them a foolish attempt to hurt their honor and legacy.

Upon returning to Little Saigon in early June of 1999, I found little evidence of the incident. Trần Trường's vacated store stood empty, and a sense of relief washed over me. The community of 15,000 demonstrators, who had participated in the largest protest in the history of Little Saigon, had resumed their daily routines. For the Vietnamese refugees, preserving the legacy of the Republic of Vietnam and protecting its history had been their mission upon arriving in the U.S. Trần Trường, in his own naive way, had challenged their aspirations and concepts of peace and identity. Through the demonstrations, it became evident to me that many Vietnamese refugees have learned how to engage in peaceful and orderly protests, leaving behind a legacy of resilience and unity.

If there is anything to learn from this incident, it's that inadvertently or not, reopening the collective wound had led the community to sorrow, protests, and then to connection. Anger on top of anger is fuming more anger. Diaspora feuding is inevitable, my father used to remind me. But with an air of optimism, he also said the time would always be a wonderful healer. When the turbulent tides began to ebb, Little Saigon residents celebrated a festive and peaceful 23rd Tết in Orange County.

THE ELUSIVE STRENGTH OF UNITY—VOICES RISING IN (DIS)UNION

Under normal circumstances, situations where there is no imminent threat to the community's existence, rallying efforts to create a single entity, a single voice, and a unified approach seem almost impossible for Little Saigon community leaders. Numerous discussions with the influential figures in Little Saigon have consistently led to the complaint that "Vietnamese people can't work together."

My father once shared an insight that one of the key factors contributing to the fall of Saigon was the constant political fissures and infighting among South Vietnamese leaders after the assassination of President Ngô Đình Diệm in 1963. Similar to the short-lived tenures of the Republic of Vietnam regimes, community leaders are determined to pursue their missions independently.

During a conversation with Tony Cao, a prominent figure and one of the first political refugees to graduate from a local university with an engineering degree, I inquired about the number of Vietnamese scientists' associations apart from the Vietnamese Engineer Association, which he founded. He sighed and replied, "I honestly cannot even count how many associations we have. There is at least one, but likely more than one, for everything and anything. There could even be multiple sub-groups for an alumni association of a high school in Vietnam."

My brother, Dương, is a local physician in Little Saigon and a former chairman of the 500-member Association of Vietnamese Physicians in Southern California. He often shares a half-joking observation, saying, "When there is only one Vietnamese, we sorely need more. But when there are two Vietnamese, there is one too many." He playfully winked and smiled at me, adding, "After all, we are the descendants of Lạc Long Quân and Âu Cơ, and they split."

The number of political associations and voluntary groups pursuing similar missions is truly mind-boggling for a community with fewer than half a million co-located members.

Chu Tất Tiến, a local anti-communist political activist, writer, and news commentator, pointed out, "Every community leader here seems to aspire to nothing less than the position of the president." Vietnamese culture, in a way, tends to avoid conflict and is hesitant to criticize. As a result, the community continues to debate exile politics strategies. Despite every community leader calling for unity and solidarity, the outcome often leads to further division, more opinions, and the formation of even more associations. Chu Tất Tiến believes that Vietnamese people, especially former officers of the SVN military, avoid facing any form of judgment as they perceive advice as critique.

Consequently, instead of resolving their differences, they tend to walk away, surrounding themselves with followers who believe their stories and views, and emotionally share past experiences.

These associations they create for themselves provide a safe space in the community to voice their thoughts and needs. "Even though no one really listens to each other, having the opportunity to speak up and voice their feelings about their loss makes them feel good. Condemning the communists back home holds significant emotional meaning for them," Chu explained with a laugh. "Whenever I publish an op-ed, I inevitably receive critiques. Some can be quite nasty. But that doesn't deter me."

The 2020 election brought four Vietnamese Americans into leadership positions on the city council of Westminster, California: Trí Tà as mayor, Charlie Nguyễn as vice mayor, and two council members, Tài Đỗ and Kimberly Hồ. However, instead of exhibiting unity in their new roles, the recent debate surrounding the creation of a war monument to honor the South Vietnamese army's hard-fought battle to recapture the ancient citadel of Quảng Trị during the summer of 1972 has revealed a toxic and dysfunctional "bro culture," leading to humiliation and harassment among the council members.

The prevailing belief is that a divided community with self-inflicted crises would inevitably lead to paralysis, which seems to be the case with the failure to advance the project. The culture of divisiveness appears deeply ingrained in the history of contemporary Vietnam, and this situation feels like déjà vu.

For many decades, the residents of Little Saigon defied this conventional wisdom. Despite having various self-sufficient political, religious, cultural, academic, philanthropic, and vocational groups with diverse missions and interests, a shared sense of nostalgia for a history erased by homeland victors, mainstream America, and the rest of the world, along with a collective dismissal of the ruling communist regime in Vietnam, have made Little Saigon unique in its cultural and social life. The countless associations and groups coexist, and their collective energy contributes significantly to the community's legacy.

Almost unanimously, the goal to reclaim their identity remains worthy and glorious to this community, even if it means encountering failures. Rivalries have surprisingly been beneficial, fostering friendly competition that pushes the groups to excel and expand the overall cause of the community.

Unfortunately, when discussing the 2021 Quảng Trị war memorial projects with some younger members of the community, the disengagement of the younger generation from the lives of the first settlers becomes apparent. The tantrum politics of the elders no longer seem to affect them, and the feuds within the diaspora appear incomprehensible to the youngest generation. With social media as an integral part of their lives, debates are expected, but it is disheartening to witness the lack of civility displayed by some netizens.

Online discussions often descend into rudeness,[1] and the ability to remain anonymous in cyberspace exacerbates this behavior. It's important to note that this lack of civility is not unique to the Vietnamese community but reflects broader societal challenges.

In my high school history classes in Nha Trang, from the perspective of any nation, I learned that the world's history has always been full of controversies. The history of this micro-cosmopolitan enclave is no exception. Even war, identity crisis, and loss of a country hadn't alleviated the ingrained culture of infighting. Perhaps the pleasure of the annoyed, I reckon. Nevertheless, the magic of Little Saigon suggests that when an argument begins to lose control, the South Vietnamese flag, not necessarily the truth, helps silence controversies. If reason does not prevail, citizens look to the flag, remembering the journey and shared responsibility for this community.

I stopped by Cô Ba & Flowers on Bolsa Avenue to pick up a bouquet of assorted roses and headed to Loma Vista Memorial Park in Fullerton. At the entrance of the Vietnamese section, where my father rests next to my mother, the Stars and Stripes and the flag with the yellow field and three horizontal red stripes fly peacefully in tandem on two thirty-foot tall poles. These flags take turns intermittently whispering with comforting sounds.

I leaned near my father, wanting to tell him that I missed our conversations about the "breaking news" in Little Saigon. If dad had been alive still, he would have called me with excitement when young Tyler Diep narrowly became California State Assemblyman in 2018. Maybe he would have laughed with happiness when saying that two Vietnamese women were running against each other for a legislative seat in 2020. *Breaking news!* Dad certainly would have shared his disappointment with the fratricide between Mayor Trí Tà and three other council members—Tài Đỗ, Kimberly Hồ, and Charlie Nguyễn.

What would dad have said when he learned that outspoken billionaire Hoàng Kiều used his wealth to "add fuel to the fire"? Maybe he would have had a few words of anger. "There will not be another loud Hi-Tek protest, but the community must take care not to fall into the trap of fake news enabled by social media," I would have said. I would have told dad that the political map in Little Saigon turned purple in 2020. "We need more discussions, Dad," I would say. But I would not have told dad that Little Saigon had two major Tết events in the same year because the organizers, distracted by infighting, had split.

The afternoon wind picked up, and the sounds of the flags grew in intensity, speaking over each other. "Sometimes history shouts its presence out loud. Sometimes it timidly murmurs. Your Little Saigon is here to stay," I told my father, turning to look one last time on my way from the memorial park.

NOTE

1. tintucthat@googlegroups.com (real news) and chinhnghia@googlegroups.com (righteous path)

Chapter 8

The Art of Mastery

SCULPTING AND RETHINKING THE IMMIGRANT IDENTITY

During my annual briefing at the Vietnamese American Chamber of Commerce of Hawai'i, I often discuss the vibrant activities in Little Saigon. The audience, filled with curiosity, frequently asks what makes Little Saigon unique. "Besides being the largest enclave of political refugees from 1975, the excellent food, and the fierce anti-communism movements, what sets Little Saigon apart?" This usually elicits smiles, nods, and comments about how they wish they could be in Little Saigon to savor the delicious cuisine. The ensuing conversations with engaged audiences delve into various aspects of Little Saigon's life and politics. It appears that perhaps Little Saigon has evolved beyond being merely a "counterpart" to the Saigon that so many had left behind. While the question may seem simple, as I ponder the complex dynamics that have unfolded over time, I realize that the answer is not as obvious as it seems.

Significant changes have occurred since the first refugees set foot in the United States, and Little Saigon has experienced profound transformations, becoming a beacon in its own right. Among the many phenomena that characterize Little Saigon, two stand out. Firstly, people of Vietnamese descent from the U.S. and around the world continue to converge and migrate to Little Saigon. It's essential to note that I use the term "people" because many new residents are not exclusively Vietnamese Americans.

"I placed an ad in the classified section of Người Việt Daily to rent my ADU home," shared Daniel Trần, an avionic engineer. He had successfully obtained a city permit to build a two-bedroom unit at the back of his rental home in Garden Grove. "My cell phone burned with hundreds of calls," he added with a nod. "Since the pandemic, it's been a landlord's market. People keep migrating to Orange County, and they desperately need a place to stay. Most of them are looking for a five-year lease contract, indicating their desire to build roots in the community."

The second prominent phenomenon in Little Saigon is the flourishing and growing number of stores with Vietnamese signs hanging above doors or framing windows. These stores are now present in all thirty-four cities of Orange County. Shopping malls in Little Saigon change ownership faster than the state average, as Vietnamese buyers actively acquire various properties, including shopping malls, restaurants, private homes, mobile homes, and vacant land. "We are not out of the pandemic yet (COVID-19), but the housing market is extremely competitive, and there aren't enough houses for anxious buyers," said Karen Nguyễn, my real estate agent. Phước Lộc Thọ has become the reference point for most properties listed on platforms like Redfin, Zillow, and others. Karen Nguyễn explained that buyers typically offer $25,000 to $50,000 above the asking price to secure an $800,000 home.

With a history of over forty-five years, Little Saigon has outlived the Republic of Vietnam. Many of the community leaders in Little Saigon were formerly part of the South Vietnamese regime that lasted thirty years (1945–1975). Hence, the question from the audience about what makes Little Saigon unique remains logical and justifiable. Perhaps, the complex answers to these questions lie within the trendsetters and the people themselves who founded the city, willing it into existence.

OFFERING IN A NATIVE LANGUAGE—A SHRINE FOR VIETNAMESE MARTYRS

Thanks to the sponsorship of a local Protestant church, my fifteen-member family arrived in Marshfield, Wisconsin, in late 1975. Pastor Smith delighted his parishioners by announcing at our first Sunday mass in Marshfield that two of the newcomers were Christians. My two oldest sisters, Minh Châu and Kim Chung, had married Catholics and converted, celebrating their weddings in Catholic ceremonies in Vietnam. Intrigued, I combed through the archives at the Vietnamese Catholic Community of the Diocese of Orange[1] and discovered that an estimated 3,000 Catholics were among the first batch of refugees to arrive in Orange County—a significantly high number given that Catholics only accounted for eight percent of Vietnam's total population. However, they made up thirty percent of the refugee population in the U.S. This influx marked the second exodus for many of them, as they had previously fled the communists from North Vietnam to the South in 1954. Fearing even harsher persecution, they were determined to escape again in 1975.

In 1978, the Diocese of Orange allocated a small dwelling to Vietnamese priests to serve as a Vietnamese Catholic center. Reverend Đỗ Thanh Hà became its first director, and the center, a modest three-bedroom residence, primarily served as housing for Vietnamese priests.

Local churches like Saint Barbara, Saint Bonaventure, St. Callistus, and others generously opened their Houses of God to the increasing number of incoming refugees. However, Vietnamese Catholics quickly realized they longed to worship in their native language, following their religious rituals and cultural customs. For them, the Vietnamese language held a deeper connection to their faith and a stronger bond to God. Lân Nguyễn, my second brother-in-law, shared, "I prefer attending mass in Vietnamese whenever possible. I understand the English version well, but there's something missing in the experience." While he didn't specify what was missing, language carries culture and identity, and perhaps it was this connection that resonated more profoundly with their spiritual selves. I couldn't help but think that the local churches in Orange County didn't have the same familiar "look and feel" of those back home—the archaic medieval French architecture, the hum of decades-old ceiling fans, and the creaking floorboards—all contributing to the indelible and unique experience of attending mass in a Vietnamese church.

Recognizing the challenges ahead, I cautioned, "Going it alone will come at a price."

"Don't worry. We can work on this. God will help us," my brother-in-law replied with a smile, his faith unwavering.

As expected, many local parish leaders initially opposed the idea of nurturing Vietnamese-style Catholicism in the U.S., fearing difficulties in controlling and understanding the Mass. They were accustomed to the federal policy under President Ford, encouraging aid agencies and institutions to help refugees integrate quickly into mainstream society. However, the growing influx of non-English-speaking Christians presented a unique challenge.

Nevertheless, the Vietnamese Catholic refugees persisted, lobbying the diocese to support their aspirations of building their church and incorporating the spirit of Vatican II, which allowed the use of "local" languages other than Latin during Mass.

Over time, the diocese shifted its position. It wasn't a dogmatic decision but rather one based on pragmatic reasons. The introduction of new rules for Mass brought joy and a surge in religious attendance, but local churches struggled with limited infrastructure and financial resources to efficiently serve the newcomers. Once again, the Vietnamese refugees showed their determination to find solutions to the challenges in their new homeland, reflecting the same spirit that led them to their new communities.

The refugee community embraced a heightened mission to address the growing needs of their community—physical, emotional, and spiritual.

Vietnamese refugees in the U.S. not only aimed to expand their base in new places of worship but also to restore the Catholic Church they had left behind in their homeland. "We must support Catholic activities in Vietnam whenever possible," emphasized my brother-in-law, Nguyễn Kế. Since his recent retirement, his home has become the gathering place for Sunday get-togethers with friends from St. Barbara Church. During these meetings, they discuss their ambitious goal of raising $300,000 to build a church in Central Vietnam and also shed light on the oppression and persecution experienced by Vietnamese Catholics. His unwavering faith, which guided him through the perilous journey to his new homeland many years ago, now fuels his desire to offer hope to others in Vietnam.

In 1988, Vietnamese Catholics overseas successfully lobbied Pope John Paul II to canonize 117 martyrs—Catholics who had faced persecution in the 18th and 19th centuries, Vietnamese ancestors of faith. They raised over $4 million to construct the Shrine for Martyrs in Santa Ana, an architectural gem with distinct Vietnamese features, adorned with a red carpet. The shrine seamlessly combines faith with culture, standing as the centerpiece of the Vietnamese Catholic Center. Its red-tiled roof, representing Catholic Vietnamese and their unwavering commitment to faith and community, crowns the building. Inside, stained-glass windows portray disciples and saints, creating an aura of serenity and devotion. In the courtyard, the Virgin Mary and baby Jesus preside, accompanied by the soothing sounds of prayers and the gentle rustle of wind and water from a nearby fountain. The community joyfully celebrated the shrine's inauguration in 1996, dedicating it to the martyrs canonized by Pope John Paul II a decade earlier.

With at least 40,000 members in fifteen parishes within the Diocese of Orange and continuously growing, the Catholic community leaders have ambitious dreams. They are currently working on a $10 million project to build the Lady of La Vang shrine on the Christ Cathedral campus in Garden Grove, a stunning example of modern architecture.

Throughout history, many Vietnamese endured persecution under anti-Catholic regimes in Vietnam. The shrine commemorates an event that holds deep significance for Vietnamese Catholics as an essential part of their healing process. My brother-in-law, a second-generation Catholic, reverently recounts the story, saying, "During the 18th to 19th centuries, Catholicism faced opposition from several dynasties, and authorities persecuted Catholic missionaries and their followers. Many took refuge in the jungles near the city where I grew up in Central Vietnam. Then, as they, the oppressed, sought safety, they witnessed the appearance of the Virgin Mary, clad in a traditional Vietnamese dress, holding the infant Jesus in the middle of the jungle. Since then, the Lady of La Vang has become the symbol of Vietnamese

Catholicism. Whenever you encounter this name around the world, you'll know it's a Vietnamese Catholic Church."

With an air of pride, my sister Minh Châu, Kế's wife, and an equally active member of the Church parish, chimed in, "Yes, but the La Vang Shrine in Garden Grove will be the largest and most expansive shrine, a future landmark not just of Little Saigon but the world." As the principal cook chef, she works alongside an enthusiastic team that assists the church in organizing annual events and private religious parties to raise funds for its missions.

As I glanced at my sister and her husband. Their eyes glint, and they smile. I initially interpreted their looks as expressions of pride, but it was more than that. Little Saigon holds a deeper significance beyond being a mere enclave of safety, self-preservation, and self-aggrandizement. Just as business owners name many shopping centers in Little Saigon after various geographical locations in Vietnam, such as Saigon Mall—Nha Trang Center or Đà Lạt Market, I presumed that Vietnamese church leaders might do the same for new churches, naming them after common names from their homeland—like the Immaculate Conception Cathedral Basilica in Saigon, the St. Joseph's Cathedral in Hanoi, or the Queen of the Rosary Cathedral in Nam Định. However, most Vietnamese churches outside Vietnam are named Shrine for Martyrs, a poignant reminder of the unwavering hearts of resistance and faith. As my sister and her husband smiled, I felt a similar sparkle in my own eyes. Little Saigon's churches, built on the foundation of faith forged through survival and perseverance, embody the epitome of the Vietnamese spirit.

Curious about the La Vang Shrine's fundraising efforts, I inquired among the Little Saigon congregation and learned that Bùi Thọ Khang, a prominent businessman who owned the first Vietnamese chain of supermarkets, eight in total, has been leading the fundraising for the Lady of La Vang Shrine. I called him, explaining my writing on Little Saigon, and he graciously invited me to a potluck-style meeting with his top business managers at his home. "I knew your family well," he said warmly. "In fact, I had my wedding at your mom's restaurant." Grateful for his hospitality, I couldn't help but feel a surge of gratitude towards my mom for her involvement during the embryonic phase of Little Saigon.

Seated in Bùi Thọ Khang's warm and welcoming living room, surrounded by his managers, delicious food, and a sense of familiarity, I eagerly listened to the discussion. "We will reach our funding target," Bùi Thọ Khang assured his team. "And even if we encounter obstacles, with the professor attending our session, I am confident we will find the necessary funding. If need be, I, along with a few close friends, will make it happen."

Curiosity piqued, I waited as Bùi Thọ Khang briefly disappeared, returning with a military-style utility box that he had carried with him during the exodus from Vietnam. Despite its age, the box remained fully operational.

With reverence, he opened the box, revealing two treasured items—a cross he carried as a boat person and an invitation card from his wedding at my mom's restaurant. The sight filled me with awe and appreciation.

Following Bùi Thọ Khang, I entered his well-appointed kitchen adorned with a decorative golden holy cross. Taking a seat at the table, he graciously offered me a cup of freshly brewed Vietnamese coffee. With a confident demeanor, he unveiled his secret for funding the project. "With the La Vang project, we are revolutionizing the approach to Vietnamese Catholicism in America. Historically, our Vietnamese communities have been self-reliant and haven't actively engaged with local American church organizations and leadership," he explained, savoring the warm, rich coffee. "Instead, we have contributed by having our Vietnamese priests and nuns serve the local Catholic communities in various capacities."

I listened intently, finding inspiration in Bùi Thọ Khang's words and reminiscing about my mother and her coffee farm.

"But this time, we have devised a financial model that not only allows us to build our shrine but also supports the operating costs of the Christ Cathedral, graciously hosting us," Bùi Thọ Khang continued, his sure smile echoing that of my sister Minh Châu and her husband. "Moreover, we are determined to contribute to the rebuilding of Catholicism in Vietnam," he added, his voice resonating with the rich and deep flavors of Vietnamese coffee.

LOTUS RISING FROM MUDDY WATERS—FILLING THE VOID

My family belongs to the approximately 70 percent of the South Vietnamese population before 1975 who identify as Buddhists and Confucianists. However, during wartime, government officials discouraged us from attending temple services. Despite this, my second sister, a member of the Buddhist student association in Nha Trang, continued to practice her faith. Unfortunately, she and her teammates were arrested and jailed for a weekend by the police for gathering without prior permission from the local security forces. Those were the last days of President Ngô Đình Diệm's regime, and as the days faded, people held onto their faith more determinedly. Without access to temples, many of us viewed Buddhism more as a philosophy of life rather than an organized religious practice. Our belief in reincarnation shaped our understanding that our present life reflects actions in a previous life, and death serves as a transition to the next life for the deceased. For most Vietnamese, regardless of their beliefs, religion serves as a guide to ethical living, providing protection and guidance from potentially harmful supernatural forces through faith in benevolent spirits.

As children, my siblings and I often stood before our highly decorated Buddhist altar, prominently hung in the center of our family room. Our mother would lead us in reciting words promising to be good people in this challenging world, seeking protection for our family.

Upon arriving in the U.S., many Vietnamese, having endured the arduous journey from Vietnam, found solace in religion. It offered them hope, community, and a place to gather. My Catholic sisters and their families joined local churches in Santa Ana and Garden Grove, finding comfort in religious practices that reminded them of home and provided a sense of continuity. The rest of my family, along with the majority of Vietnamese refugees—Buddhists, Taoists, Caodaists, or practitioners of ancestor worship—sought ways to reinforce their faith, but often lacked local congregational support.

Before 1975, my sister Hải wasn't particularly devout in practicing Buddhism. However, witnessing our family's ordeals during the exodus and settlement in a new land instilled a deep faith in her. Buddhism became a source of hope and comfort for her, and like my Catholic sisters, she has become a fervent practitioner. It has provided her with insight and understanding, offering solace for all that we have experienced.

I met Master Quảng Thanh during one of the most challenging times of my life—the darkest hour, as my father's life on earth was coming to an end. It was then that my mother sought the presence of a "respected monk who knows what he is doing" to bring solace to her heart. Taking on the responsibility, I set out to find such a monk.

As my father's funeral unfolded, I witnessed Master Quảng Thanh officiate the ceremony for the first time in Orange County, with a deep voice, spirit-filled chants, eloquent prayers, and sincere empathy. His presence and guidance provided us with essential healing during our time of grief. Amidst the service, my gaze caught the sight of the water in the lotus pond at the Bảo Quang temple courtyard, and I recalled a lesson I learned as a child. The muddy water in the pond symbolizes our pain, suffering, and despair, but within that mud, the lotus flower finds nourishment and grows to bloom beautifully. Buddhism, I realized, is akin to the lotus rising above the mud, representing inner peace and spiritual growth. Thanks to Master Quảng Thanh's prayers and the symbolism of the lotus pond, I found the words to bid farewell to my father.

In the wake of my father's passing, my mother became a devoted supporter of Master Quảng Thanh. While a monk's usual duties revolve around preserving and disseminating Buddha's teachings and offering spiritual guidance to laypeople, Master Quảng Thanh extended his role, becoming a lifelong champion for his people in Little Saigon. Like many of the first Vietnamese temples in the enclave, Master Quảng Thanh's place of worship began as a modest residential dwelling, with the living room transformed into a prayer hall where he offered his wise counsel. However, through his entrepreneurial skills and fearless community leadership, he successfully raised funds, and Temple Bảo Quang flourished into one of the largest in the area during his time.

Even as Temple Bảo Quang prospered, Master Quảng Thanh continued his tireless community work. He took on the role of teaching local monks and became instrumental in revitalizing Vietnamese Buddhism in the community. Although deeply connected to his congregation in Little Saigon, he never forgot his homeland, Vietnam. Master Quảng Thanh extended his support to the monks back home, bridging the healing and compassion of his works for the Vietnamese people across oceans and lands.

One afternoon, in my exploration of faith, religion, and the Vietnamese community, I decided to visit Temple Diệu Ngự on Chestnut Street in Westminster. This impressive 20,000 square-foot structure with its distinctive pagoda-style architecture had opened its doors to worshippers in 2008. As I arrived, I noticed a group of elementary school children filling the courtyard. Around 200 students stood in formation, led by a young woman in her twenties who spoke to them in both Vietnamese and English, mentioning they would review lessons on manners and etiquette.

Curious about their Sunday activity, I approached the team leader to ask a few questions. However, to my surprise, she politely declined, stating that they were not allowed to talk to strangers and suggested I speak with her supervisor standing by the temple gate. As I glanced over, I saw a man holding a cigarette and didn't find him approachable. Deciding not to disturb their worship, I drove away, leaving them to their activities.

Later, I decided to search for Vietnamese temples in Orange County using the Yelp.com app. The listings revealed thirty-five temples, some of which were grand structures like Temple Diệu Ngự and Temple Huệ Quang in Santa Ana. These temples were planned and built with proper permits, a significant contrast to the first-generation temples hastily created in small residential houses that often caused inconvenience to neighbors.

It had been over twenty years since I last met Master Quảng Thanh. I entered his temple with a warm greeting, noting that the monk had aged, but he still wore the same saffron long-sleeved robe. His eyes sparkled, and his voice retained the authoritative tone that had provided me solace during my father's passing. I expressed how my sisters often saw him at various events, and he acknowledged the same, mentioning my frequent travels.

As one of the first fully ordained leaders, Master Quảng Thanh had a dual mission for the temple: to function as a monastic center for teaching Buddhism and as a lay center serving the spiritual needs of the community. He spoke about the challenges they faced without the support that the Catholic Church received from the Vatican and local dioceses. Some political refugees in Little Saigon still suspected temples of being communist hubs in disguise, which he found to be a lingering mistrust. This reminded me of the infamous monk burning protest in 1963 when Venerable Thích Quảng Đức immolated himself to protest the persecution of Buddhists by President Ngô Đình Diệm's South Vietnamese government. Master Quảng Thanh expressed his efforts to prove that their temple had nothing to do with politics, but "politics keeps chasing after me."

According to my records, Reverend Thích Thiện An, an exchange philosophy professor who arrived at UCLA from Huế in 1966, played a pivotal role in establishing the first Vietnamese Buddhist center near Los Angeles. His efforts eventually led to the creation of the International Buddhist Meditation Center in Los Angeles in 1970, and he later opened a second center to support refugees in 1976. However, Reverend Thích Thiện An passed away in 1980, before witnessing the blossoming of Vietnamese Buddhism in America within a more tolerant environment.

Another influential figure in the Vietnamese Buddhist community was Đỗ Ngọc Yến, a journalist and founder of the largest Vietnamese newspaper and the first bookstore, Tú Quỳnh. After leaving Camp Pendleton, he established the first lay center by collaborating with a monk to sublease a room in his bookstore, thus creating the very first Vietnamese Buddhist venue, Trúc Lâm Yến Tử, located on First Street in Santa Ana.

Master Quảng Thanh shared with me his affection for the International Buddhist Monastic Institute in San Fernando, which is more than just an ordinary temple. The institute serves as a hub for training monastic members based on pre-1975 Buddhist teachings and functions as a publishing house, as well as providing guidance and practice to the Buddhist laity. This institute plays a crucial role in Vietnamese Buddhism's exile, overseen by the Vietnamese American Unified Buddhist Congress.

Inspired by Master Quảng Thanh's tireless efforts and the establishment of his temple, other communities have followed suit, resulting in a proliferation of Vietnamese temples across the United States, particularly in regions with significant refugee populations. As the residents become more prosperous, they are revitalizing old temples, giving them much-needed facelifts, while new temples are sprouting up across Orange County, offering solace and healing to the newer generations.

During our meeting, which lasted almost two hours, the master kindly showed me around his museum and signed several of his books for me. He wanted me to stay as if he longed to share more stories about his journey. I sensed a melancholy in his eyes as if he knew this might be our last encounter. Sadly, a few months later, Master Quảng Thanh passed away unexpectedly from a sudden illness. His demise left a significant void, as he had not even considered succession or having a bucket list; he was full of life and energy.

His memory will forever be cherished by the community, as he was a charismatic spiritual leader who made remarkable contributions to the development of Buddhism in the diaspora.

Master Quảng Thanh's life was a mesmerizing tale of compassion and dreams, faith and survival, and ultimately, destiny and death. His legacy will be difficult to match. Nevertheless, the growth and advancement of self-disciplined and scientific Vietnamese American Buddhism is a testament to the leaders' care and nurturing, akin to the lotus flower rising above muddy waters.

SINGING WITH HEART AND SOUL—BEYOND THE CULTIVATION OF HOMESICKNESS

Before my parents passed away, my first cousin, Bùi Đức Lân, a retired government official from Saigon residing in Manitoba, Canada, would often visit my family in Fountain Valley during the Christmas holidays. In our family, Bùi Đức Lân was like an eldest brother, having been raised by my parents after being orphaned at a young age. He pursued a career in public administration, and before returning to the cold winters of Canada's prairie province, he made it a tradition to stop by Thúy Nga Productions and Tú Quỳnh bookstore in Little Saigon to explore their latest CD or DVD albums. This ritual seemed deeply ingrained in many Vietnamese visitors to Little Saigon.

Similarly, my college classmate, Nguyễn Phương Liên, a retired bank executive from Geneva, Switzerland, followed the same tradition. I teased her, saying, "Every year, I see you buying the same albums." Nguyễn Phương Liên defended her shopping spree, rebutting, "These songs bring back happy memories. I don't mind supporting the artists."

In Little Saigon, two prominent media production companies, Thúy Nga Productions and Asia Entertainment, have become the focal points of Vietnamese diaspora cultural consciousness, serving as living repositories of nostalgia through their record labels, song titles, and book collections.

Located just beside the Asian Garden Mall, Thúy Nga Productions appears tiny and unassuming, but since 1989, it has served as the headquarters for one of Little Saigon's most dazzling family businesses. I had the opportunity to meet Tô Văn Lai and his wife, Thúy Nga, in their small shop back in 1988 when they had just released their fourth signature Paris By Night 4 VHS music video.

Recognizing the global potential of Little Saigon, Tô Văn Lai and his family left Paris and relocated to Orange County. In a short time, their privately-held family business turned Paris by Night variety show into a juggernaut of secular Vietnamese culture overseas. Over the last three decades,

Paris by Night from Little Saigon has brought a mix of nostalgia and pre-war culture, reminiscent of Las Vegas-style productions, to Vietnamese audiences both abroad and at home.

In its 40th year and 136th edition, Paris by Night performances are highly regarded for their sophistication and Hollywood-style productions. While Paris by Night DVDs used to sell in over 300 stores worldwide, DVD sales have now significantly declined, with DVD stores at Phúc Lộc Thọ closing one after another. Adapting to the COVID-19 pandemic, Thúy Nga Productions has turned to YouTube channels and introduced its concept of the "music box."

While Paris by Night shows have amassed millions of views on YouTube, a majority of the audience has shifted to Vietnam, resulting in limited income. As the audience outside Vietnam ages, Thúy Nga Productions now seeks to target Generations 1.5 and 2.0. In its fifth year, young hopeful Vietnamese from all corners of the world sign up for V-Star, a show that aims to bring together the youth of Vietnamese origin while discovering fresh young talents.

The Paris by Night series has always had a strong focus on preserving the best of Vietnamese music and culture, especially songs that evoke feelings of longing for Vietnam, nostalgia, and homesickness. However, renowned songwriters Anh Bằng and Trúc Hồ chose a different path. "We had a clear mission in mind when creating Asia Entertainment programs," Trúc Hồ explained from his CEO office at SBTN. "Our entertainment programs are meant to remind our audience that we are political refugees and to honor those who fought for South Vietnam." Trúc Hồ's tone softened, but his resolve remained unwavering. "I would rather do something that preserves the heart and soul of our Vietnamese refugees than just focus on entertainment."

And indeed, Trúc Hồ followed through with his vision. In 2002, he left his popular and acclaimed show to dedicate himself to his cable Saigon Broadcasting Television Network (SBTN), a 24/7 Vietnamese language television network offering a wide range of programs, from news and talk shows to documentaries, dramas, and kids' programming. "I want to be community-centric and serve the political refugees here in Little Saigon, across the U.S., and around the world," he emphasized. The beloved musician and producer transitioned into an unexpected role as a television producer with a sense of purpose. "I see a mission in what I am doing, even if it is a much harder business endeavor."

I expressed my support, acknowledging Trúc Hồ's principled stance. "It's truly heroic. You are a man of principle, and it's great to see you also serving the second generation," I said.

"In Vietnam," Tô Văn Lai explained, "our DVDs and CDs are officially banned from selling because we refuse to submit our products for government pre-screening and censorship." However, nowhere but Vietnam does the impact of their million-dollar shows, featuring lavish spectacles akin to French cabarets, Las Vegas extravaganzas, and sophisticated staging orchestrated by Emmy-winning Hollywood choreographer Shanda Sawyer, resonate more powerfully. Despite being pirated and freely available on the streets and illegal websites, the videos attract eager viewers in public places like nail salons, barbershops, restaurants, and electronic stores, resulting in lost business for Thúy Nga Productions.

While Thúy Nga Productions increasingly relies on corporate sponsorships from Vietnam to cover rising production costs, SBTN has chosen to distance itself from business relations in Vietnam. Their focus lies in bridging the gap between Generation 1.0 and the American-born and raised Vietnamese Americans, targeting the next multicultural and multigenerational generation.

When I mentioned that I teach "Digital Transformation in Business" to MBA students, Trúc Hồ showed me a pilot-stage app on his smartphone. "We need to find a way to reach out to our constituents differently," he said.

Encouragingly, I replied, "Video-on-demand and interactive TV would definitely be worth trying."

"I hope this will turn our financial situation around," Trúc Hồ said softly, nodding.

For music lovers who are not fans of "nhạc vàng" (contemporary and popular music) and its commercialization, Little Saigon continues to be a fertile musical hub, catering to every conceivable taste. Musical events are abundant, taking place throughout the year in the enclave.

A few months before the COVID lockdown, I had the pleasure of attending the annual Christmas concert by the Vietnamese American Philharmonic at the Diamond Seafood Palace III. The program featured a rich international repertoire, including compositions by American, British, French, Italian, Mexican, and Vietnamese composers, all conducted by twelve talented conductors, with Lê Văn Khoa leading the orchestra as the director.

In the late 1950s, Lê Văn Khoa, after winning several music awards, recognized that Vietnam lacked a philharmonic orchestra. Despite receiving advice to pursue other avenues from popular composers of his time, he chose to focus on symphonies.

After the Christmas event, Lê Văn Khoa kindly invited me to his residence. In his living room, next to his baby grand piano, he proudly showed me a large poster in Russian. "It took me a decade to compose 'Vietnam 1975,'" he said. "In 2007, the Kyiv Symphony Orchestra in Ukraine finally premiered my piece." Subsequently, to the delight of his dedicated fan base, he conducted the "Ca Đoàn Ngàn Khơi" (Thousands Seas Chorus) and collaborated with the Pacific Symphony in Orange County to introduce Vietnamese music to a broader audience.

After shaking hands with Tô Văn Lai, Trúc Hồ, and Lê Văn Khoa, I felt a sense of puzzlement. I asked them how they envisioned the future of their musical legacies. My academic background led me to consider suggesting that they innovate their music production creatively. However, it became evident that the preservation of cultural roots through music and shows had magically bonded Vietnamese refugees for a generation.

But the magic is slowly but surely fading. Fans like my cousin, Lân, from Canada were no longer around, and those like my classmate Nguyễn Phương Liên had grown tired of the repetitive songs and styles year after year. Generation 2.0, represented by my two children, were more inclined towards their identity as Asian Americans than Vietnamese Americans. They craved creative spaces with multicultural expressions. As I contemplated these thoughts, it dawned on me that if Little Saigon sought creativity and innovation in ethnomusicology, it must be these veteran game-changers who lead the way.

HOME IS WHERE ART AND CULTURE ARE

During a visit to one of Frank Jao's offices in Huntington Beach to discuss a startup business, I couldn't help but notice a captivating two-foot-wide round contemporary abstract metal sculpture by Ann Phong hanging on the entrance wall. I had previously met Ann Phong at an interview dinner with the executive leaders of the Vietnamese American Arts & Letters Association (VAALA) at the Brodard Chateau in 2018. As I sat down with Ann Phong, Ysa Lê, and Julie Vo, I was deeply impressed by their dedication to enriching the community's cultural life and promoting art and culture for the Vietnamese diasporas.

These leaders, part of the 1.5 generation, may appear to be ordinary Vietnamese women juggling demanding jobs and private lives, but their involvement with VAALA is far from ordinary. They rely on limited financial support to organize remarkable events such as art exhibitions, book signings, music recitals, plays, musicals, and the acclaimed Vietnamese Film Festival. As I listened to their passion and dedication, I felt they deserved the utmost recognition and appreciation from Little Saigon residents.

Ysa Lê, who took over the helm of VAALA to honor her father's passing, famed author Lê Đình Điểu and co-founder of the association, shared her excitement about VietFilm Fest, the largest international Vietnamese film festival in the world. Starting in 2003 with a small audience at UCI and UCLA, the festival has grown tremendously, showcasing movies and documentaries about Vietnamese voices and stories. With over 3,500 attendees and panel discussions on important topics like "Vietnamese Women in Film" and "Immigration and Displacement," the festival has been a remarkable achievement.

With many directors of Vietnamese descent residing in seven different countries, the collection of films enraptured audiences with a world of despair and glamor, portraying agitated generational fights and emotionally moving assimilation of generations 1.5 and 2.0. "I have college students taking their parents to the festival with a simple mission: communicate with them by watching the films together," Ysa Lê said, referring to Kady Le's *Like Mother, Like Daughter* and Loan Hoang's *First Generation*.

Looking at the enthusiasm of the VietFest Film attendees, most of them generations 1.5 and 2.0, I understood how Little Saigon could affirm its identity. Instead of focusing on lost glory and enduring pain, the documentaries shown over the last ten years at the film festival have achieved something that their elders in Little Saigon did not: uncovering and exploring diaspora identity through their people's daily lives. These films present alternatives to idealistic but mostly hostile and radical political discourse. The conveners of VietFest shared their stories with a younger audience, less divisive in identity politics, and united through cinematographic arts.

"You're doing something marvelously unique," I told the three VAALA executives. "It seems like you have helped your constituents find the road to ultimate freedom through arts." Ysa Lê looked at Ann Phong and smiled at her. "We also gave an award to 'sister' Ann for her lifelong contribution to arts and the community," she said.

Ann Phong, who defied the difficulties of being a new immigrant, chose to be a "poetic" painter—the term coined by Mat Gleasong, an internationally acclaimed art critic and curator. As a so-called boat person who had survived the cruelty of the high seas and the struggle to assimilate into a new land, Ann Phong used the magic of her brush strokes to create two avant-garde and profoundly emotionally significant art collections. Looking at her *Immigrant* collection, she shared with me the recollection of her long and unimaginable ordeal at sea through eye-captivating and imaginable paintings. I could not take my eyes off the dreadful "Crossing the Pacific Ocean," the hopeful "Angel in the Sea," and the painful "Memories of Saigon." I felt gratified being in the presence of an exceptional artist able to piercingly expose the pain of the hundreds of thousands of people who fled war by boat. Yet, her facial expression became stern when she explained how she painted "Human Traces on Earth" and "Oil in the Ocean."

Many Vietnamese households in Little Saigon have a heartwarming tradition of adorning the walls of their homes with cherished memories from their lives back home in Vietnam—faded photos captured before 1975, wedding pictures showcasing family bonds, and joyful reunions with friends. These homes are infused with nostalgia, preserving a piece of their past. Despite the sweet reminiscences, haunting memories of the past, marked by the horrors of war, would inevitably resurface. As I stood there hearing Ann Phong discuss her artistic process for "The Ocean in My Heart," I felt healed and liberated, a sensation of unbounded freedom. Her artistic messages hold the key to unlocking hope and peace for those still haunted by the echoes of war. As I reflect on this experience, I can't help but wish that her art's transformative influence could extend its embrace to all those in need, offering them a path towards healing and renewal.

The Inheritance of Knowledge—Generations Rising

"Who will take care of your business the day you decide to retire?" A question that I often asked during light moments of interviews, playfully emphasizing the significance of family succession planning. "At this stage of my life, I just want to focus on projects related to healthcare and education," 74-year-old Frank Jao said. He is one of the most prominent businessmen in the community. "My daughter Felicia has taken most of the managerial responsibilities. It has been a few years."

Quách Nhứt Danh, who opened the first pharmacy on Bolsa Avenue, Westminster in 1978, and one of Frank Jao's once-business partners, expressed pride in his children's accomplishments. Thủy Linh, a pharmacist working at a hospital, successfully runs an online store selling herbal medicine, while her brother, Nhất Trí, opened a medical office adjacent to their father's pharmacy. "I am not sure if they know that I count on them to take over my investments. I am spending more time now on jogging and meditation," he said.

Succession stories like these are woven into the aging fabric of Little Saigon. Nguyễn Tâm Jr. graduated from medical school under the pressure of his parents. But he decided to take the helm of the family business after his father, the founding member of the Advance Beauty College, had a heart attack and retired.

Family business succession has never been easy in any society, culture, or phase of economic development of a nation. It is even more challenging for Vietnamese refugees, as generation 2.0 does have a fundamentally different choice: to immerse entirely into mainstream America. Tâm Nguyễn Jr. plans to grow his father's legacy with new programs and new locations, a move that his father was reluctant to do. "My dad just wanted to help my mom and the refugees to find a decent job. What he did with the school was a stroke of unbelievable entrepreneurship. But managing growth was something he did not set his heart on," he said. Tâm Junior sat next to his dad. "My dad was so excited that you came and visited us. He dressed exceptionally well today for the occasion." He recorded the conversation. "My dad would enjoy listening to it again, and listening to him telling you the journey of his life to the U.S. tells me that I made the right decision in sustaining his legacy."

Generation 1.5 marches to the beat of their own drummer, heading in new directions. Sonny Nguyễn of 7-Leaves Cafe of Garden Grove chose to leave his much-envied position as the State regional manager of Bank of America in 2011 to start a business with his three brothers. His loving parents opposed the idea. "I never felt 100% happy. I needed to find my own identity beyond being the siblings of refugees with a nostalgic soul. Because of my MBA education and daily reading, I discovered a glocalization vision—a business strategy that takes into consideration both local and global market trends—to help me extend the success of Vietnamese coffee," Nguyễn Tâm Jr. said.

Nguyễn Tâm Jr. introduces himself on LinkedIn as a change agent. He teamed up with his three brothers, Quang, Hà, and Vinh, and three additional investors to launch a coffee shop specializing in artisan gourmet teas, coffees, and pastries with an Asian spin. The shop doesn't merely target millennials. Seven years later, 7-Leaves has sixteen stores in Orange County and plans to open one in Las Vegas. The award-winning entrepreneur by the City of Westminster and the "North Star of Little Saigon" aims higher. "I want to be the Asian Starbucks with a target of 200 outlets in the next decade," Sonny Nguyễn said, with one eye observing his staff's handling the order line and the other smiling at me.

I interpreted Sonny's statement slightly differently. Like Nguyễn Tâm Jr., Sonny, the daring entrepreneur, wanted to show his parents he could achieve greatness. The second generation of entrepreneurs and community activists look to their parents with gratitude. The success or failure of Little Saigon family businesses depends on intergenerational transition. The first generation of Vietnamese Americans engaged in business with limited skills as a necessity to survive, and their offspring pick up the baton with skill sets and language acclimation they did not have. The first generation paved the paths to success for their children and successive generations.

As I reconnected with Tâm Nguyễn Jr. and Sonny Nguyễn the next day at a joint-family breakfast at Cafe N T in Fountain Valley, Tâm graciously introduced me to other family members, including their adorable toddlers. "We are proud of our families. Being connected with friends in the community moved us forward," Tâm acknowledged with genuine appreciation for the support they receive. Meanwhile, Sonny seemed to politely acknowledge the need to adapt to the new realities of the ever-changing business landscape. "We have our own way of doing business," he asserted, highlighting their willingness to embrace innovation while honoring their roots.

I can't help but extend my heartfelt congratulations to these game-changers. Despite facing countless challenges, they have achieved remarkable success in diverse areas such as establishing churches, temples, meditation houses, music chambers, art galleries, and transformative cuisines. These endeavors are no longer mere replicas or nostalgic recollections of the past; rather, they reflect the proactive nature of the citizens of Little Saigon, who refuse to be defined solely by historical circumstances.

Indeed, the people of Little Saigon now wield the power to shape their lives according to their renewed needs and aspirations. They have transcended the role of helpless victims, forging ahead with determination, and embracing opportunities for growth and progress. The community's vibrant spirit and resolute resilience showcase a remarkable transformation that celebrates both their heritage and their commitment to a dynamic, promising future.

Sitting at my desk, I reviewed the notes I drafted and the photos I took for this chapter. I became hypnotized by the radiant yet serene, peaceful but animated smiles of the people I talked with over the month. In their own creative and artistic way, they have created a means to preserve memories, yet they are free from the past as they aim for a new identity. I remember I had to write an essay in my Philosophy class in my middle school in Nha Trang. "What did Jean-Paul Sartre mean when he said, 'Freedom is what you do with what's been done to you,'" the prompt read. I struggled as a teenager with this question. I still struggle now. Yet, what I've learned from these game-changers in Little Saigon has given me a more complex understanding of Sartre's quote. Little Saigon recognizes itself as a Vietnamese American cultural enclave with its own unique personality. Perhaps it is a personality that is ever discovering itself and its limitless possibilities through the spiritual, creative, artistic, and entrepreneurial spirit.

Tre già, măng mọc (As bamboos grow old, young shoots spring up)—As elders wither, youth rise.

NOTE

1. Cộng Đồng Công Giáo Việt Nam Giáo Phận Orange

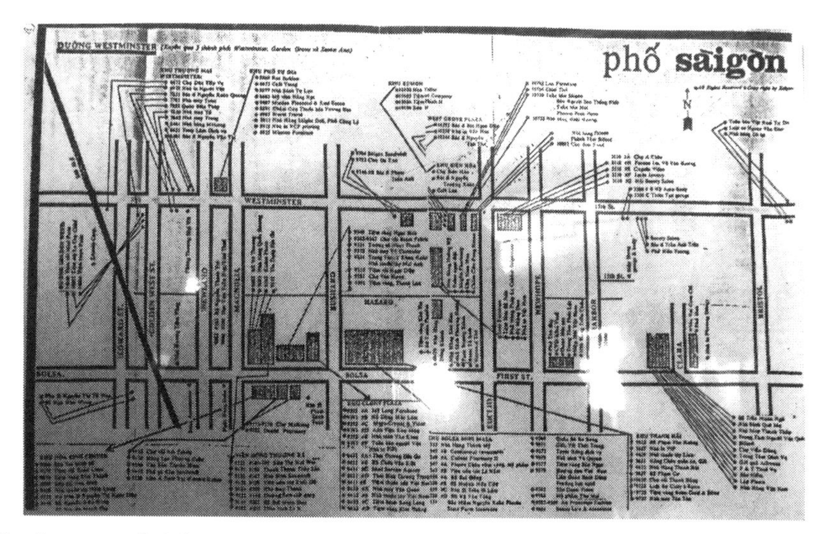

The first map of Little Saigon (courtesy Du Mien, 1980.)

The Bui family, Haiphong, 1954.

The Bui five brothers: Quinn, Tung, Duong, Mai, Truc, Westminster, 2019.

Bui's second generation: Victoria, Tung, Mickey and Ren, Huntingon Beach, 2019.

Tung, Quach Nhut Danh and Nguyen Manh Tien, Westminster, 2018.

Tran Du at his Delta Foods Co., Westminster, 2018.

Tam Nguyen Jr., Tam Nguyen Sr. with spouse, Tung, Westminster, 2018.

Trong Minh, Santa Ana, 2018.

Dinh Xuan Quan, Tung, Chu Tat Tien, SBTN, Garden Grove, 2018.

Huynh Thi Ngoc, San Juan Capistrano, 2019.

Master Quang Thanh, Bao Quang Temple, Santa Ana, 2018.

Front: Thuy Vo Dang, Nha Ca; Back: unknown, Peter Arnade; Tung, Westminster, 2018.

To Van Lai, Westminster, 2018.

Truc Ho, SBTN, Garden Grove, 2018.

Tung, Ysa Le, Ann Phong, VAALA, Santa Ana, 2018.

Quynh Vo, Ann Phong, Tung, Viet Bao, Westminster, 2018.

Tung and Kathy Buchoz, Phuc Loc Tho, Westminster, 2018.

Tony Quang Lam, Westminster, 2018.

Sunny Nguyen (second from right) with family and friends, Fountain Valley, 2018.

Tony Cao and Vivian Cao at their Machine Shop, Santa Ana, 2018.

Du Mien (center) at the Vietnamese Library, Garden Grove, 2018.

Frank Jao, Huntington Beach, 2018.

Bui Tho Khang (front, center) and colleagues on La Vang fund raising, Fountain Valley, 2018.

Sunday youth gathering, Asian Garden Mall, Westminster, 2019.

Chapter 9

Emergence

BUILDING A NEW HOME

Months after the first refugees left Camp Pendleton in 1975, the prevailing sentiment among my mother, father, other family members, and friends was a feeling of being uprooted, disoriented, and rootless. Despite my attempts to offer words of comfort, I, too, felt disoriented, even from my school in Switzerland, as I witnessed the changes in my homeland from afar. In 1977, the late poet Du Tử Lê eloquently captured the sentiments of so many refugees in a poem: "When I die, take me to the ocean . . . so that my body can return home."

Many dreams of their stay in this vast and foreign land as a temporary situation, with the hope that one day, Vietnamese refugees, forced to flee their beloved country, could return to their homeland. As Vietnamese Americans, with one-half of their heritage rooted in Vietnam and the other in America, they find places they can call home, their sense of belonging transcending borders. The U.S. is an enormous land, approximately twenty-nine times larger than Vietnam, with California alone covering about 20% more area than Vietnam.

Among the first Vietnamese refugees, generation 1.0, including Du Tử Lê, many planted themselves in Little Saigon and chose to remain there throughout their lives. They extended their sense of home, family, and community by bringing relatives and friends to this new place they built. Only a small fraction of the Vietnamese refugee population left Orange County to resettle elsewhere. The vast majority of Little Saigon residents kept their eyes and hopes firmly focused forward on a high-spirited and possible dream.

Each person carries a unique and deeply personal journey, and we are storied selves, full of diverse experiences. The emotionally tumultuous and piercingly unreal journey from Vietnam to Little Saigon was laden with trauma, sorrow, and jubilation. When Little Saigon residents graciously welcomed me into their homes, allowing me a few hours to hear their stories, I listened attentively. Just like their families who gathered around, captivated by the narratives they shared, I too was drawn into a state of contemplative enthrallment as they recounted the richness and fulfillment of their lives. Their stories, infused with passion and humility, offered a human perspective that allowed me to appreciate the future of Little Saigon through their loving eyes.

A LONG JOURNEY INTO THEIR NIGHT: OUR HEROES, REST NOW

My father instilled in me many lifelong habits, but one that stands out and continues to be a daily practice is reading the morning newspapers during breakfast. I recall him sitting in his favorite spot in our small kitchen alcove, wearing his glasses on the slope of his nose, carefully reading each news article. Today, I carry on this inherited routine with my iPad, scrolling through local and worldwide news, even though recent research from Harvard warns that "three minutes of bad news would lead to eight hours of grumpiness."

However, a surprising headline in the local newspaper, the Honolulu Star Advertiser, brought me solace and lifted me from the predicted grumpiness. It was about United States Marine Corps (USMC) Colonel (Retired) Gene Castagnetti, someone I hadn't seen in a while. We usually met during the annual Tết gatherings at Kapiolani Park in Waikīkī, where around 8,000 Vietnamese living in Hawai'i gathered to celebrate.

Seeing Colonel Gene Castagnetti brought back memories of an interview I had with his boss, U.S. Army Chief of Staff General Frederick Weyand, in 2005 at VN Television of Hawai'i, which was directed by Nina Nguyễn. As the TV host of her show, I had used the one-hour-long episode to ask General Weyand about his life and role during the Vietnam War.

In the tumultuous days of April 1975, President Ford had sent General Weyand back to Vietnam to assess the military situation on the ground. Weyand reported to Ford, urging urgent U.S. intervention to reverse the dire situation in South Vietnam. Unfortunately, the request fell on deaf ears in a democratic-led Congress, ultimately leading to the fall of Saigon. After we went off the air, General Weyand confided in Colonel Castagnetti and me that he would spend the rest of his retired life in Hawai'i with his comrades who fought in Vietnam. Eleven years after his passing in 2010, General Weyand would be pleased to hear that Castagnetti had worked tirelessly to bring closure to tragic events for a few comrades.

On December 11, 1965, 81 personnel of the 72 Airborne Battalion of the Army of the Republic of Vietnam (ARVN) with four American airmen set off for Tuy Hòa airbase from Phú Yên, a highly contested area. Their mission was to assist an outnumbered Korean battalion against northern forces. However, tragedy struck as the northern troops shot down their U.S. military plane C-123B. Bad weather and treacherous terrain made it challenging for search teams to locate the crash site.

A year before the end of the war, South Vietnamese troops found the crash site and collected the bone fragments, which were eventually returned to the U.S. Army Central Laboratory in Bangkok, Thailand, and finally to Hawai'i. DNA analyses revealed that 95% of the bone fragments belonged to the Vietnamese soldiers. The U.S. military stored the remains in the Defense POW/MIA Accounting Agency's laboratory at Joint Base Pearl Harbor-Hickam in Honolulu, Hawai'i.

In 2017, Vietnam veteran James Webb, a former California senator and Navy secretary under President Ronald Reagan, learned about these lost men and was deeply moved by their narrative of being nameless and lost to their loved ones. This led him to found the Lost Soldiers Foundation, with the aim of taking care of these "men without a country." Webb strongly believed in the utmost respect for these soldiers. His convictions were inspired by the philosophy of care advocated by William Ewart Gladstone, a career politician who served as the United Kingdom's Prime Minister for twelve years in the late 19th century. Gladstone argued that the measure of a noble country is the value and respect it shows its people and extends to how a country cares for its dead.

Webb collaborated with the Family of the Vietnamese Red Berets in Little Saigon to bring the soldiers "home" to their comrades living in exile. Utilizing his connections, he sought help from Richard Spencer, then Secretary of the Navy, and another retired officer of the Marines, FedEx Chairman Fred Smith. Together, they obtained government approval to release the soldiers' remains from Hawai'i to California.

The process to bring the remains of the Vietnamese soldiers to their new home proved to be a complex and bureaucratic journey. Despite the challenges, the petitioners persevered and finally received federal permission. However, they encountered another unexpected hurdle, needing authorization from the California Department of Health to bring the foreign remains into the state for burial. Col. Gene Castagnetti shared his experience, and eventually, he escorted the soldiers' remains on an Air Force C-17 cargo aircraft from Hawai'i to March Air Reserve Base in Riverside, California. The story is somber, filled with loss, but its ending is a triumph—reuniting the deceased Vietnamese soldiers with their people in a new homeland.

On a memorable Saturday, October 26, 2019, more than 2,000 people gathered at Sid Goldstein Freedom Park in Westminster to attend the Lost Soldiers Ceremony, more than half a century after the plane crash. There, they solemnly honored and buried the remains of the 81 soldiers while flags rustled in the breeze.

Witnessing the emotionally charged veterans during the memorial services, it was evident that this had been a long journey "home" for these paratroopers. The residents of Little Saigon hadn't witnessed such an inspiring and tearful moment in a long time. As seven United States members of the Honor Guard fired 21-volley shots, the sorrow pierced the air, but the sounds were somehow soothing.

Among the 81 paratroopers killed in action, only three were identified, including Second Lieutenant Dương Văn Chánh. His elder brother, Dương Văn Hoa, and his family had never found closure after learning about Chánh's tragic death. Until the U.S. military released the DNA analyses, they had held onto hope that their missing loved ones would return one day.

At the memorial services, Dương Văn Hoa and his family finally bid farewell to Chánh and the "soldiers without a country." The service brought many to tears, and afterward, more than 500 members of the Family of the Vietnamese Red Berets gathered to light candles and perform traditional Vietnamese rituals to honor the heroes. Dương Văn Hoa expressed his gratitude for the epic crusade that had finally reunited families. Tears flowed down his cheeks without shame as he said, "Finally, after fifty-four long years, our Chánh and his 80 comrades received the farewell they deserved. We are relieved and grateful that my brother and his fellow soldiers can warmly rest in peace here in this capital of Vietnamese refugees."

His words resonated deeply with the mourners, and the service and candlelight vigil allowed for catharsis within the Little Saigon community—a river of emotions that flowed back to Vietnam, connecting and rebuilding communities.

"To my brother, Chánh, welcome to your new home, a place to rest, at last," Dương Văn Hoa said with a joyful smile, infecting those around him with tears of both love and loss. Many participants at the farewell dinner, in their late 70s, wore long-stored uniforms, carefully dry-cleaned and pressed for the occasion. Despite the range of emotions on their faces, anger was absent.

The next day, before leaving for Toronto, Dương Văn Hoa, his wife, Minh Châu, and two close friends, Dr. Vinh Chánh and Pham Tín An Ninh, who were also paratroopers and now freelance writers, returned to Westminster Memorial Park. Their faces radiated an undefined mixture of love and loss as they wept, touching the marker erected to remember the fallen soldiers. "At last, we have found closure for our family's tragedy—a tragedy that impacted a whole country that saw disrespect bestowed on its fallen soldiers. Rest in peace," Dương Văn Hoa said with heartfelt emotion.

The pain and suffering of the community are ever-present, both as a historical burden and an ongoing struggle. During the interview process for this project, I witnessed tears as people delved into their memories. A public health worker revealed that mental health issues stemming from war trauma still afflict many Little Saigon residents. While the healing process may span generations and many more years, a glimmer of hope emerged with this watershed event, indicating that intergenerational recovery from the deep and profound trauma of war had finally begun. For a fleeting moment, pure joy washed over me, a rare occurrence during this project.

THE KINSHIP FACTOR

As far back as French colonial rule, Saigon proudly bore the title of "The Pearl of the Orient." It was a city exquisitely crafted by those who adored it, including myself when I visited for the first time at twelve years old. Coming from Nha Trang, I saw Saigon through the eyes of a child, dazzled by its vibrant shops in District 1, the bustling sounds of people and motorcycles, and the ceaseless allure of the city. For the Vietnamese refugees of 1975, Saigon remains an everlasting symbol, unchanging and deeply cherished in their memories.

Now residing in Little Saigon, these refugees have tenderly embraced their memories of Saigon, treasuring them alongside their most prized possessions. The name "Little Saigon" holds profound meaning, a testament to their heritage and history. Du Miên, one of the first local journalists who advocated for the name "Saigon Town," expresses the depth of emotion tied to this name, a beacon of their heritage. Saigon is a static image caught in last ruminants of a gloaming light, a light that mellowed with the streetlights lighting the Saigon night.

Vietnamese refugees have carefully wrapped the memory of Saigon, placing it where they keep their most cherished belongings, and now they shine their love on Little Saigon. The beloved namesakes carry the dreams of those who founded it, lovingly. "Calling the place where we live 'Little Saigon' means a whole world to me," Du Miên, 73, said. He is one of the first local journalists who lobbied for the name Saigon Town. The name is an emblem of heritage and vessel of history.

If culture is a river, Little Saigon's culture resists the flow of change, returning, instead, to a Vietnam of the last century. This Vietnam no longer exists. Nevertheless, the stories carried by immigrants have evolved to include leaving Vietnam and arriving in the United States. Nathalie Trần, 45, grew up in Orange County with her mother, a first generation Vietnamese American. Mother and daughter first set foot in Connecticut thanks to a family who sponsored them in Vermont. But the North East's long winters were too cold for them, and they soon sought out warmer climates and a Vietnamese community. Nathalie Trần is currently an Associate Professor at California State University at Fullerton. "I forsake the opportunity to take some interesting job offers elsewhere so that I can be here. Looking at the second and third generations of Vietnamese Americans, I want to be part of their future," Nathalie Trần said. "Fullerton is the right choice for me."

Much like Nathalie Trần, Vũ Lê, 44, a well-to-do business executive, lives and thrives in Little Saigon. Soon after graduating with a business degree (and through professional networking during his college years), one of the top seafood exporters from Vietnam offered him a country manager position. His accounts include Costco and Wall-Mart, but no business accounts with Vietnamese companies in Orange County.

In a trendy Vietnamese-French Cafe & Te restaurant in Fountain Valley, I sat across from Vũ Lê as we engaged in our conversation. I had asked him why he chose to live near Little Saigon, and he took a moment to reflect, a hint of a knowing smile gracing his lips—a familiar response that many residents had shown during this project when speaking from their hearts. "I don't know these people," he gestured towards a group chatting at a nearby table.

Listening carefully, I nodded and jotted down notes, sensing where the conversation was headed.

"I don't have any business with them, and I probably won't in the future. I'm not fond of their loud chit-chatting," he explained. However, he continued, "But sitting here, just a few feet from their tables, I somehow feel at home and complete." His words emphasized the essence of home. Though he could afford to live anywhere, such as Bellevue, Malibu, or SoHo, where most of his corporate contacts resided, he chose to make his home near Little Saigon. Despite owning a residence in NewPort Coast, a bit of a drive to L.A., he embraced this community as his true home, a place that embodies the culture, values, and strong sense of community cherished by countless Vietnamese living outside of Vietnam.

Without uttering a word, I understood his sentiment. Placing my pen on the table, we both glanced over the menus presented by the server moments before.

Vũ Lê, true to his identity and connection with the culture, chose to order the Vietnamese beef shank stew served with a freshly baked French baguette. The delightful aroma of star anise, lemongrass, and cinnamon wafted around our table, heightening the experience. The baguette, an epitome of flaky perfection, sat before us like a work of art. I couldn't help but envision some Instagram star capturing the essence of this meal through a photograph.

In that moment, it became evident that the combination of flavors and atmosphere surrounding us mirrored the deep-rooted connections that Little Saigon provided to those who embraced it as home. The allure of this community transcended any geographical boundaries, and for Vũ Lê, it was a place that perfectly encapsulated the spirit of Vietnamese culture and the sense of belonging that thrived within its boundaries.

As I witness the sunset of Generation 1.0, I observe their once fervent desire to return to Saigon slowly fading. The quasi-utopian idea of reclaiming their homeland now seems to slip away. Instead, they find comfort and belonging in Little Saigon, coming to terms, perhaps, with Thomas Wolfe's notion that "You Can't Go Home Again." Home, as they remember it, exists only in the realm of memory, and reality can never fully match those cherished recollections.

For Generation 1.5 and 2.0, the pull of Little Saigon remains strong. They seek proximity to their aging parents and find ways to live and work within this vibrant community. Little Saigon, to them, is the home of their childhoods, a place that resides in their hearts and memories, forever shaping their identities.

Take my niece, Sissi Nguyễn, and her husband, Philip, for instance. Both children of first-generation Vietnamese refugees in Little Saigon, their paths converged at Fountain Valley Regional Hospital. Sissi, as the attending pharmacist, was taking care of Philip, who was suffering from food poisoning.

"It was a rather peculiar situation," Sissi recalled. "Philip's sister was observing me intently while I explained what was happening to him. It turned out she was looking for a potential match for Philip."

Initially finding the situation unusual, my niece eventually found herself marrying Philip, embracing the beautiful intertwining of both families. "Having relatives from both sides around us feels wonderful," Sissi shared. "Living and working in Orange County gives us the best of both worlds—our daily professional lives à la American, while being surrounded by our fun-to-be-with brothers, sisters, cousins, and the 'weird' uncles and aunties. Not to mention, the delicious Vietnamese cuisine that makes it all complete."

I examined my genealogical tree and found that Sissi and Philip stand out as one of the two couples within their generation who are of 100% Vietnamese descent. The changes in our family tree tell the story of leaving Saigon and settling in the U.S. This narrative continues with my nephew, Danny Trần, 32, who has made his choice clear when it comes to where he and his newly wedded wife want to live. His wife is of half-white and half-Japanese heritage.

"I hear my parents talking about Vietnam every day, and my retired dad speaking about vacationing in Vietnam more often, but we will be living in Orange County," Danny confidently states. A data scientist working for a market research firm, he and his wife, an optometrist, recently purchased a home in Huntington Beach, not too far from his mother's house. The housing market in Orange County may be overheated and on fire, but Vietnamese Americans and Vietnamese seem willing to pay the high prices to stay close to home and family.

Much like Lê Vũ, this couple has numerous options for living and working due to their successful careers. Yet, they have intentionally chosen Little Saigon as their home. "My parents and siblings live here. We can have the best of both worlds—working in the mainstream U.S. economy while also experiencing a taste of Vietnam whenever we crave it." Clearly, they have fallen in love with the place and the community it offers.

Another example in our family is my son, Mickey, who called me on a pleasant Sunday during the Spring of 2019. He asked me to check my calendar to see if I would be available to attend his wedding later in the year. Raised in the U.S. with little parental pressure, Mickey still followed the Vietnamese tradition—graduate first, marry next. Although this advice is given by families in many cultures, Vietnamese parents tend to emphasize the importance of a good education before considering marriage and starting a family. My parents had twenty-six grandchildren from their ten children, including my two children. Mickey became the fifteenth in his generation to get married, joining twelve out of fourteen of his first cousins who married inter-ethnically. His then-wife-to-be, Ren, is of Italian descent.

Vietnamese wedding traditions, at their most splendid, are steeped in richness and elaborate rituals. The process involves a pre-wedding meeting, during which the groom expresses his intentions and formally asks for the bride's hand in marriage. Following this, meetings are held to decide on the engagement and wedding ceremonies, accompanied by formal gift offerings to the bride's family. On the wedding day itself, tea and candle ceremonies pay homage to ancestors, preceding the joyous and colorful wedding reception.

Having grown up in a family with Northern traditions, which are known for their formality compared to Southern Vietnamese traditions, I vividly recall my aunt Ký Phương, my mother's eldest sister, saying, "Rể là khách, dâu là con," meaning "We treat a son-in-law as a valued guest and a daughter-in-law as a daughter."

In traditional Vietnamese families, daughters-in-law are expected to embrace their husbands' extended families as their own. This embrace often includes taking care of the husband's parents when needed. It is also customary for in-laws to become integrated into the family and kin networks.

As many second-generation children marry inter-ethnically, my siblings and I feel blessed that our family and kin networks remain a loving and supportive haven. Our parents' descendants have found ways to maintain strong family relationships, even while speaking in English, creating family group chats, gathering during holidays, and affectionately discussing their Vietnamese-born parents' cultural traditions with a sense of honor and respect. Despite the blending of cultures, their Vietnamese heritage remains a cherished part of their identity.

In my extended family, the act of code-switching from our Vietnamese to English has not diminished the intensity of our dialogues or conversations; if anything, it has made them more direct and sometimes even brutal. My sisters have never been shy or diplomatic in poking their noses into their children's lives, and their use of English only amplifies their straightforward inquiries.

When my son, Mickey, got married, he and his bride chose a Vietnamese American wedding planner to incorporate our cherished traditions. Yet, I couldn't help but notice that some of our rituals seemed to slowly fade away, despite the effort to preserve them. However, Mickey's wedding ceremony was still incredibly moving, bringing tears to the eyes of many attendees. The whole extended family was present, offering their heartfelt congratulations. Seeing Ren, my new daughter-in-law, in an elegant and graceful Vietnamese red wedding dress, was a poignant reminder that certain traditions withstand the test of time.

After the wedding, I visited my parents' resting place at Loma Vista Memorial and shared the joyous occasion with them. I felt the peace and beauty surrounding their final resting place as I contemplated all the changes our community has faced.

In a lighthearted moment, I playfully joked with my parents, imagining them laughing along, saying, "Mom and Dad, on my way home from Mickey's wedding, I thought of modifying the old Vietnamese adage 'Rể là khách, dâu là con' (we treat a son-in-law as a valued guest, and a daughter-in-law as a daughter) to 'Dâu rể ngoại quốc là khách, dâu rể người Việt là con' (we treat non-Vietnamese children-in-law as valued guests, and Vietnamese children-in-law as children)." In a way, it reflects how our social concept of the extended family has evolved with the small "army" of grandchildren and their non-Vietnamese spouses. Despite the changes, the essence of our extended family is beautifully preserved, if not reinforced, in its own unique way.

METAMORPHOSIS

In 2018, during a city council meeting, Phạm Hoàng Bắc proposed a visionary idea that received unanimous support from the Westminster city council. His proposal involved developing a mega center called Saigon Xưa, meaning "Retro Saigon," at the prominent corner of Bolsa (officially known as King Trần Hưng Đạo Avenue) and Brookhurst. This ambitious $120 million project, occupying a six-acre lot, was set to become the community's next iconic development after Phước Lộc Thọ Center.

I had the opportunity to meet with Phạm Hoàng Bắc a few months prior to the council's decision. In his small office on the second floor of the Ramada Plaza in Garden Grove, which he had acquired in 2013, Bắc exuded the determination and resilience characteristic of many within the Central Vietnamese community and diaspora. He struck me as a quiet yet no-nonsense businessman. His family's journey to Orange County and their path to success through hard work was a familiar tale in this close-knit community. As an engineer, Bắc had toiled diligently, while his wife, Joann Pham, contributed to their family's prosperity as a mortgage lender. They expanded their businesses, including two hotels catering to Little Saigon tourists in Westminster and Garden Grove. Now approaching retirement age, Phạm Hoàng Bắc and Joann Phạm were eager to leave a lasting legacy to the community they both built and cherished.

During our conversation, Phạm Hoàng Bắc shared his reflections on the past and his exciting plans for the future. He leaned over his desk, pointing out blueprints laid on a wooden table. As I moved closer, Bắc Phạm spoke calmly and passionately about each detail of the project. His vision aimed to recreate nostalgia for the community by designing a hotel and residential structure reminiscent of the historical Continental Hotel and a 48,000 square-foot shopping arcade inspired by the iconic Bến Thành Market tower. "Mesmerizing and brilliant," I exclaimed, realizing the historical significance and cultural impact of this endeavor. My words seemed to strike a chord with Bắc Phạm, who managed a modest yet gratified smile.

The blueprint for Saigon Xưa revealed Bắc's thoughtful plan to reconstruct lost elements of the past while incorporating modern and local adaptations. The Continental Hotel, a colonial gem dating back to 1880, holds a special place in the hearts of visitors to Vietnam. Glamorized by Graham Greene's The Quiet American, the hotel's allure remains intact for tourists who visit. Alongside it, Bắc plans to include the iconic Bến Thành market, a symbol of vibrant international trade, built in 1912, as well as a touch of Hội An town market's charm.

As I flipped through the blueprints, Bắc Phạm elaborated on his vision for the mixed-use property. He intended to house high-end and luxury boutiques within the Bến Thành market wing, while the interior court would come alive with nighttime culinary and cultural activities. To further enrich the experience, Bắc planned to introduce the Wyndham Grand, a 5-star modern hotel, and a collection of luxury condominiums comprising 200 units, providing residents with a tangible link to their cultural heritage while embracing the conveniences and luxuries of the present.

In the early 1980s, the first Vietnamese refugees wrestled with how to build modest commercial centers. Quách Nhứt Danh, who was among the handful of major investors, remembered the time well, reliving it during one of our conversations. "At that time, the only thing I wanted was to find an inexpensive—I meant very cheap—shopping plaza with affordable leases, which would bring Vietnamese businesses into a communal location." Subsequently, the first new Vietnamese stores were quickly constructed in the new retail and commercial space, with little thought to architectural styles.

What Little Saigon lacked, as Nguyễn Thiện, 33, a project manager of a multinational corporation, pointed out, was an indelible picture of community triumph. "Phước Lộc Thọ is a great venue for local bargain-hunting shoppers, killing-time retirees, and curious visitors. But there is nothing spectacular about it—nothing architecturally that I can show to my colleagues at work." Perhaps Saigon Xưa, once completed, will provide this elusive representational belonging that Đặng Võ Thủy, the UCI library curator, referred to earlier. Little Saigon slowly crafted and continues to create its own identity, founded with an intriguing mix of cultural heritage and an embrace of contemporary life in a Western environment.

Scheduled to open in mid-2022 and fully constructed by 2023, Phạm Hoàng Bắc's Saigon Xưa has already garnered praise from the local community. The project is poised to reinforce the cultural identity of Little Saigon, and the properties surrounding the area have seen an increase in value. Nevertheless, with a venture of this magnitude, rumors abound, and some suggest that Phạm Hoàng Bắc may have solicited investments from Vietnam, a decision that has sparked controversy among a few local political activists.

Undergoing a series of facelifts, Little Saigon exhibits an unstoppable trend of urban renewal, almost akin to the community's own metamorphosis. As I lay before me a collection of pictures taken over the years, the transformation becomes apparent—Vietnamese restaurants and shops have evolved, storefronts have changed, and the faces of the individuals running the stores differ. The early designs have vanished, replaced by sleeker two- and three-story structures that have replaced the once modest one-story buildings from the sixties. Little Saigon's atmosphere now boasts updated architecture, epitomized by the Mall of Fortune in Garden Grove, which, after its renovations, now showcases upscale aesthetics and expanded spaces compared to its pothole-ridden, unimpressive past.

The expectations of the younger generation no longer align with the first waves of Vietnamese shops. Little Saigon faces a rapidly changing demographic, and new restaurants like Earth Delights Deli, Little Sister, The Vox Kitchen, and other newcomers embrace a more European design. Departing from the plain strip mall appearance reminiscent of pre-1975 Saigon's mom-and-pop shops, these young entrepreneurs have distinct visions for their businesses. As their grandparents and parents sought to recreate a community reminiscent of the one they lost, the newer generation has its own aspirations. The business signs now reflect more artistic and less chaotic elements, as the next generation—young and diverse—brings their dreams to life.

The prevailing motto of local business developers and owners in Little Saigon is "growth." It's all about bigger commercial centers, larger shops, and expansion. Mayor Michael Vo of Fountain Valley proudly showed me the new trend when he took me on a city tour. Vietnamese businesses are increasingly moving to Fountain Valley, bringing with them a significant boost in residential demand. To maintain the city's integrity and compliance with regulations, Mayor Vo has spent considerable effort reminding Vietnamese homeowners to adhere to building codes and obtain necessary permits when renovating their properties. Thanks to this influx of newcomers, real estate in the city has seen an impressive appreciation of at least 20% in 2020–2021, proving to be a win for the city's coffers and the mayor alike.

Amidst this dynamic growth, a more subtle yet transformative change has emerged in Little Saigon. Many second-generation businesses have embraced modern business practices, transitioning from a cash-based economy to a technology-assisted business environment. Sleek credit card machines like Clover have become commonplace, while wireless and online platforms handle restaurant reservations and food orders. Younger and bilingual waitstaff now meet service standards expected in upscale venues, and second-generation individuals, educated and trained in the U.S., now staff most medical offices in the community. These shifts represent a quieter, but no less impactful, revolution in Little Saigon's business landscape.

NEW WAVES

During one of my stopovers at Los Angeles International airport, I encountered a Vietnamese family at the boarding gate. It's a common sight to see Vietnamese American travelers at major airport hubs with flight connections to Orange County. Nguyễn Phượng and her family were welcoming seven members of her husband's family to Little Saigon, including two married sisters-in-law and their siblings. "It took nearly thirteen years to sponsor my husband's family to emigrate to the U.S.," Nguyễn Phượng shared, a sense of relief evident in her voice as her husband assisted his arriving relatives with their luggage.

As we continued our conversation while moving towards the boarding area, I learned that this group represented the third wave of immigrants from their family. Nguyễn Phượng's mother was a "boat person" who survived three harrowing escapes on the open sea before arriving in Pulau Bidong,

Indonesia, and eventually settling in Louisiana and Orange County in 1978. Her mother then petitioned for Nguyễn Phượng to join her in Little Saigon in 2002, and now, in 2019, they were joyfully welcoming new members into their family circle. "It feels like a dream come true. My sisters-in-law have been patiently waiting for decades, saving every penny they could back home, and now they are looking forward to building a new life here in Little Saigon. We are reunited again."

Nguyễn Phượng then asked me with an anxious voice if I knew anyone who offered rental sharing. "For the last three months, after I got word that our relatives successfully passed the interviews at the U.S. General Consulate in Saigon, my husband and I have been searching for a rental for them. But it has been in vain. The available rentals are either too far from Bolsa Avenue or simply too expensive."

In addition to the continuous flow of immigrants from Vietnam, brought to the U.S. through family-sponsored petitions and other avenues, Little Saigon has also attracted other immigrants, contributing to the town's growth. "I hear you," I responded. "I'm sorry. I don't have knowledge of the rental market in Little Saigon. But, I'll ask someone who might be able to help."

A few days later, as I headed to breakfast with Nguyễn Văn Trác, a long-time acquaintance who had migrated from San Jose to Orange County to retire, I couldn't help but inquire about housing. Nguyễn Văn Trác had been a versatile entrepreneur in the Little Saigon community, trying his hand at various businesses, including a mini supermarket, a real estate agency, a mortgage lending brokerage, and a tax preparation service.

During our meeting, Nguyễn Văn Trác surprised me with his down-to-earth approach to retirement. He shared that he had rented out his Victorian home in San Jose and opted for a mobile home, which he parked at a convenient mobile home park near Little Saigon. "The weather here is quite pleasant, and I find it very comfortable. I'm enjoying my time in Little Saigon," he said with a chuckle. "Interestingly, some of my neighbors are Vietnamese from Houston, Texas."

His decision to retire in a mobile home park seemed to offer a sense of freedom and the opportunity to engage with fascinating neighbors. Nguyễn Văn Trác had clearly found a little piece of heaven in this setting, and perhaps it was providing him with a sense of adventure in his retirement years.

Considering my own future retirement from academia, I reached out to Shirley Nguyễn, a local real estate agent, to assist me in finding a "great deal" home in Orange County. I soon realized that the timing for this venture was rather off; the community was experiencing a surge in housing demand. Despite the country's success in keeping COVID-19 at bay in recent months, the housing market was booming. "It's a seller's market," Shirley explained over the phone. "Low-interest rates, limited housing supplies, rising lumber costs for new constructions, and concerns about the stock market's stability are driving buyers to offer prices that often exceed the seller's asking price by 5 to 10%."

I was prepared to hear some news about the housing market, but it still came as a shock. Shirley Nguyễn explained that finding a bargain in Orange County was challenging due to the presence of numerous affluent cash buyers, many of whom were Vietnamese, and some even coming from Vietnam. The influx of newcomers from Vietnam has significantly impacted the housing market in the area.

Curious to understand the motives behind this wave of immigrants, I asked if Vietnamese individuals were primarily coming to Orange County to purchase residential properties. However, I soon received the answer to this question from a different source. My brother Dương, a gastroenterologist, approached me with an investment opportunity in a commercial building. He was looking to lease a facility for his clinic as his current contract was expiring soon. During our search, Lê Tân, a real estate broker from Garden Grove, showed us some commercial buildings. However, the values of these properties had appreciated considerably in recent years. Lê Tân mentioned that they had observed significant interest from investors in Vietnam, as properties on the market were often quickly acquired by buyers of Vietnamese descent. Moreover, the Korean community in Garden Grove and Buena Park appeared to be gradually selling their properties to Vietnamese buyers.

The Vietnamese community in Little Saigon is a haven, calling all to its shores.

THE BRIDGE

There should be only one recipe to make "authentic" phở, yet every Vietnamese restaurant boasts of having the best in town. Curiosity got the better of me after hearing a friend rave about Hạt Ngò in Fountain Valley, known for its authentic northern-style phở made with premium Japanese Kobe beef. The allure of trying this succulent dish was simply irresistible.

As I entered Hạt Ngò, I was greeted by a clean and functional interior adorned with white decor and glass structures. While waiting for my order, I overheard a conversation at a nearby table by the coffee machine. Six middle-aged men, dressed in golf attire, were placing their orders with a young waiter. Their distinctive Northern Vietnamese accents caught my attention, and I couldn't help but eavesdrop on their conversation. They had just returned from a golf session at the David Baker par-62 Executive golf course on Edinger Ave in Fountain Valley. I presumed they were from Hanoi, given their accents. They spoke fondly of their second residence in Orange County, where Little Saigon was their place for business, relaxation, and recreation.

In 2020, Vietnam boasted a trade surplus of $69.65 billion with the U.S., a remarkable achievement considering the earlier years of bilateral exchange. As a result, a portion of this surplus is expected to be reinvested in the U.S. economy. The rapid growth in Vietnam, estimated by Forbes to be just ten to fifteen years behind China, is also benefiting the sustainability and prosperity of Little Saigon. Forty-five years ago, it would have been unimaginable for this enclave that the economic achievements of "victors and former enemies" now contribute to the growth of Little Saigon, showcasing a pragmatic partnership, a workable marriage of reason.

Whether embraced or not, Little Saigon is poised to play a pivotal role as a bridge between two nations. According to Đinh Quân, a retired economic advisor from the United Nations Development Programs (UNDP) and now a news commentator for various local media channels, certain sensitive topics are better left untouched—such as the flag, corruption, and the communist party. Despite his extensive global experience, advising government officials of developing nations in cities like New York, Paris, and Geneva, Đinh Quân has chosen to savor his retirement in the vibrant atmosphere of Little Saigon. With his adeptness in conveying complex political and economic matters to the general public, he finds fulfillment in contributing to the community during his leisure time. He believes that any other mutually beneficial discussions are welcome.

During our discussion about the future of Little Saigon and the increasing presence of Vietnamese from Vietnam, Đinh Quân expressed optimism about the possibilities of this union. The long-standing crusade against communism, nurtured for over four decades, is likely to continue under the next generation's leadership out of respect for their elders. However, the new generation will likely bring a more "mainstream" approach to business practices.

I recently had dinner at Fogo de Chão Brazilian Steakhouse in Irvine and met Tony, a Vietnamese student studying at California State University, Long Beach. Among the twenty-thousand Vietnamese students attending American universities, over 6,000 are living in California. Tony shared that his parents advised him to come to California due to the presence of a third cousin living and working here, offering a sense of comfort and assistance in a foreign land. "They said they would feel more comfortable to have someone to assist me in a foreign land. I seldom meet my cousin, but the good news is it is relatively easy for me and my friends to find a job here," Tony explained.

The connection to Vietnamese culture remains strong in Orange County. Bùi Thọ Khang, the owner of fourteen supermarkets in the area, mentioned that his stores carry various items imported from Vietnam, including popular items like instant coffee, dried foods, bakery products, and household appliances. The presence of these products further solidifies Little Saigon's identity as a Vietnamese community, even in the eyes of non-Vietnamese residents.

I had a breakfast gathering with a group of scientists and business people at a European-Vietnamese restaurant near the University of California, Irvine. Among them was Nguyễn Phú, a Vietnamese citizen and a Ph.D. graduate from UCI, conducting research at the UCI Center for Hydrometeorology and Remote Sensing alongside other Vietnamese American colleagues. We discussed the continuous flow of entrepreneurs between Vietnam and California, noting that the academic and scientific communities are also involved in this exchange.

Efforts are being made to formalize collaborations between the Vietnamese scientific communities in America, including Orange County. Frank Jao, who serves on the University of California, Irvine Foundation Board of Trustees, envisions UCI as a hub for facilitating science and technology transfers and exchanges between the two nations. This reflects the growing ties between Little Saigon and Vietnam, paving the way for potential future partnerships.

Frank Jao's philanthropic and community work is nothing short of awe-inspiring, painting an unusual picture of the intricate bridge between Little Saigon, a haven for political refugees, and present-day Vietnam, embracing economic reforms (đổi mới) forged by the Hanoi government over decades. His dedication to the Vietnamese American Oral History Project at UCI, generously funded through his personal foundation, captures the poignant stories of first-generation Vietnamese refugees and immigrants, allowing their diverse experiences to shine brightly.

Moreover, Frank Jao's unwavering commitment to education and science in Vietnam during his tenure as chairman of the Vietnam Education Foundation (VEF) from 2002 to 2009 is truly encouraging. His passion resonates deeply as he also contributed to the governing board of Fulbright University, a Vietnamese institution empowered by a U.S. special fund, expected to ensure a brighter future for generations to come.

As I delved into the repercussions of the trade dispute between the Trump administration and China's Xi Jinping, my heart raced with curiosity, seeking to understand its impacts on Little Saigon. A conversation with Tiffany Nguyễn, a community-centric real estate agent who travels to Vietnam looking for buyers, revealed an undeniable truth—the Vietnamese from Vietnam are flocking to the land of opportunities, eagerly seizing every chance to prosper. While her statement may be slightly exaggerated, the overwhelming anecdotal evidence leaves no doubt.

The numbers, shared by a visa officer at the Vietnam Consulate General in San Francisco, evoke a sense of amazement—out of half a million visas issued in 2018, a staggering 400,000 were granted to Vietnamese Americans.

The profound transformation from three decades ago is no less than spectacular, reminding me of a poignant tale shared by a colleague who once shunned partnership with an outstanding software engineer due to the painful scars of Vietnam's past. His poignant question, "Why did you return to a country that tortured my parents?" lingers in my heart, revealing the complex and ever-evolving dynamics between Little Saigon and Vietnam, entwined by history and ever-changing perspectives.

GREAT MINDS—MORE THAN DREAMS OR NIGHTMARES

When Catlin Trần, a determined sophomore at the University of California, Irvine, reached out to me for advice, I was immediately drawn to her passionate pursuit of a different path. Despite her mother's strong desire for Catlin to study biology and pursue a medical career, Catlin had a unique dream of her own. While juggling her classes, she found herself concocting an ambitious business idea centered around the commercial food and beverages industry.

Reflecting on my own past, I couldn't help but marvel at Catlin's ambition and drive. While I was once solely focused on acing exams, she has her sights set on disrupting current food production and delivery systems with her ambitious and original venture. There's no doubt that she has a challenging road ahead as she prepares her business plan for fundraising, but I have no doubt that her passion and vision will pave the way for success.

A few months earlier, Frank Jao and I helped Hoài Khổng Anh, a denture specialist, work on a business model for his new invention. He developed magnetic technology that would replace current tooth implant technology. Khổng Anh also dreams big. "This is a billion-dollar industry. I have a proprietary technique that is so cost-effective and much less painful for the patient. We could be another Vietnamese-owned Robinson Pharma for the Little Saigon community," he exclaimed.

Witnessing these emerging entrepreneurs and inventors, I can't help but be reminded of my mother's generation of business people in Little Saigon. They persevered with small enterprises, and their ingenuity, exemplified by pioneers like Trần Dũ's Delta Foods and Quách Danh's groundbreaking pharmacy, laid the foundation for the vibrant imagination and boundless creativity that flourishes in today's generations.

Catlin Trần and Khổng Hoài Anh stand as encouraging examples of the possibilities that lie ahead. Catlin envisions a national food distribution network, leveraging the Internet of Things (IoT) technologies, while Khổng Hoài Anh dreams of a manufacturing facility that rivals the impressive 400-employee robot-powered manufacturer of dietary supplements at Robinson Pharma, owned by Tom Nguyễn in Santa Ana. Their aspirations know no bounds, and it is heartening to witness the potential they hold to shape the future. I wish them the best of luck in their endeavors.

The arts and humanities in Little Saigon also shine brightly, thanks to pioneers like Ysa Lê and her dedicated colleagues who work tirelessly to organize the annual Viet Film Festivals. Despite the challenges posed by COVID-19, they fearlessly embraced virtual platforms to share Vietnamese arts and culture with a global audience. This bold experiment led to a hybrid version in 2023, celebrating the 20th anniversary of Viet Film Fest with a two-day in-person gathering at the Frida Cinema in Santa Anna, followed by a two-week virtual showing.

As I reflect on these second generation aspiring stars and daring minds, I can't help but feel a surge of excitement and hope for the future of Little Saigon. The determination and creativity of this new generation promise to propel the community to greater heights, embracing change and forging a brighter path forward.

Speaking of political leadership, Tony Lâm, the first Vietnamese elected councilman for the city of Westminster in 1992 at age fifty-six, had to navigate a delicate balance between governing the city and addressing the concerns of exiled refugees. Fast forward to 2020, the community has over twenty-two Vietnamese Americans elected to various official functions in Orange County. These young leaders, in their late forties, center their agendas on the future of Little Saigon and the cities they serve. They are old enough to cherish Vietnamese traditions and young enough to breathe new life into the community. The political landscape of Little Saigon has evolved, no longer solely driven by nostalgia.

The media's perception has also shifted, as they now refer to Little Saigon as the Vietnamese American community, seldom mentioning the label of political refugees. Time has indeed changed Little Saigon and its people, ushering in a new era of growth, diversity, and potential. Little Saigon will undoubtedly continue to shape its destiny, perhaps embracing a more "mainstream" American approach while retaining its unique and vibrant identity.

THE FUTURE IN TRANSIT

As I sit here reviewing the diverse perspectives on the future of Little Saigon, I can't help but feel a mix of emotions. The recent waves of immigrants have undoubtedly transformed this community, redefining the meaning of "little" in Little Saigon. It's fascinating and heartwarming to see how this once modest enclave that my parents called it home has grown and evolved into an ever growing and dynamic place, attracting people from all walks of life.

I find myself smiling at the complexity of the situation. It's as if the community itself reflects the diversity of opinions and values it holds. There is no single answer or common strategy that can guide the future of Little Saigon. Yet, amidst the cacophony of voices, one thing remains certain—the boundless imagination and potential that its multi-generational inhabitants envision for their home.

Little Saigon has come a long way since its humble beginnings in 1976, now almost ten times larger than it was back then. Despite its remarkable growth, this dynamic community remains renowned for its diversity of opinions, conflicting values, and unclear visions. It's a place where people passionately disagree on various matters, and seeking a single answer has always been a challenging task. Yet, amidst the spirited debates and differing viewpoints, the resounding and jubilant voices of its multi-generational inhabitants might signal a future full of boundless possibilities.

When I posed questions about the future of the enlarged and segmented Little Saigon community to Trần Dạ Từ, the accomplished novelist, poet, and managing director of Việt Báo Daily, his response was both insightful and thought-provoking. With a warm smile, he shared, "I do not worry much about a segmented, or some might say, fractured community. To me, diversity is a strength, and diversity is good." As he held a lit cigarette in his fingers, his contemplative demeanor added weight to his words. He went on to mention that while there may be disagreements among the people here, the continuous influx of individuals to this place, including many Vietnamese from Vietnam seeking to emigrate, hints at something being done right.

Curious about my perspective as both an insider and outsider of Little Saigon, Trần Dạ Từ turned the tables and asked me the same question. The unexpected exchange left me pondering.

As a trained economist, I've learned to approach the future of Little Saigon with caution, knowing that its dynamism and diverse perspectives defy any simple predictions. There is no one-size-fits-all strategy to sustain and nurture this extraordinary community. Instead, we find ourselves traversing uncharted territory, where uncertainties abound. While I could have offered a standard response like "the future of Little Saigon is at a crossroads," I chose a different path, one that my late father would have advised me—seeking wisdom from the experiences of other immigrant groups that came to the U.S. before the Vietnamese in 1975.

Over the generations, ethnic enclaves seem to experience shifts in their demographics and vibrancy. Take, for instance, Little Italy in New York City, which saw its population decline significantly since its inception in 1926. At its peak, the neighborhood boasted around 10,000 residents with Italian ancestry, spanning a 12-by-10-block area in Lower Manhattan. However, in the early 21st century, the numbers dwindled to just about a thousand, now occupying approximately 14 city blocks, representing a little over 8% of the area's population.

Similarly, Little Tokyo in downtown Los Angeles experienced its heyday when Japanese immigrants arrived in the late 1880s. The community flourished with restaurants, grocery stores, businesses, and churches, swelling to an all-time high of 30,000 residents within a three-square-mile area. However, World War II led to the forced relocation of Japanese ancestry citizens to internment camps on the West Coast, followed by community redevelopment in the 1960s. Today, the population stands at around 3,500, with only 39% being Asians, occupying just four blocks in downtown Los Angeles.

Before I respond to Trần Dạ Từ, I contemplate whether Little Tokyo can reclaim its former prominence or if the process of assimilation is already complete. After carefully examining census data, it appears to me that the process is indeed underway. Both Little Italy and Little Tokyo have managed to preserve their historical identities, attracting tourists seeking to immerse themselves in their unique food, commodities, and cultural festivals. However, their socio-demographic landscapes have undergone significant shifts. While Little Italy still stands as a low-income community, Little Tokyo has transformed into a luxurious high-rise residential area catering to affluent young professionals and seniors, with a majority of non-Italian and non-Japanese residents, respectively. The opposite evolution stands as a testament to the ever-changing dynamics of urban life and the rich assortment of diverse cultures now thriving in these neighborhoods.

As history often repeats itself, I can't help but wonder about the path that lies ahead for Little Saigon. Will it follow a trajectory similar to that of Little Italy or Little Tokyo, or will its unique character and heritage lead it towards a distinct future? Having endured almost five decades, this enclave has already taken on a life of its own, shaped by countless independent and divergent forces that intertwine to bring about change.

As newcomers continue to flock to this diverse enclave, tensions between stakeholders are inevitable. Yet, I see it as a celebration of diversity, an opportunity for the next generation to forge creative spaces of equity and inclusion.

Throughout my journey in writing this book, I sat with each person, witnessing their stories firsthand. It became clear to me that the best way to predict the future is to actively create it. I humbly extend my gratitude to the first-generation Vietnamese refugees for their indomitable dreams, unwavering courage, and visionary foresight. As I think of the young people, I feel warmth in my heart, eagerly waiting for their voices to rise and their stories to unfold.

In response to my dear friend Trần Dạ Từ, I share these heartfelt words: "As we usher in a new era, Little Saigon is poised to blossom into an even more vibrant tapestry, adorned with captivating narratives. Each resident within this community will hold their own unique and compelling stories, contributing to the richness and beauty of our shared journey."

Chapter 10

A Voyage into the Unknown

In 1986, as my mother prepared to celebrate her 71st birthday, my sisters urged her to consider retirement. Our family-owned restaurant had been a successful venture, not only providing livelihoods for family members in need of money for schooling but also serving as a significant source of community engagement. However, with the impending opening of Phước Lộc Thọ mall, a timely decision had to be made. Little Saigon's dynamics were changing rapidly, and my mother foresaw that the center of attraction was shifting away from her restaurant, particularly after Governor George Deukmejian inaugurated the Little Saigon Exit, directing drivers in the opposite direction.

Fortunately, my parents embraced retirement with joy. The latter years of their lives were marked by tranquility, contentment, and a sense of fulfillment. The heart of our family activities shifted to their living room, becoming the cherished gathering place for the "Bui's clan." Weekends were filled with joyous parties and celebrations, providing us with ample reasons to come together. Whether we commemorated the anniversaries of grandparents' passing, honored our parents' birthdays, celebrated graduation ceremonies, or observed special occasions like Father's Day, Mother's Day, New Year's Day, Christmas parties, and Tết New Year, each gathering was an opportunity to create cherished memories and strengthen our familial bonds.

Trọng Minh, the journalist who proudly showcased the "Pride of Vietnamese [Americans]," once imparted a valuable lesson to me: "Don't miss dinner time with your children, and speak to them in Vietnamese," he wisely advised. Without knowing Trọng Minh, my parents wholeheartedly embraced this guidance. They not only cherished family meals together but also made a conscious effort to communicate with their American-born grandchildren in Vietnamese, passing down their cultural heritage.

Amidst conversations with their friends, who often discussed events in Vietnam, such as the "Đổi Mới" economic reform policy and the forever tension between China and Vietnam, my father had a simple yet powerful reaction, "Is there anything else to talk about? Why not find a way to teach your kids Vietnamese?" He believed in the importance of preserving our language and identity for future generations.

During their leisure time, my father immersed himself in reading and watching tennis tournaments on cable television, while my mother enjoyed visiting her friends and attending their gatherings. At these gatherings, two prevalent themes graced the dining tables: fond memories of the yesteryears in Vietnam and the vibrant community life in Little Saigon. Naturally, my parents also took pride in sharing the achievements of their children and grandchildren, reveling in their successes.

Additionally, my mother dedicated a significant portion of her time to community service, with a particular focus on Monk Quảng Thanh's temple. Her dedication exemplified the spirit of giving back to the community and contributing to the well-being of others. It was through her involvement in community service that she continued to strengthen her bonds with the people around her. In essence, my parents' actions spoke volumes about their commitment to preserving our cultural heritage and fostering a close-knit, supportive family and community. Their unwavering dedication serves as a guiding light, inspiring me to carry on these traditions and values for the next generation.

During my visits to my parents' home, I often slept in a spare bed in my father's bedroom. One day, I mustered the courage to ask, "Dad, do you still experience the nightmares you used to have in Nha Trang?" His surprised expression showed that he didn't expect me to recall those moments when he would wake up in the middle of the night, drenched in sweat and calling for help. In his high school years, he endured the harrowing experience of being captured and tortured by both the French police and the Việt Minh. They suspected him of being involved in the student movement for national independence, and that fear left a lasting mark on his psyche for decades.

To my relief, my father replied, "I think they are gone," suggesting that the nightmares might have finally subsided.

However, despite their resilience, the weight of old age was something my parents, like many of their friends, couldn't entirely escape. Life took a challenging turn when doctors diagnosed my father with terminal colon cancer. Every weekend, I drove the long distance home from the Silicon Valley area, covering 400 miles each way, just to be by my father's side. I couldn't shake the feeling of helplessness, knowing that my sisters, who lived nearby, were the devoted caretakers providing the constant support he needed.

Over all these years, I only witnessed my mother cry on two occasions. The first time was the day I boarded an Air France flight to Bern, Switzerland. My mother traveled from Ban Mê Thuột to Saigon to bid me farewell. Typically, my mother, belonging to a generation where physical affection was restrained, didn't hug me often. However, at the airport, her tears took me by surprise, revealing a mix of pride and relief in her eyes. The country was still recovering from the devastating 1968 Tết Offensive that caused widespread casualties. Amidst the tense atmosphere, with military police stationed at Tân Sơn Nhất airport, it was evident that Vietnam was still embroiled in war.

Despite my own worries about the future, both mine and that of our country, I assured her, "I will do well. Don't worry, Mom." She wept but smiled, expressing her happiness for me and the knowledge that I would be safe outside Vietnam. Her affectionate words and tearful farewell were etched in my heart.

The second time I saw my mother cry was many years later, outside the doctor's office in Little Saigon. The doctor's words weighed heavily upon us as he said, "Get ready to say farewell." Silently, we gently guided my father out of the doctor's office in a wheelchair. Each of us, with tender care, placed our arms around his body, carefully lowering him into the back seat of the station wagon. After closing the car's solid door, I turned to my mother. She leaned onto my shoulders, her emotions overcoming her as she tried to hide her tears from my father. With profound sadness, she whispered, "Give your dad the best farewell, will you?"

Her words resonated deeply within me, carrying the weight of a lifetime of love and sacrifice. I vowed to honor her request and be there for my father during his final moments, cherishing the time we had left together as a family.

The temple overflowed with mourners at my father's funeral, a testament to the impact he had on friends, family, and the community. In a touching tribute, my mother requested the mortuary to drive my father on a final tour of Little Saigon. The car slowly traversed Bolsa, Westminster, and Magnolia Avenues, symbolically bidding farewell to the cherished neighborhood he called home, a place filled with memories of his life in exile. We laid him to rest in the Vietnamese section of Loma Vista Memorial Park in Fullerton, California—his last wish, fulfilling his eternal connection to this beloved community.

Over thc years, while living and working in various places across Europe, North America and Asia, I held the opinion that Little Saigon's architecture should embrace modernity, reflecting an urban and twenty-first-century identity. However, my perspective shifted when Councilman Tony Lâm adorned Little Saigon with French Antique street lights. Initially, I didn't fully grasp the significance, but as these lights illuminated the center of Little Saigon, I began to see their deeper meaning. They symbolized the warmth of connections forged between the people who built and nurtured this high-spirited community. At my father's burial, one of his friends placed a South Vietnamese flag on his casket, embodying his unwavering loyalty to history, memories, and the community. In that moment, I realized that my father, too, was a guiding light in the heart of Little Saigon.

My mother led a healthy life, diligently taking care of herself. She often reminded me to start my day with a full glass of water. After my father's passing, she immersed herself in volunteering at the temples, dedicating her time and energy to the community. However, our fears materialized all too soon, and she fell seriously ill, succumbing to leukemia less than nine months after my father's departure. It felt as though she, too, longed to be reunited with him, ready for her eternal rest. Looking at photographs from her funeral, I recognized familiar faces—individuals from this book, who, like my mother, found solace and belonging in Little Saigon, creating homes and families in this nurturing community.

My mother left us with one final decision and a heartfelt request. "Do keep Mom's house as a family gathering place. I know you all have your own homes, but Mom's wish is for the family to remain united and stay close to each other," she earnestly expressed. With her words etched in our hearts, we honored her wish, and for a quarter of a century after her departure, her home served as a cherished gathering spot. It remains a welcoming place for out-of-town family and friends to stay, preserving the bond she cherished so dearly. When I visited Little Saigon, I found peace in staying at my parents' home, surrounded by the memories that shaped our lives. The walls echoed with the laughter, love, and shared experiences of our family, leaving an indelible legacy that warmed my heart.

As I embarked on the journey of writing this book, I had the privilege of visiting many of the first-generation Vietnamese Americans mentioned in its pages, right in the comfort of their homes. Immersed in the presence of remarkable individuals like Huy Phong, Tony Lâm, Tâm Nguyễn, Lê Văn Khoa, I witnessed a beautiful scene—their homes filled with the warmth of love and the laughter of their children and grandchildren, encircling these beloved elders. It felt as if we had all gathered together to listen to the tales of history and wisdom imparted by our revered elders. Each story shared with me became a precious archive, not only reflecting who we are as individuals but also portraying the essence of Little Saigon as a tight-knit and resilient community.

As I concluded the interviews, these cherished community members bid me farewell with words that filled my heart with joy. "I have great memories of your parents. You look like them. Let's meet again when you can to talk about the community. For now, I am getting ready to have dinner with my children and grandchildren." In these heartfelt goodbyes, I sensed a profound sense of accomplishment and a burning desire to continue living life vibrantly. It was evident that the bonds of family and community were cherished and nurtured, representing a legacy that carries on through the generations.

After returning to my eldest sister's house, her second son, Đức, asked his cousins to take me to "Garlic & Chives," a restaurant that symbolizes the wave of new Vietnamese eateries with Western names. These places offer a delightful blend of traditional dishes and Asian fusion. As I explored Little Saigon, I couldn't help but notice the evolving identity of its restaurant owners, expressed through names like "Phở Saigon," "Phở Hà Nội," and "Quán Huế," connecting the community to various geographical locations and hometowns in Vietnam.

Little Saigon's historical ties to Vietnam are again intertwined with a unique and novel flair for diverse cuisine, evident in the names of establishments like "Another Kind Café," "Nep Cafe and Brunch," "Bamboo Bistro," "Le Kitchen Phở and Rice," and "Paper Rice — Spring Rolls & Bowls." It's heartening to witness the younger generation, like Sonny Nguyễn, co-founder of 7-Leaves Café, finding inspiration in culture and embracing diversity. Their determination to succeed by serving Vietnamese American millennials while reaching out to other ethnicities reflects their desire to carve a path of their own and make their parents proud.

In conversations with my nephews and nieces, we effortlessly switch between English and specific Vietnamese vocabulary, sprinkling our speech with exclamations of "nước mắm" (fish sauce), "tương ớt" (chili sauce), or "đi chùa" (visit a temple)—a beautiful connection between food and prayer that binds our generations. Like Đức and many of the generation 1.5 individuals, they have established their careers in the mainstream American economy but have intentionally chosen to work and reside in Orange County, close to their parents and siblings. Take Vũ Lê, for instance, a successful young businessman who could easily live in Bellevue or Los Angeles where his clients are, but instead, he chooses to stay in Little Saigon. "I feel at home here, hearing people around me speaking in Vietnamese, even though I may not know them personally," he eloquently expressed.

Little by little, Little Saigon's commercial centers are embracing the twenty-first century, undergoing facelifts that approach the architectural standards of shopping centers owned by larger corporations. Evolution is not only about adapting to the times but also about preserving the essence of the community while progressing toward a brighter and more inclusive future. Although much of this effort remains to me a work in progress, the commitment to revitalizing and preserving the spirit of Little Saigon is however palpable.

With a touch of wry humor and a hint of poetry, Chu Tất Tiến shared with me his prediction, "Only ten more years," and Little Saigon, the Vietnamese refugee capital, will bid farewell to the first-generation settlers, and will likely blossom into a major hub for Vietnamese communities living overseas. As the next generation comes of age, they will come to know Vietnam and its history through the memories passed down by their grandparents and parents. Little Saigon propels forward on its journey to modernity, while securely carrying the treasured memories of the first generation's profound transition from war to a vibrant community, paving the way for the generations to come.

As I review my interview notes, I find myself sentimentally attached to the first-generation residents of Little Saigon. Perhaps it's because I no longer have my parents, and the people here serve as poignant reminders of my own mother and father. Through this work, I have come to appreciate the innocence and unwavering faith in the future displayed by the next generation of Vietnamese Americans. Observing young individuals like Đức and his friends fills me with a reassuring sense of hope for Little Saigon's future, despite the uncertainties that the post-pandemic world presents.

Du Miên, now 73, reflects on life during our last conversation, sharing his primary goal of staying healthy as he battles with leg pain. The community continues to flourish, and the first-generation retirees enjoy a well-deserved rest. Though Little Saigon may not have grown in the exact direction Du Miên once aspired as a South Vietnamese in exile, it has undeniably thrived. If Trọng Minh were to continue writing volumes about "The Pride of Vietnamese (Americans)," he would undoubtedly need a full staff to publish the countless success stories emanating from this vibrant town. Many years ago, Monk Quảng Thanh worried about not having enough disciples as he sought to soothe the souls of a community in exile. Today, the countless temples and pagodas scattered all over Little Saigon stand as a testament to harmonious worship and a thriving community center, a living testament to the strength and resilience of this extraordinary community.

Sitting in front of my desktop, and weaving these evolving stories together, a sense of momentum pervades my writing. Little Saigon, with its complex history and ever-changing demographics, may never find a single shared community aspiration—and that's perfectly alright. It has never been a place of uniformity. As I sat beside Frank Jao's pool, contemplating these notions, I couldn't help but ask him about his plans. "My daughter, Felicia, has taken up the reins of managing my business. Now, I am solely focused on two areas: education and healthcare. They are noble causes that can also be profitable," he shared with a sense of purpose.

The unwavering dedication and labor of the first settlers have left an indelible mark on Little Saigon, shaping it into the vibrant community it is today. Their tireless efforts, laced with a profound sense of nostalgia, both enchantments and disenchantments, and unwavering aspirations, have been lovingly passed down to subsequent generations. This transfer of values and experiences has laid a solid foundation for the cherished community we know today. Their endeavors went beyond constructing mere homes; they created something truly unique—a Little Saigon that stands as a testament to the spirit of resilience and unity.

As time continues its march, a new generation of young and ambitious residents emerges, poised to carry on the legacy. In ten more years, these future local generations may find themselves missing the firsthand history of the settlers, just as I cherish the memories and stories shared in this book, remembering them along with my own individual journey.

Little Saigon's tapestry of narratives continues to unfold, and I am grateful to have been part of capturing a glimpse of its richness. As the community progresses, embracing its complexities and diversity, I take solace in knowing that its essence will endure through the passionate efforts of those who call it home.

PART II

Voices of the Movers and Shakers

By its very nature, history is personal and political, and personal accounts connect to lived experiences and human emotions. We acknowledge that every little Saigon resident has a valuable story to tell. But, inevitably, we could only choose a few life stories. We were looking for a kaleidoscopic recall of the making of Little Saigon and sharp reflections of its future.

When approaching each interviewee as historians in the making, we ensured that the narratives unfolded naturally. And the people we interviewed delivered more. They revealed their lives and opened their hearts. Their stories unfurled with their voices, and we remained silent and eager to hear, with genuine respect for their past. We loved every moment, as the conversations always lasted longer than the time allotted.

The interviewees, in this section and throughout the book, had a sense of shared fate, empathy, and for-better-and-for-worse kinships. The first waves of refugees and now proud first-generation Vietnamese Americans share stories of survival, extraordinary sagas of resettlement, (dis)enchantments and aspirations for a futurity built on prosperity and community. The second-generation Vietnamese American have chosen their own identity. They carry their dreams boldly shaping their own future and that of Little Saigon of tomorrow. These stories belong to the history of America. During the darkest nights, these Vietnamese became Americans; these vanguards lead future generations of Vietnamese Americans as stars that illuminated the path to freedom and equality.

This town is the stories of those who labored to erect a new community, and it is narratives of sadness, anxiety, and resilience from Vietnamese artists, writers, intellectuals, community organizers and, first and foremost, the uprooted refugees who reflect on heritage and identity—vivacious and complex identities. By including only a few stories, we certainly must have missed so many others. Each of the engaging residents of Little Saigon is a building block of the long roller-coasting emotionally charged soul searching and relentless community building process.

My deepest appreciation goes to my colleague, Dr. Vo Huong Quynh, who has spent long hours, playing, rewinding, and playing again the recording of the interviews I conducted. Through the transcribing of the narratives, she has reconstructed their stories as if she is visiting Little Saigon through time and space from its inception to the ongoing endeavors with multiple pairs of eyes. I recognize that truths are mostly relative and memory is known to be selective. Yet, the voices of the charismatic movers and shakers constitute the souls of the enclave. What people say and do reflect who and what they are.

Chapter 11

Flourishing Amidst the Trials

The Triumph of Economic Tenacity

QUÁCH NHỨT DANH, A CHARMED LIFE

I met Quách Nhứt Danh in the waiting area of his modest pharmacy, which bears his name, "Danh's Pharmacy." The choice of location for our meeting was apt for the purpose of the interview. Situated in the first shopping center of Little Saigon on Bolsa Ave, it has retained much of its original design from 40 years ago. Despite his age of 80, Mr. Quách appeared sprightly, exuding an athletic allure. His eyes were vibrant, his mind inquisitive, and above all, he possessed a sharp memory of his charmed life. The interview was conducted in Vietnamese.

When Quách Nhứt Danh first arrived in Orange County, he learned from earlier Vietnamese refugees that the city government provided more favorable conditions for those seeking refuge. With this knowledge, he immediately envisioned a new haven for the Vietnamese American community.

Within the residents of Little Saigon, Quách Nhứt Danh has become a symbolic figure representing his time and place. He holds the distinction of being the first Vietnamese refugee to own a pharmacy, not just in Orange County, but in the entire United States. Like other prominent figures in Little Saigon, Quách Nhứt Danh dedicated himself wholeheartedly to his endeavors. At the core of his remarkable success lies a powerful trifecta of virtues: optimism, resilience, and ambition, which he continues to embody tenaciously to this day.

Living in America has always been seen by Quách Nhứt Danh as a blessing rather than a misfortune. Looking back, he expresses only one sentiment: "gratitude." This profound appreciation for the United States has been deeply ingrained in him throughout his life. Quách Nhứt Danh recounts how Americans established hospitals in South Vietnam before their departure, saving countless lives, including their own. Despite feeling abandoned, he recognizes the tremendous impact of these well-equipped medical facilities, witnessing firsthand the magic of American medical supplies during critical moments like the Tết Offensive of 1968. Without such advanced medical stations, the tragedy could have been even more devastating for pro-American Vietnamese.

Unlike many first-generation refugees who faced immense challenges of displacement, resettlement, and assimilation, Quách Nhứt Danh experienced a life that was relatively privileged, with more opportunities than hardships. Growing up in poverty and lacking education in Sóc Trăng, a province in the Mekong Delta during the French colonization of Vietnam, he witnessed the dire consequences of starvation that claimed the lives of two million people and left corpses scattered everywhere. During those difficult times, Quách Nhứt Danh would ride his brakeless bike to school or go barefoot. However, his circumstances began to change when his family moved to Saigon. There, he attended Petrus Ky School and honed his English skills at the Vietnamese American School, an esteemed language institute. After earning his Bachelor of Science in Pharmaceutical Sciences (BSPS), Quách Nhứt Danh secured a position at American Medical Logistics, where he oversaw 12 southern provinces in Vietnam with the support of six American advisors and 13 Korean assistants. All of these experiences occurred prior to his flight to the United States.

Quách Nhứt Danh was part of a fortunate group of individuals who fled Vietnam just one week before the fall of Saigon on April 30th, 1975. Like many of the first-wave refugees, predominantly affluent families who left out of fear and a hidden hope of eventually returning to their homeland once peace was restored, Quách never had the opportunity to go back. While stationed in the US base on Wake Island, located in the western Pacific Ocean between Vietnam and the US, amidst a sea of desolate refugees mourning the loss of their homeland, Quách weathered the melancholy with the spirit of an optimistic prophet, envisioning his own future. He vividly remembered the collective tears shed during that moment of calamity and despair in the camp before his family was sponsored to Arkansas, then Connecticut, and finally Nebraska.

Determined to continue his medical career, Quách enrolled in Medical School in Nebraska, where the Dean, who had known him from Vietnam, waived certain credits for him and provided generous support. In 1978, while his wife pursued her pharmaceutical degree, Quách fervently sought employment to support their family. Through his network of connections, he secured a position at a mental hospital in the region while awaiting his wife's graduation. Subsequently, their family relocated to California, a destination sought after by many Vietnamese due to its sunny weather and better social welfare opportunities.

For the second generation of Vietnamese Americans who were born and raised in America, the journey of their parents from refugees to the bourgeoisie is nothing short of legendary. Firstly, their pilgrimage across the ocean was a heroic feat, as many lost their lives before reaching the shores of their new home, while others were separated from their families and struggled to reunite in the aftermath. Secondly, those who successfully established themselves in their new homeland endured years of grief, longing, and isolation, as their descendants often chose to assimilate into the mainstream culture, adopting new values and distancing themselves from their roots. However, all, or almost all, of the initial inhabitants, like Quách Nhứt Danh, shared a collective aspiration to revitalize their lost homeland, lost memories, and lost traditions in their beloved new haven, affectionately named Little Saigon.

Within this romantic space of the lost homeland, Little Saigon, communication between the first generation and their younger counterparts often feels futile, as silence prevails. Those who lived through the war, scarred and traumatized, have no desire to relive those memories. Sharing war stories is akin to pouring salt on old wounds, causing them to fester anew and making the healing process even more challenging. Who wants to disturb the ashes? For those who witnessed and buried countless deaths during the war or endured the brutalities firsthand, the pain is piercing. Quách Nhứt Danh left Saigon out of a profound fear that the imminent battles would endanger his family. With only their basic belongings, they left behind all their properties and possessions, silently holding onto the hope that once the war ended, they could reclaim everything that belonged to their family—everything they struggled to accept was gone and lost.

Yet, the prospect of resettlement in a new land of freedom was more enticing to Quách than the temptation to return home. This is precisely why Orange County became the most compelling destination for Vietnamese refugees. Only within this Vietnamese enclave could they freely speak their mother tongue, Vietnamese, whenever they sought help, needed a service, or wished to express the emotions bottled up inside them. These displaced individuals preferred doctors, pharmacists, restaurant waiters, barbers, dressmakers, and others to communicate with them in Vietnamese. Many of them, having arrived in America after spending half their lives in Vietnam, struggled to read or understand English. When Quách Nhứt Danh sold medicine with English labels to his fellow countrymen, they faced great difficulty. Understanding this plight, Quách made a request to the California State Board of Pharmacy, urging them to allow Vietnamese translations on medicine labels for the Vietnamese community. However, when inspectors visited his store, their response was dismissive, asking, "Why don't you guys just go back to where you came from?"

Why did titans like Quách Nhứt Danh become fearless and resilient in the face of such hostility from Americans? The answer is simple. Once they had fiercely survived the deadly war and swam resolutely to these shores, nothing could scare them anymore. Nevertheless, coping with the realities of starting anew was initially challenging for Quách, especially when he became the first licensed Vietnamese pharmacist to open a pharmacy in the US. It was a difficult period for his family when he established his first medical business in Orange County. His wife had to commute 80 miles each day to her workplace in Riverside to support him financially. However, between 1979 and 1980, Vietnam faced a severe medicine shortage, and Quách's business thrived. Since medicine could be exported without a doctor's prescription, he sent one thousand pounds of medicine to Vietnam every week. His store was constantly bustling with people who packed their own supplies and clothes to be shipped alongside the medication. Through his medical parcels, countless lives were saved in Vietnam during that wretched time.

When President Bill Clinton lifted the U.S. trade embargo against Vietnam in 1994 and the two countries reestablished full diplomatic relations, Quách sensed the fierce competition that would arise. As a result, he decided to discontinue his business dealings with people back home. Shortly thereafter, Triệu Phát (Frank Jao) approached Quách Nhứt Danh with a proposal to jointly purchase land with the support of the Mayor of Westminster. They invested in Ward and Bolsa, which were completed in 1984. However, Quách Nhứt Danh harbored more skepticism than confidence regarding the future of this project that he and Triệu Phát were striving for. "It was the bleak and dilapidated Chinatown in the vicinity that painted a grim picture for me about the future of a similar township for the Vietnamese," Quách Nhứt Danh recalled. He observed the younger generation of Chinese Americans choosing to leave Chinatown and seamlessly assimilate into mainstream culture without looking back. He worried, "What if our Vietnamese youth would do the same?" Quách Nhứt Danh fretted about the potential abandonment of Vietnamese descendants who were born and raised in the US and might not prioritize preserving their cultural heritage. He was particularly concerned about his own stake and influence in the community.

Against all grim visions, the Vietnamese business quarter invested by Triệu Phát and himself quickly flourished due to the continuous influx of Vietnamese migrants who chose to make Little Saigon their home. This homey and romantic enclave of Vietnamese people attracted more and more Chinese Americans back to Chinatown, which soon regained its abundance and excitement. "The first supermarket in Little Saigon was opened by a Vietnamese Chinese owner," Quách Nhứt Danh recalled. Later, he moved his business to Cherry Street, just across from Westminster airport, where he dreamed of a more vibrant community in the future. However, when

Quách and Triệu Phát initially entered the project, they were plagued by worries. Would they be able to handle the substantial bank loan? Would other Vietnamese business owners show interest in their project? These fears weighed heavily on them, and they explored various strategies to sustain their dream. Initially, Triệu Phát had to rely on insurance companies that provided loans without requiring credit but at high interest rates. They also engaged in pre-leasing at the construction site to secure support.

Quách Nhứt Danh had vague concerns about the generation gap between himself and the later generations, who may be less aware of their roots and identity. However, he still held hope that the community would endure and thrive for many years to come. "We, Vietnamese people, are more resilient and traditional than other ethnic communities like Koreans, Japanese," Quách Nhứt Danh reflected. "We know how to teach our children and pass on traditional values to them." He observed with delight Vietnamese families dining at Vietnamese restaurants on weekends and celebrating Vietnamese festivals such as the Mid-Autumn Moon Festival and Tết (Lunar New Year). While parents may shield their children from the melancholic aspects of their past for the sake of their peace of mind, they have continued to cultivate Vietnamese culture, traditions, values, and beliefs among the younger generation. This is achieved by actively involving them in Vietnamese festivals and cuisine, which naturally imbues their mindset and enriches their sense of Vietnamese identity.

The first generation of renowned and successful businessmen like Quách Nhứt Danh and Triệu Phát were titans, with shoes that no one in the younger generation could fill. They were not ordinary individuals, but invincible and ambitious figures whose work was revered. They rarely faltered and shared an unwavering optimism for creating a vibrant haven for the Vietnamese community from the very beginning. Their path to realizing their dreams was crystal clear, much clearer than that of many Vietnamese residents in the community. They were unafraid to toil for their dream project: the establishment of a homey space they named Little Saigon. What is even more remarkable is that their ambition and enthusiasm for Little Saigon have not diminished over time. As their plans and ideas have matured and solidified, they have continued to pass on these visions to their descendants.

TRẦN DŨ | EQUILIBRIUM

Note: When I contacted Trần Dũ for an interview, he immediately recognized my voice. "You sound just like your brothers. Please come," he said warmly. Trần Dũ had been a long-time business partner of my mother, and I was excited to reconnect with him. Even at the age of 80, he was still actively working. I met him in the midst of his bustling activities, as he shared the remarkable story of his resilient life and his reputation as a cornerstone of the early businesses in Little Saigon. Despite his financial accomplishments and ownership of properties, Trần Dũ continues to make his home in a mobile home he purchased decades ago, originally intended for his late mother. This abode carries deep significance for him, providing a space where he can hold dear the memories and strong attachment he shared with her. The interview was conducted in Vietnamese.

It was a serene spring afternoon, and yet the gentle sunshine cascaded upon Moran Street, just a block away from the iconic Phuoc Loc Tho. Trần Dũ donned a plaid shirt, adorned with thick blue and dark gray stripes, accompanied by navy blue stretch corduroy pants. He exuded an air of ease as he greeted us cheerfully at his front desk. Leading us through a labyrinth of boxes and shelves brimming with fresh produce and an assortment of supplies for the restaurants of Little Saigon, Trần Dũ unveiled the bustling heart of his domain. Positioned behind his desk was a 3-by-4-feet black and white map of Orange County, while a sizable monthly calendar adorned the right wall. On the eve of his birthday, Trần Dũ remained spirited, deftly managing sales orders, effortlessly preparing invoices without the aid of a calculator, and adeptly loading goods single-handedly. Each day, he toiled with fervor at the store until 2 p.m., only to hasten home thereafter, immersing himself in the soothing embrace of news broadcasts on the television and engaging in late-evening conversations with his beloved wife. Within his realm, tranquility reigned supreme, devoid of extravagance. And in the waning hours of the afternoon, he would embark on leisurely strolls, often lost in the embrace of nostalgia, reminiscing about his past in Vietnam while relishing the richness of his present life, his accomplished children, and his cherished pets.

Everyone in the first wave of exodus or belonging to his generation knows him well. For the HO immigrants who arrived on the shores of America long after the fall of Saigon, disheartened and desperate, Trần Dũ stood as their benevolent savior. He toils relentlessly, capitalizing on his position as the pioneering food distributor for Vietnamese-owned restaurants. Embracing a humble existence, he nurtures his family alongside his caring housewife and six children. Diligently, he invests his hard-earned money. Moreover, when approached, he selflessly bestows lands upon those seeking to build their homes, pays rents for aspiring artists, and extends employment opportunities to the unemployed. In times of prosperity, he sustains destitute dreamers and ensures the dignified burial of the homeless departed. "All our fellow countrymen . . . I have endured the same agony of displacement," Du affirms, forging an unbreakable bond with each and every one of them, be they men or women.

When Trần Dũ finally settled in San Diego in 1976, after enduring four unsuccessful attempts to flee from communist Vietnam, he left behind a miraculous life. Having grown up as a destitute Chinese Vietnamese, he managed to rise as a prosperous entrepreneur during the war. Carrying the weight of a large family, Trần Dũ embarked on his journey to America with a mere $200 and an uncertain future looming ahead. In a testament to unwavering determination, his brother-in-law, then a bus driver, tirelessly knocked on doors and sought help from acquaintances to secure a rental payment of $375 for Du's family. Thus, eight individuals found themselves crammed into a modest dwelling—their newfound home in America.

Resolute in his resolve to start anew, Du enrolled in an electronics course at a community college, harboring dreams of a brighter future for his family. His wife, too, toiled through night shifts while attending classes alongside him during the day. "Who doesn't need a technician?" Du mused, reflecting on his college days—challenging yet imbued with a profound sense of pride in his chosen path, one he believed to be the most promising for fellow refugees. "Even before graduating, I secured employment with an American proprietor who operated three radio/TV repair stores, earning a wage of $6.75 per hour." However, as the business's efficiency waned, the owner was left with only a solitary store, relocating it near the Mexican border. Sensing the winds of change, Trần Dũ astutely hedged his bets.

Unlike some individuals who, in the midst of exilic tragedy, lost their sanity, lashed out at their families, turned to heavy drinking, or even succumbed to the depths of despair through suicide, Trần Dũ transcended his misfortune. A born trader, he embarked on a path of resilience by selling persimmons harvested from the very gardens of the churches that provided support to his family. With determination, Trần Dũ diligently packed and sold 100 boxes, each weighing 50 lbs, amassing a daily earnings of $5,000. Life became somewhat less burdensome for this resilient individual, who had once presided over a colossal factory employing a thousand workers, producing bicycles for export. Unfortunately, the tides turned against him after the unification, resulting in the loss of everything he had built. Yet, undeterred, he persevered by engaging in the sale of persimmons, oranges, and morning glories at Dân Tiếp Vụ—the inaugural Vietnamese market in Orange County.

Trần Dũ doesn't simply set aside his memories; he cherishes them, layering one photo upon another, story upon story. Through these mementos, he breathes life into each moment, reliving them with vibrant clarity. Whether it's reminiscing about hosting the former president of South Vietnam in his home, sharing meals with artists, or recounting his travels to Hawai'i, he narrates his experiences with such vividness that it feels as though he's projecting the movies of his life onto the screen of our imagination. His appreciation for friendship knows no bounds, his devotion to family is unwavering, and his affection for his pets knows no limits—it is unconditional love. Whenever someone is in need, Trần Dũ generously extends his helping hand, never expecting anything in return. He speaks with pride about his collaboration with Kiều Chinh, the renowned actress of the Vietnamese community, who is also recognized for her role in Amy Tan's "Joy Luck Club." Trần Dũ provided financial support whenever Chinh embarked on journeys to aid other refugees still stranded in Hong Kong or Thailand. Furthermore, he offered crucial support to Vietnamese newspapers during their initial struggles with financial instability. Remarkably, Trần Dũ never boasts about his moral deeds; his humility is the source of his extraordinary strength.

For Trần Dũ, conducting business in the 1980s in Orange County was smooth sailing. In early 1982, he established Delta Foods, the first wholesale market, as a tribute to his roots in the Mekong River Delta in South Vietnam. With the profits from his distribution business, he ventured into the realm of real estate, seizing lucrative opportunities. Reflecting on his journey, Trần Dũ remarked, "My success can be attributed to my honesty and audacity. Since I didn't speak English, having a trustworthy American neighbor as my broker was a true blessing."

During the pinnacle of his business in 2003, he acquired properties in Chinatown, Los Angeles, followed by the expansive area of Westminster and Saigon City Market. However, in 2018, he tragically lost all of them. It was a year of despair, as he found himself burdened with immense debt and unable to secure bank loans. Despite his valiant efforts to fulfill mortgage payments, Trần Dũ received no financial support from those he had once assisted, and one by one, the banks foreclosed on his properties.

Although his failure was substantial, so was his resilience. His once expansive business dwindled down to groceries alone. Exiting the real estate market and relinquishing his markets liberated Du from the burdens, frustrations, and outbursts that often plagued him upon returning home for family dinners. "My children wanted me to work less, as they couldn't bear witness to my anger at home," confided Trần Dũ. Consequently, he relished a more harmonious familial atmosphere. "These are truly the best days of my life. I need to unwind and relax. Every day, upon returning home from the shop, I express gratitude to my wife. She prepares a refreshing mixed fruit juice that rejuvenates my spirits, and for many years, I have never fallen ill."

"Đất lành, chim đậu" (Birds land on good land), Trần Dũ remarked, unaware of when his emotional attachment to Little Saigon took root. He firmly believes that this place continues to captivate Vietnamese immigrants, no matter what. "The soul of Vietnam resides here, and it will endure eternally." Those, like Dũ, who arrive and never leave, find solace in Little Saigon—a cathartic space for their nostalgia, a wellspring of inspiration, a comforting embrace that Vietnamese Americans, both young and old, simply cannot resist. In this exilic realm where estrangement is the norm, one finds Vietnamese restaurants emanating the tantalizing aroma of their cuisine, the mother tongue resounding melodiously, and a congenial atmosphere that feels like home. It is this cultural vitality that keeps Trần Dũ firmly anchored in Little Saigon.

"When we acquired this establishment, the neighborhood was still devoid of life. However, over time, shopping malls and business centers sprouted one after another along Bolsa Avenue, giving rise to a thriving community," Trần Dũ reminisced, speaking like a seasoned local who recalls the distinct personalities that inhabited this enclave.

It hasn't always been smooth sailing. The history of Little Saigon encompasses fragmented and contentious narratives, steeped in acrimony, antagonism, and hostility. Some tales are mere rumors, while others emerge from collaborative conflicts and personal perceptions. When Frank Jao acquired vast land in Little Saigon and called for collective investments, not everyone placed their trust in him. Trần Dũ was among the skeptics. "He constructed his shopping centers and restaurants through connivance and deceit," Trần Dũ remarked, recollecting how some investors shared stories of losing their properties due to Jao's disreputable machinations. While Trần Dũ never became directly involved in Frank Jao's projects, he harbored lingering resentments towards him, fueling loose conversations. Vietnamese refugees, even as they depart their homeland, carry certain cultural traits that have firmly entrenched themselves in their minds. Many remain entangled in egomania and repulsive desires. This darker side, silently and insidiously, drives people apart.

Of Chinese heritage but Vietnamese at heart, Trần Dũ wholeheartedly embraced Vietnamese culture and values while consciously distancing himself from pessimistic traits. If asked about the "magic" behind his ability to thrive and overcome tragedy, he would recount, endlessly, his glorious days in Vietnam before his escape. "Looking back, I'm immensely proud of everything I had done for them. They revered me like a saint." Even the most dangerous criminals who ravaged markets in Saigon would soften in Trần Dũ's presence. "I never resorted to violence against them. Never." Benevolence was Trần Dũ's strength. He never relied on hostility or belittled anyone he knew.

Many people have tested his saintliness. They knock on his door not only for financial assistance but also for wisdom. "Rise when you fall," he would say, "resilience and loyalty are inevitable virtues in the business world." Trần Dũ, an ocean-hearted, humble, and mighty man of Little Saigon, bestows his genuine gift of compassion upon everyone, regardless of their poverty or vulnerability, without expecting anything in return. If someone inquires about his unwavering benevolence, Trần Dũ simply smiles quietly and replies, "You know, when I'm no longer here, nothing else matters."

TÂM NGUYỄN | NAILING DOWN THE BEAUTIFUL DREAM

Note: I was introduced to Tâm Nguyễn Senior by a colleague and co-author of mine who has known the family for decades. When I arrived at their doorstep in Little Saigon, Tâm Nguyễn Senior, his wife Kiên, and their son and heir, Dr. Tâm Nguyễn Junior, warmly welcomed me. Tâm Nguyễn Senior was dressed in a light beige suit and tie, exuding the air of a distinguished elder. Tâm Nguyễn Jr. greeted me with a smile and remarked, "My dad was really looking forward to meeting you. It's been a while since I've seen him dress up like this." I smiled gratefully in return. Tâm Nguyễn Jr. requested to record the interview, saying, "My dad doesn't talk much at home, so my family and I might learn something new as well." The interview was conducted in Vietnamese.

On a sultry and dreary early summer day in 1975, a penniless, forlorn, and frazzled former lieutenant colonel of the Army of the Republic of Vietnam (ARVN) arrived in Los Angeles with his pregnant wife and young son. They felt bewildered and lost in the vastness of their new homeland and uncertain about their future. Just a few months prior, Tâm Nguyễn held a high-ranking position in the Army of the Republic of Vietnam (South Vietnam), but life was far from better. In fact, it was bruising and wretched. As a military technician, Tâm Nguyễn did not engage in battle nor qualify for battle welfare. His meager earnings were not enough to support his family, so he had to take on various moonlight jobs, some of which were even hazardous.

During the war, in order to pay off debts while building his first house, Tâm Nguyễn worked as a restaurant manager from 5:30 p.m. to midnight every day. He recalled being targeted by disabled veterans who demanded money, but he managed to persuade them to leave him alone by explaining that he was only a hired manager, not the owner. Tâm Nguyễn understood that his power in the army was a hollow glory that concealed lurking dangers.

Fleeing communist Vietnam by boat and plane when Saigon fell, his family eventually reunited in the new land of freedom after months of transitioning from one camp to another. They had lost everything, but Tâm Nguyễn did not mourn for long before he swiftly embraced creative changes. Unlike many embittered Vietnamese veterans displaced to the US, Tâm Nguyễn persevered with tolerance, grace, and hope. He founded the manicure industry and elevated it to an art form, establishing the first beauty college called TAM's Beauty College, cleverly coining the acronym "Technical Arts Management System." The college created hundreds of thousands of jobs for Vietnamese refugees and immigrants in the US, earning him the title of the Godfather of manicure, which has become the most lucrative and sought-after industry for Vietnamese Americans.

While other veterans were still caught up in the illusion of reclaiming the lost nation, Tâm Nguyễn tirelessly traversed the intersections of Santa Cruz, distributing leaflets to promote his wife's hair services. With a newborn baby in a stroller on one side and another young son on the other, Tâm Nguyễn let go of all the fame, power, and glory of the past. He focused on promoting his wife's expertise, as she was the only one with a hair certificate, and the couple had just found a station for their business.

"It was a quiet fabric store, so we knew the owner would have no reason to hire us if we applied for a job there. We asked them to allow us to place a chair in the store for our business," his wife recalled with pride. Their humble business experienced rapid growth each day as more Vietnamese customers sought out a Vietnamese stylist for their hairdressing needs. On occasion, Vietnamese concerts would take place in the area, attracting performers who would flock to Tam's. The landlord became even more thrilled as their store gained numerous customers.

Both Tâm Nguyễn and Kiên, his wife, were unconventional pragmatists from the early days of their marriage. In Vietnam, Kiên worked as a secretary at the Ministry of Health, but she found the job underpaid, unpromising, and tedious. Eventually, she decided to leave the position. Influenced by the harsh realities and the people around her, Kiên ventured into less glamorous but more lucrative jobs. She vividly recalled how professions affected the quality of life during the war and how these experiences shaped her outlook.

Kiên remembers an example of one of her husband's colleagues, a colonel, whose wife was a teacher and could only afford to have sticky rice for breakfast every day, while a doctorate scholar married to a dressmaker enjoyed a bowl of Phở (Vietnamese noodle soup) each morning. Reflecting on this, Kiên thought, "Why not switch to a more profitable job?"

Tâm Nguyễn initially wanted his wife to become a dressmaker, but she preferred to be a hairdresser because she believed it would provide more interaction and companionship with customers compared to a dressmaker who would mostly receive clothes from customers and work alone. Tâm Nguyễn was convinced, especially since it meant their children could stay at home with their mother.

The mystery of their success is not elusive. Tâm Nguyễn and his wife did not romanticize their glory in Vietnam or lament their challenging lives in the US. Instead, they adapted to the circumstances. When their children were still young, Tâm Nguyễn worked as a social worker for the United States Catholic Church (USCC), which provided childcare for his children while he assisted in the resettlement of new Vietnamese immigrant families. Life was still a struggle, and Kiên had to work hard, often witnessing the family facing financial difficulties.

Tâm then enrolled in Hacienda La Puente Adult Education Cosmetology to obtain his hair certificate. Years later, their children, Tâm Nguyễn and Linh, also attended the same school and learned the trade from their father's former instructors, who reminded them of his extraordinary resilience.

Tâm Nguyễn was not only resilient but also wise and daring. He seized every opportunity that could bring more food to the table for his family. Whenever someone inquired about beauty school, he would direct them to Hacienda La Puente and negotiate a commission of $100 per student with the school. This deal brought him good income, but unfortunately, it didn't last long as the school broke their commitment and turned away from him once they had a large number of students. This setback crushed him deeply.

Despite his bitter disappointment, Tâm Nguyễn took legal action against the school, but he couldn't find anyone willing to testify on his behalf, and he ultimately lost the case. Filled with bitterness and sadness, Tâm Nguyễn decided to start his own school: Tâm Nguyễn's Beauty College, becoming the very first beauty school run by a Vietnamese American in the US. His vision was not only to provide beauty training services but also to establish manicure as an industry. Although the startup was ambitious and overwhelming, Tâm Nguyễn's audacious business model proved rewarding and thrived within the community.

No ordinary man, Tâm Nguyễn referred to himself as a "bold pioneer." He firmly believed that one can never attain good fortune unless they believe in it right from the beginning. When he established the school, Tâm Nguyễn charted his own path to success. Despite having a modest budget, he managed to recruit his former military comrades as teaching staff, including a former lieutenant colonel who had served as the chief of the military women's regiment, and a major from his own cohort, both of whom were veterans of the ARVN. Tâm Nguyễn took care of everything else, from designing flyers to writing newspaper ads. His message was clear and enticing: "lowest tuition, basic English." Remarkably, his strategic approach yielded results. Tâm then embarked on extensive travels to promote his beauty programs, which quickly garnered the interest of thousands of students across all age groups.

The prevailing inclination was that many of his students, after honing their skills at the school, would go on to start their own businesses and become owners. "It's the common nature of Vietnamese people," Tâm Nguyễn said. "They all aspire to be their own bosses." When news reporters interviewed him about his experience of establishing the manicure industry in California, Tâm often likened his Vietnamese students, who joined the programs with dreams of becoming bosses, to blind men touching an elephant. They were driven by their own imagination, which could sometimes be misleading, as the realities of the industry presented more complexities and nuances.

The emergence of Tâm Nguyễn's business in the Vietnamese community led to his reluctant involvement in state politics. The increasing number of Vietnamese immigrants in Orange County prompted the state to include more Vietnamese officers in the system. When the state initiated a training program for a group of 30 individuals of Vietnamese origin, including doctors, lawyers, engineers, and scientists, Tâm Nguyễn was among them. Charismatic yet level-headed, Tâm tended to distance himself from conflicts and rumors within the group.

During the training period, the general director of the volunteering organization approached him and appointed him as the director of the HO immigration program for the state. "We need someone with leadership ability," she explained. "And no one but you can handle the current turmoil." Despite the position's requirement of two bachelor's degrees and one year of experience, Tâm, with his humble high school education, became the remarkable leader of those highly educated professionals. "Power just came out of the blue," he remarked.

Struggles seemed never-ending. Unable to juggle between Tâm Nguyễn's Beauty College and the HO program, Tâm Nguyễn nominated Bửu Hồ, who had obtained a PhD degree in sociology, to replace him as the HO program director so that he could fully concentrate on his school. The secret to his success is quite simple: he values his job. In a community that still places importance on social status based on education and professional standing, Tâm Nguyễn recognized the value of his work in the manicure industry. It not only secured his family's financial well-being but also allowed others to thrive. To him, a profession is just a name, and what truly matters is the wealth it generates for society. He recalled how many individuals were unable to practice their previous professions due to limited English proficiency and unqualified expertise. Some doctors who had earned easy money in Vietnam were rendered useless in the US, often only allowed to treat minor ailments like influenza or nasal congestion. "Some former military officials, who were once powerful lions on the battlefield, now had no choice but to take on menial jobs," Tâm Nguyễn remembered, recounting an experience of assisting a former major in applying for welfare at the Human Services Department while the man tried to hide his identity with sunglasses and a cap.

Running the school, Tam encountered people from all walks of life, and he inspired them through his passionate dedication to the manicure industry. Some individuals developed close relationships with him and expressed interest in franchising Tâm Nguyễn's Beauty College in other states. Tam trusted them without hesitation, but their ventures only lasted briefly due to mismanagement and a lack of creative technological development to meet the growing market demand. While they could have applied Tâm Nguyễn's business model by showcasing his manicure techniques, they failed to adopt his enduring strategies, such as competitive tuition rates and constant innovation, as well as the inspiring articles he personally crafted and disseminated in the media. "My dad has that flair. He wrote influential pieces about manicures, and newspapers even sought him out to write about it. So the school gained an enormous reputation," shared his son, Tâm Nguyễn Jr.

"Everyone in my family shares one name: Tâm," Tâm Nguyễn proudly declared. In Vietnamese, it means "conscience." As a child, he was initially named Diễm (Beauty), but one of his uncles later renamed him Tâm. His son also carries this name. And this meaningful name, "conscience," has become the motto of Tâm Nguyễn's business. Americans refer to them as Tâm Senior and Tâm Junior. Fortunately, the two generations of Tâm Nguyễn share the same traditions, values, and business philosophy. "We are so grateful to our parents. They worked tirelessly for their children, and now we can handle the business without any worries about loans and debts," said Tâm Jr. Since his father had a stroke in 1999, they have taken over the business while also upholding their parents' work ethics, which prioritize the community over profits. Tâm Jr.'s wife has also left her lucrative job as a pharmacist to assist her husband and sister-in-law in running Tâm Nguyễn's business. Many families have enrolled their entire households in courses at the school.

Tâm Senior has transitioned into the twilight of his career, passing on his lifelong business to his children, Tam Junior and his sister Linh, who have restructured the college and renamed it Advance Beauty College. There has been a significant transformation in scope and system, but the second generation is equally determined. Unlike their parents, who had limited knowledge of legislation and were taken advantage of by consultants, Tâm and Linh have obtained membership and are protected by professional associations. Their parents relied solely on the selfless devotion of their former colleagues and comrades to sustain their business. These like-minded individuals shared a belief in the value of manicure, which was considered unconventional in a culture that often looked down upon such work. It is no surprise that Tâm Nguyễn's children continue to express their utmost admiration for their parents, standing on their shoulders and realizing their beautiful dreams. Indeed, they have every reason to be proud of their parents, who humbly bowed their heads so that their children could hold theirs high.

Chapter 12

The Unbreakable Splendor

Resilient Pride

TRỌNG MINH | GLORIOUS BELONGING

Note: I have known Trọng Minh for years. We first met in 1996 at the annual meeting of the Vietnamese Association for Computing, Engineering Technology, and Science (VACETS). Whenever I stopped by Little Saigon, he would often invite me to his show on SBTN. Recently, I visited him at a retirement home where he now resides. In the living room of his one-bedroom apartment, Trọng Minh proudly displayed a large poster featuring the cover of his book series: "The Pride of the Vietnamese." During our conversation, conducted in Vietnamese, he expressed his satisfaction with his retirement community and shared how the Vietnamese community in exile has been an integral part of his life.

"Homecoming is no longer a desire that grips me," says Trọng Minh, a retired journalist who founded one of the first Vietnamese newspapers in the US and authored a pentalogy titled "The Pride of the Vietnamese," as we discuss the concepts of "home" and "return" at his apartment in Santa Ana. His modest yet newly decorated condo, still retaining a hint of charm, is imbued with a sense of serenity on this tranquil afternoon. It is neither an extravagant community nor a desolate neighborhood. In the fading light, a couple of middle-aged residents quietly depart in their aged sedan, leaving behind the fluttering flag of the Republic of Vietnam on the terrace, swaying lightly in the breeze.

At 80 years old, Minh walks with an upright posture, his memories of bygone days still vivid, and his recounting of historical tales filled with fervor. Looking back, he no longer harbors regrets. "It's my destiny," Minh reflects, having reached a moment of epiphany. "I would have never made it here if my life had been smooth in Vietnam during the war." He reminisces about his glorious days working for a newspaper in Saigon, his voice tinged with nostalgia. "It was a time of luxury for me: I wrote fiction, graphic novels, news . . . I miss that euphoria." Overflowing with affection for the past, Minh slowly recounts his journey from war-torn Vietnam to Orange County, the place he would come to call "home" for the remainder of his life.

"During the atrocious battle of 1968, I served as a warfront journalist, and it was there that my fate took a twist," Minh recalls, his voice trembling with emotion. Memories flood his mind as he recounts his experiences. His life is intertwined with the word "because": because he left his comfortable job at the newspaper office, because he ventured into the warfront, because he crossed paths with those American sailors . . . and thus, he was not only saved but warmly welcomed on board, escaping the chaotic night before Saigon fell on April 30, 1975. He left behind a sea of people crying out desperately for a final rescue. The weight of that moment still lingers, forever etched in his heart.

Following the initial wave of Vietnamese refugees striving to escape communist Vietnam, Trọng Minh arrived in Fullerton, where he reunited with his sister and resided for many years before eventually moving to Santa Ana. During his time in Fullerton, Minh dedicated himself wholeheartedly to anti-communist protests. In 2004, he led a group of political activists who fought against General Nguyễn Cao Kỳ, the former premier of the Republic of Vietnam. General Kỳ had returned to Vietnam on a three-week peace mission, responding to an invitation from the communist government. It was reported that he even played golf with communist leaders. As Minh reminisces about those fervent days, a momentary gleam of pride flickers in his eyes, only to be replaced by a fleeting shade of wistfulness.

"We aspired to create our own newspaper even when we were on the boat, floating in the choppy ocean," Minh opens his heart. Other first-generation exilic reporters, such as Du Tử Lê and Đông Duy, renowned for their literary and artistic work before 1975, wasted no time in pursuing their ambition as soon as they arrived in Orange County. Quê Hương (Homeland) became the first newspaper to satisfy the thirst for news among the Vietnamese community who couldn't read English. However, due to insufficient funding, this newspaper had to cease publication after just three issues.

At the age of 38, Trọng Minh decided to temporarily set aside his dream of journalism and made a living as a room cleaner in Anaheim and Costa Mesa. But after years of toiling in a foreign land, his passion for writing was reawakened, and Minh embarked on starting his first newspaper with vim and vigor. He collaborated with other journalists, namely Đinh Việt Phương, Hoàng Phương Hùng, and Nguyễn Ngọc Luận, to launch their own newspaper, Phục Quốc (Nation Reclamation). While initially focused on disseminating stories about Vietnam and expressing their frustration at losing their country, Minh eventually took the lead in all anti-communist activities in the county. Through the analytical articles of this newspaper, readers were convinced to believe in the superiority of a liberal society. Minh single-handedly handled everything, from drafting to the final copy, typing every article, and manually pasting every title. However, financial stress eventually led to the discontinuation of the publication after 12 issues.

"A thriving community would keep newspapers alive," Minh concludes, reflecting on how he supported and sponsored Hoài Diệp Tư, one of the first journalists to run the newspaper Mai (Tomorrow). Minh could never forget the day when Diệp Tư cheerfully showed him the first $20 he earned from selling ads. This made Minh realize that newspapers needed to be nurtured by selling advertisements and had to adopt a commercial orientation. Newspapers and commerce had to be interdependent. Soon after, Vietnamese newspapers began to proliferate one after another, and they all thrived by promoting commercial products and services. These newspapers did not propagate any specific ideologies or imply a political agenda. Vietnamese newspapers, then and now, primarily cater to the readers' demand for news from Vietnam. Vietnamese newspapers in the United States flourish without a specific political mission, as Trọng Minh witnesses, but they adapt, evolve, and transform alongside the ever-changing political landscape of the United States. This political current is always precarious, mutable, and unpredictable. The enduring truth, as Trọng Minh asserts, is that "whenever a Vietnamese community exists, Vietnamese newspapers will never die."

At the sunset of his life, Trọng Minh reflects on his past with a sense of contentment and pride. If one day he must close his eyes forever, his magnificent legacy—the compendium of The Exceptional Vietnamese—will live on. Crafting the first book in 1987, it was not until 1991 that he could have it published, followed by four more volumes. "I know the books are not flawless," Trọng Minh confesses modestly. He was plagued by the humiliation of others, burdened by feelings of inferiority, and driven by Vietnamese pride. Trọng Minh recounts the unforgettable incident that compelled him to write his five-volume book series about the glorious Vietnamese people. It was during a period when he had given up on journalism and was residing in Las Vegas. While wandering in casinos, he observed card players, most of whom were foreigners, openly displaying their contempt and hostility towards Vietnamese refugees. They stared intolerantly into their eyes and hurled insults like "barbarians" and "bastards" who were ruining their country. Trọng Minh chose not to engage in an argument. Instead, he expressed Vietnamese exceptionalism through his books.

He approached 400 outstanding Vietnamese figures from various domains, engaging in conversations with them about their journey from "refugee to bourgeoisie," and celebrated their lives in his books. As he speaks about them, his face lights up, and his eyes shine with a unique sense of pride.

"They represent us, the Vietnamese people, and they are magnificent," Minh expresses with unwavering belief in his fellow countrymen. If there's anything that vexes him about the community, it is the lack of profound appreciation for Vietnamese consciousness and history, with historians providing shallow analyses of Vietnamese legends. "When we equate our King, Quang Trung, with Emperor Napoleon, we are diminishing the greatness of our King," Trọng Minh emphasizes. While Napoleon won and lost battles, our King triumphed in every combat. "Can you find any other women warriors in this world who were as valiant, fearless, and victorious as our Trung sisters?" Minh asks passionately. "In other countries, even powerful ones, women didn't have rights. I haven't seen any women in this world who fought off enemies and then reigned over their own country like our Trung sisters." Minh firmly believes that if Vietnamese people learn to appreciate their glorious history and honor their ancestors, they will never be defeated.

The first generation of Vietnamese refugees, including Trọng Minh, brought with them the traditional mindset of raising their children to become doctors, pharmacists, and other esteemed professions. Many of them succeeded in realizing these dreams. Minh sees this achievement as a long-standing tradition that has been passed down through several Vietnamese generations, marked by wars and displacements. "If our children become doctors, they can withstand any historical turmoil. They are needed, not just in times of war but also in times of peace," Minh explains.

However, in the present day, Vietnamese people no longer prioritize specific careers for their children. Instead, they encourage them to pursue their passions and thrive in their chosen fields. Minh believes that the success of Vietnamese individuals is largely attributed to the culture of "parental support," which he considers a form of sacrifice. Unlike American children, who are often expected to become independent at the age of 18, Vietnamese youths are typically sheltered by their parents until they can establish themselves. "Why should we turn them into tenants in our own house? We should protect our children and nurture their potential," Trọng Minh insists. He firmly believes that if they possess resilience and academic passion, they will undoubtedly flourish and, in turn, help their fellow Vietnamese.

Musing on his aggressive and fearless youth, Trọng Minh has, for a long time, shrugged off all grudges, vendettas, and hostilities from his mind and soul. "We all need to make Vietnamese people, whether communist or liberal, exceptional individuals." Within him, at this moment, remains only the Vietnamese consciousness. He trusts that many other Vietnamese in the diaspora, including himself, want to support their compatriots back home in one way or another due to their sense of kinship, shared mother tongue, and Vietnamese identity. "Some people are pompous and irresponsible. Those windbags should be more humble and contribute more sensibly to the Vietnamese community." Trọng Minh admires former generals of the Republic of Vietnam, whose quiet repentance maintains their dignity and integrity. Trọng Minh is proud of Little Saigon, yet he hopes for a more harmonious collaboration among its residents, who built their homes and businesses from car cemeteries and strawberry farms. "We must not rest on our laurels but work for the collective prosperity of Little Saigon with genuine hearts."

Trọng Minh has lived long enough to understand his Vietnamese peers. He knows that there are many selfish people who, in pursuit of fame and wealth, ignore their flaws and hide their past. This flawed mindset only alienates them from the younger generation, who look down on them while observing their behavior. "I'm not pretentious," he affirms, referring to his belief in Vietnamese Exceptionalism. "I wrote my books with conscience and responsibility. I have no remorse." Trọng Minh is confident in himself and firmly believes in the future of Little Saigon. "The younger generation will never forget their Vietnamese heritage and culture as long as we maintain our family meals," Minh reflects, imagining family stories exchanged around a dining table and the sustenance of familial bonds. "The younger generation of Vietnamese should reserve their mother tongue," Trọng Minh concludes, "for our language will keep our community alive."

Meditating on death, Trọng Minh has his own philosophy, which is truly simple: he does not expect his children to build a splendid mausoleum for him, as many Vietnamese people desire. "How can I leave that burden to my descendants?" Trọng Minh sounds peaceful. "Then every year, they will have to return from everywhere only to see that heap of soil." So when he dies, Minh just wants his body to be cremated, and his ashes to be scattered in the ocean. Until then, Minh will not return to Vietnam but will stay with his family in the United States. He has his own version of Hermann Hesse's quote, "Home is not here or there. Home is transient, wherever we truly belong." As he walked me out to the building lobby, Trọng Minh shook my hand and said, "Where we call home or want to belong is no more important. We all, eventually, will die." I smiled back at him and replied, "I surely would like to see you again and again before you go away."

CHU TẤT TIẾN | THE VANITY WAR

Note: I met Chu Tất Tiến at a Vietnamese restaurant near his real estate office in Huntington Beach. To make a living in Orange County, he takes on various office jobs and, in his retirement, owns a real estate business. However, Chu Tất Tiến is more than just a versatile worker. He is considered the voice of the generation of former officers from the Army of the Republic of Vietnam

(ARVN) who immigrated to the U.S. under the Humanitarian Operation (HO) program. This program was an agreement between Washington and Hanoi to release approximately 100,000 prisoners from reeducation camps and allow them, along with their family members, to emigrate to the United States.

In addition to his work for income, Chu Tất Tiến is a writer, poet, news reporter, martial arts master, and community activist. Among his many publications, "The Legend of Boat People" (a collection of poems published in 2000) and "Is Anything Worth Talking About in Bolsa Ave?" (Paris có gì lạ không em?) (published in 2009) are perhaps the most recognized by his fellow Little Saigon residents. The interview was conducted in Vietnamese.

Why Orange County? One might question the reasons behind Vietnamese exiles choosing this location. Little Saigon has become a "Vietopia" for many Vietnamese refugees, where their resettlement has transformed their lives from chaos to serenity, from war to peace. However, it is also within this Little Saigon that one can witness violence, turmoil, madness, and calamities that divide the community. Anyone familiar with the struggle for democracy and human rights within the Vietnamese American community would likely know Chu Tất Tiến, a veteran and a crusader for the Humanitarian Operation (HO), whose strong voice prevails in every political forum. He can be found at various events, reciting his passionate poems, singing fervent songs, and delivering political speeches, all with a resolute stance against communism. A dissident at heart, his social activism has garnered him a multitude of enemies.

Poor Chu Tất Tiến. He is met with little respect. One political opponent dismisses him as an "opportunist." Another labels him a "womanizer." The online community that follows his social activities even refers to him as a "windbag." In his moments of contemplation, he reflects on his isolation, describing the community as heartless, delusional, and divided. His downcast eyes and trembling voice betray the weight of his emotions. Chu Tất Tiến has no patience for cryptic silence or indifferent apathy. Upon arriving in Orange County under the Humanitarian Operation (HO) in the 1990s, Chu Tất Tiến and other veterans who had endured years of detention in communist prisons were not greeted with the warmth they had anticipated and imagined before leaving Vietnam. Unlike other artists and singers who had escaped earlier and received flags, flowers, and cheers from a community that had yearned for their performances, Chu Tất Tiến and his comrades arrived with an unwelcome reminder of tragedy and a set of non-marketable skills. When he reached out to people for support, they would brazenly ask, "Who cares about you, dumbass?"

Chu Tất Tiến will never forget the scorching summer of 1990 in California, when he tirelessly went door to door, under the blazing sun, to raise funds for the first HO Spring Tree celebration, commemorating the arrival of ARVN veterans in Orange County. However, he was met with cruel rejection, treated like a "wild dog." A representative from Người Việt Newspaper dismissed his audacious plan, deeming Chu Tất Tiến a "nobody" destined to fail. Unfazed, he defiantly declared, "Why do I need to be anybody? I'll do what I wish to do. So never mind." Chu Tất Tiến took matters into his own hands and printed flyers himself.

Unfortunately, empathy was scarce. The owner of Van But restaurant threw a flyer in Chu's face and cursed at him. Another pharmacy owner pushed him away, telling him it was too early in the morning. Doctors, lawyers, traders, reporters—all turned him away. But there were also benevolent individuals. Phở Hòa, for example, generously donated $500, and a bank contributed $1,000. In the end, he managed to collect a total of $15,000. The gathering at Westminster City Council was unforgettable, with an abundance of food, including Vietnamese sausages, rice, and other dishes. Chu's face lights up with joy as he recalls how one "brother" gave them a car, while two others offered bicycles.

As an organization head without a bank account, Chu Tất Tiến had to borrow one from Mai Công, who was the community president at the time, in order to collect the money.

For the HOs who immigrated to Little Saigon later, Chu Tất Tiến is their confidant and savior. He played a crucial role in commemorating all the commandos who were neglected and enraged upon their arrival in Orange County. These commandos had suffered through hardships and humiliation in prison. In Little Saigon, they felt the public's indifference, which further fueled their anger. Chu Tất Tiến took it upon himself to appease them by visiting their homes and listening to their thoughts. He remembers his fellow veterans, many of whom live in poverty and despair, with some even resorting to death as an escape.

One commando confided in Chu that he had been imprisoned for 23 years, yet his arrival in Orange County went unnoticed, making him feel invisible in both spaces. Chu promised to make his presence known and acknowledged in his new home, Little Saigon. In 2014, during a meeting with lawmakers in Washington DC, Chu highlighted the case of the commandos, emphasizing that the American government had abandoned these brave warriors who fought in their war. He denounced the treatment of ARVN veterans, stating that after years of torturous imprisonment, they were given the cold shoulder. As soon as the newspaper article was published, the government approached the "invisible veteran, Đinh Hồng Nhi," to interview him and bring his story to the attention of Congress. Subsequently, Đinh Hồng Nhi and others like him received $40,000 each in recognition of their sacrifices.

For veterans of the Army of the Republic of Vietnam (ARVN), their pride remains unwavering. Chu Tất Tiến is part of this illustrious group. Even after the communists took control of Vietnam, he carried his pride with him into the prison walls, where he would fantasize night after sleepless night about the day he would bask in the light of freedom and transform his life in a "heavenly" place. The days spent in the communist prison were nothing short of traumatic. In an instant, Chu Tất Tiến went from being a courageous warrior who had shed blood and bones for his nation to a despicable outcast.

Chu Tất Tiến's eyes darken as he recalls the deep forests, treacherous cliffs, hunger, and torture that failed to break the prisoners' dignity, oaths, and dreams. Despite enduring the harshest torments from nature and their captors, Chu Tất Tiến and his fellow prisoners waged an ideological war against cowardice. They steadfastly labored with their backs and heads held high, refusing to bow down to anyone, even when their lives were in peril.

Musing over the Vietnamese refugee experience since 1975, Chu Tất Tiến's face radiates with satisfaction. "Vietnamese Americans have remarkably surpassed other ethnic groups. We have achieved more success than even Europeans who arrived 100 years ago," Chu exclaims. However, in his anthology titled "Forty Years of Vietnamese People in the United States," Chu Tất Tiến delves more into themes of loss, trauma, hatred, treason, and jealousy within the Vietnamese diaspora rather than their triumphs. The community he inhabits and observes has caused more destruction than support among its members. "We lack solidarity. It is the self-centeredness and self-importance that erode our collective progress," Chu Tất Tiến concludes.

Jealousy hinders collaboration for the betterment of the community. Despite the numerous individuals who excel in their respective professions, their achievements remain isolated. "We have 'somebody' in various fields, from business to politics, but Little Saigon has yet to emerge as an economically vibrant community," laments Chu Tất Tiến, recalling the lackluster support from the community for his petition against the UN's ratification of Vietnam as a member of the UN Human Rights Council. He sent out 4,000 emails, hoping they would go viral, but only 48 thousand people signed, which was barely enough for a "case number" but lacked the necessary strength to give the community a powerful voice against the UN's decision. "After three years of investigation, the case was eventually revoked. Those prominent groups demonstrate their collective politics of anti-communism, but there is no harmony among them," sighs Chu Tất Tiến, reflecting on the ongoing war they continue to fight: a vanity war.

Chu Tất Tiến's life, since his arrival in Little Saigon in the early 1990s, has been marked by significant setbacks. He lost out on business opportunities in San Jose, where he could have run a profitable restaurant for his brother, and realized the American dream. However, if you were to ask him about that incident, he would simply smile with a sense of nostalgic contentment, as he had dedicated those early years to fulfilling his filial duties to his mother before her passing. "So I missed out on the chance to get rich," reflects Chu Tất Tiến, recalling how he embarked on his new life with little money and a hazy vision of the future. After four years of pursuing a degree in automobile mechanics while making ends meet, he found himself unemployed. "I made the wrong choice. Employers looked at my frail body, tested my muscles, and never called me back," Chu half-jokingly remarks, recalling his struggles with soil engineering that ended up overwhelming his mind with "rocks and stones and soil," instead of providing him with a "fishing rod." Eventually, he decided to quit.

In Chu Tất Tiến's life, a combination of three jeopardies—racism, abuse, and resentment—often left him feeling like he was constantly on the run. One day, his son asked him, "Your background is English, why don't you continue with it here, dad?" This question served as a wake-up call, leading Chu Tất Tiến to resume his studies in American literature and Psychology, pursuing double majors. He also obtained two additional pedagogical degrees in English and Vietnamese, preparing himself for a teaching career.

Despite his English proficiency being sufficient for ENG100, Chu Tất Tiến was dismissed from class by his white teacher due to his resistant behavior and unusual reaction to an "odd" assignment. The assignment asked students to reflect on a story about an adulterous sexual encounter, which went against Chu Tất Tiến's moral code and the influence of Confucian culture. The dean, recognizing that Chu Tất Tiến was yet another victim of pernicious racism, encouraged him to take legal action against the teacher. However, in the end, Chu Tất Tiến decided to drop the class instead.

Another incident, similar in nature, dealt a final blow to Chu Tất Tiến's teaching career. It occurred during a nightmarish 11th-grade class, which ultimately sealed his fate. "Many of the students were single mothers. One lady introduced me to her child, and another male student reached into my blazer pocket, asking where I came from," Chu Tất Tiến recalls with a somber expression. The memories of his former students mocking him still linger. They booed and jeered at him, but he remained composed, drawing on the resilience he had developed during his years in jail.

After the first class, the principal rushed out to meet him, expressing concern about any trouble caused by the students. Unfortunately, the challenges persisted throughout the entire first semester. A rebellious female student fabricated a story, accusing Chu Tất Tiến of insulting her in class. As a result, he not only lost his job but also faced additional repercussions from the false accusation.

Leaving his teaching job for an administrative position turned out to be jumping out of the frying pan and into the fire. In 2000, when Chu Tất Tiến was in his fifties, he surpassed more than 400 individuals to become one of only four people selected as California state executive board examiners.

"However, I eventually had to quit," Chu Tất Tiến reveals. It was not because he was incompetent or irresponsible. "My female director had been harassing me for many years. I couldn't tolerate her any longer," Chu Tất Tiến recalls with sharpness, remembering how that white lady would frequently wrap her arms around him while typing on his computer, press her chest against his shoulders, and whisper softly in his ears . . . all to no avail. Eventually, one day, she fired him without any valid reason.

In her naiveté, she never realized that Chu Tất Tiến had meticulously recorded every moment, every inappropriate action she initiated, waiting for the right time to report them to the general director. "How could they dismiss me? I was the only Vietnamese employee who had been dedicated 'Employee of the Year' in Sacramento," he reflects. They asked him to sign a document agreeing not to sue the State, and he reluctantly did so. Chu Tất Tiến vividly remembers that time after the incident when his troublesome director was finally removed from his sight, but he felt isolated by the distant gazes of his female colleagues in the office. Disheartened, Chu eventually left this job, brooding over yet another disappointment from an employer.

Chu Tất Tiến's commitment to social activism for human rights and the recognition of ARVN veterans has been unwavering, paralleling his professional aspirations. He embraces both struggle and futility as catalysts for aspiration and change. Reflecting on his past in Vietnam during the war, Chu recalls joining the ARVN without being drafted. "My brother was already in the army, so I was exempt," he explains. Witnessing the devastating sight of communist tanks rumbling through the streets, the loss of lives, and the destruction of homes, these atrocities compelled him to join the warfront.

Chu Tất Tiến underwent training by the US Army in Texas and Georgia after being enlisted. Graduating as the valedictorian from the Academy of National Politics, he was then recruited to train soldiers in Thu Duc. His anti-communist spirit has grown stronger over time. Although Chu doesn't belong to any specific associations, he has his own political path focused primarily on human rights and veterans' causes. "I have provided financial assistance to them," Chu Tất Tiến passionately states. He often gives each veteran between $200 and $500. Additionally, he interviews them all, translates their stories into English, and submits them to the National Assembly. Chu has even been invited to speak at the National Assembly, where he delivered a three-minute talk. "At the last minute, I shouted, 'Long live the Republic of Vietnam!' The audience was left in awe."

"My futile struggle here [in Little Saigon] is to unify all associations," laments Chu Tất Tiến. He has observed a relentless competition among individuals and groups to become the "president." This pursuit of power is characterized by malignancy, treachery, and rampant hostility. In an attempt to ease the tensions within the community, Chu has intervened as a peacemaker, but his efforts have often backfired. The desire to become president fuels constant fighting, growing more intense with time.

Chu Tất Tiến has written numerous articles, urging people to abandon these divisive skirmishes that only harm the community. He emphasizes that the title of president holds no real profit or benefit. Despite his appeals, the fighting persists, and the community becomes even more divided. "Everyone yearns for fame, a mere vanity," Chu Tất Tiến denounces these individuals in newspapers. However, his outspoken stance has earned him more enemies. The word "president" itself has become a curse to him, reminding him of President Hồ Chí Minh and the slogan, "The great President Hồ Chí Minh will live forever in our hearts," which Chu Tất Tiến finds intolerable.

At one point, Chu Tất Tiến attempted to unite two associations without the consent of other members. In response, they attacked him, exposing his personal life and disparaging his entire family. The experience left him shattered and deeply affected.

What, then, is more perilous for Little Saigon: an articulate leader who vigorously transforms the community, or a group of shaky narcissists who hold complete control over the community, where malignancy, resentment, and violence prevail?

HUỲNH THỊ NGỌC | WHITHER VIETNAMESE?

Note: I was introduced to Huỳnh Thị Ngọc by one of my sisters, Bùi Phong Thu. Huỳnh Thị Ngọc is a co-founder of the Hồng Bàng Cultural Center, and my sister Thu has served as the center's principal since 2012. The center, as a nonprofit after-school organization, welcomed its first students in 1993. With a focus on teaching Vietnamese language, the center's mission is to preserve Vietnamese heritage and culture. I met Huỳnh at my brother's office in Westminster, as her route home coincided with the location of my brother's office. Our conversation took place in Vietnamese, although we also enjoyed exchanging a few words in French, as I learned that she attended a French-speaking school in Vietnam.

Nurturing the mother tongue among the Vietnamese diaspora is like navigating a rickety boat on choppy waters, as Huỳnh Thị Ngọc, a full-time emergency technician at a local hospital and the volunteer principal of Hong Bang Cultural Center in Little Saigon, reveals. "It's quite a challenging task," she says, "especially when we are part of a fragmented community with divided allegiances." Nevertheless, Huỳnh Thị Ngọc has dedicated most of her life to a single endeavor: preserving the Vietnamese language for the community. What sustains this 70-year-old woman in such a noble pursuit is not fame or fortune, but the pride she feels in her cultural roots. Moreover, she confesses,

"I yearned for the opportunity to speak Vietnamese because I attended French-speaking schools in Vietnam, where we were required to speak French. It was only within my family that I could use my mother tongue."

Becoming the custodian of the Vietnamese language has been a serendipitous journey for Huỳnh Thị Ngọc. Upon her arrival in the US through the first Ordinary Departure Program (ODP) to reunite with her father in 1989, Huỳnh Thị Ngọc immediately volunteered to teach the language at Hồng Bàng Vietnamese Language Center for over three years. Unfortunately, the center had to close its doors due to a lack of teachers. Encouraged by concerned parents, Huỳnh Thị Ngọc took the initiative to establish and lead a new center, Hồng Bàng Cultural Center, dedicated to preserving the language for their children.

The name "Hồng Bàng" in Vietnamese refers to a mythical giant bird from Vietnamese ancient history, dating approximately between 2789 BC and 259 BC. Despite lacking prior pedagogical training or formal language teaching methods, Huỳnh Thị Ngọc, fueled by her passion, resilience, and vision, embarked on the arduous journey of nurturing the Vietnamese language with audacity and empathy. She sees herself as the "glue" that holds people, staff, and parents together in their collective effort. While some parents assisted in finding a suitable location, others volunteered to run classes alongside her.

In 1993, the Hồng Bàng Cultural Center began with an initial enrollment of only 60 students, who were taught by 10 dedicated volunteer teachers. Those who have persevered through challenges over the years share a common philosophy of serving the school, not for personal gain, but out of a commitment to cultivating the Vietnamese language and culture for the community. Huỳnh Thị Ngọc emphasizes that their dedication is not driven by self-interest but by a promise to fulfill this arduous obligation.

Despite not having a permanent campus and receiving no government benefits throughout their 20 years of existence, the center has had a significant impact on the community. Their collective efforts and shared aspirations have drawn more Vietnamese immigrants, who seek a sense of belonging in this new and exotic environment. The center continues to provide a homey experience for those who are eager to connect with their cultural roots.

Mobility has become a way of life for the Hồng Bàng Cultural Center. Despite the constant relocations, parents, students, and teachers always make the move together. "We have been nomads since the center's inception," Huỳnh Thị Ngọc explains. Nevertheless, the number of students continues to grow, reaching 800 in total. Classes are held every Saturday, from 1 p.m. to 3:30 p.m., for a duration of two and a half hours.

The center offers a comprehensive K–8 curriculum that covers a wide range of subjects, including Vietnamese ethics, mannerisms, history, geography, literature, and culture. Adult classes are also available, focusing on equipping participants with the necessary language skills to communicate effectively within the Vietnamese immigrant community. Huỳnh Thị Ngọc emphasizes the importance of Vietnamese professionals such as doctors, lawyers, and pharmacists being able to communicate fluently in Vietnamese. Failing to do so may lead to customer dissatisfaction and the loss of clients who specifically seek out Vietnamese businesses to overcome language barriers.

People often hesitate when faced with various options. When the school boards of Garden Grove and Westminster incorporated Vietnamese into dual language education for all schools, many students decided to drop out of Hồng Bàng Cultural Center. Their parents hoped that the mainstream curriculum would adequately provide Vietnamese language education for their children. The availability of extra Vietnamese classes became a point of consideration. Some parents opted for bilingual programs at their children's schools.

However, despite the competition, Hồng Bàng Cultural Center still stands out among the 90 Vietnamese language centers in California, boasting an impressive number of students and staff. Huỳnh Thị Ngọc proudly states, "We go beyond what the mainstream curriculum offers to our students." The center is dedicated to teaching not only the Vietnamese language but also cultural etiquettes, values, and traditions. They emphasize the importance of celebrating one's heritage and ancestors, teaching children how to show respect and greet their elders when returning home from school, and guiding them in remembering and expressing reverence to parents and teachers on special occasions.

There were similar initiatives in the past that aimed to incorporate Vietnamese language into mainstream programs. Quyên Di Chúc Bùi, a lecturer in UCLA's Department of Asian Languages and Culture, and Kim Oanh Nguyễn Lâm, an ESOL teacher and former member of the Orange County Board of Education, took the initiative. However, only a few students chose Vietnamese as their second language because their parents, upon arriving in the new country, wanted their children to assimilate into the target culture, making English the more desirable choice at the time.

Despite the challenges, Huỳnh Thị Ngọc has persevered in nurturing Hồng Bàng Cultural Center and advocates for a collective commitment to preserving Vietnamese culture. Her mature and reasonable approach has paved a solid path for the center, even in the face of unexpected changes. Over the course of 20 years, the center has graduated 400 students, many of whom have excelled in their professions, demonstrating fluency in both English and Vietnamese.

Ultimately, Huỳnh is deeply passionate about her role as the navigator of HBCC. However, her emotions can be contradictory, often oscillating between gleeful pride and intense pressure without finding a stable balance. The feeling of pride prevails when young parents, who themselves are unable to speak Vietnamese, choose to enroll their children in Hồng Bàng Cultural Center. Moreover, witnessing the success of more and more graduates from the center who have excelled in their careers brings her immense joy. Huỳnh Thị Ngọc beams with pride as she recalls reading social media posts from former students expressing how their Vietnamese language skills acquired from the center have facilitated and enhanced their professional lives. She celebrates their achievements vicariously, as she believes their success validates her dedication to the center despite the numerous challenges it faces.

She acknowledges that since the work at the center is voluntary, there are instances where teachers and parents may miss classes without prior notice, leading to chaos. Unlike other centers that hire teachers based on contracts, Huỳnh Thị Ngọc runs the center based on a covenant-commitment of the heart. However, hearts can have unpredictable reasons, and the constant turnover of volunteers creates a nightmarish staffing problem that she must contend with.

Work dissent is inevitable as not everyone shares Huỳnh Thị Ngọc's selfless philosophy. For some, monetary concerns take precedence. Some colleagues detach themselves from HBCC and start their own school, such as Vietnam Cultural Center, where teachers are paid for their lessons. In contrast to HBCC, which has two voluntary teachers in each class, Vietnam Cultural Center only has one teacher per class. One may question why Huỳnh persists with voluntary mechanisms. "Money cannot retain people," she argues.

Despite the challenges, Huỳnh Thị Ngọc remains self-effacing, congenial, and empathetic, skillfully engaging engineers, doctors, pharmacists, and other intellectuals in the collective effort to preserve the Vietnamese language. Without any financial support to promote their programs, aside from a symbolic tuition fee of only $217 for the entire year, which covers the costs of uniforms and facility rentals, Huỳnh has encouraged all staff members to participate in street marches during festivals to advertise the center. They have tirelessly knocked on every door, from city to district, seeking support, only to be rejected with the simple reason that it is not their language or culture, so the preservation efforts must be undertaken independently.

Huỳnh Thị Ngọc and other seniors at the center are less optimistic and more ambivalent about the younger generations who remain silent when asked to carry on with the center's mission. "They don't have childhood memories in Vietnam. That's why," she explains. Despite these moments of melancholy, Huỳnh Thị Ngọc remains hopeful that the Vietnamese language will never vanish.

The essence of a polarized community, according to Huỳnh Thị Ngọc, lies in the tendency for easy assimilation among young people who effortlessly speak English, juxtaposed with the stubborn mentality of seniors who struggle with the language. This divide will only deepen if the Vietnamese language is not preserved and nurtured. "Many elderly individuals still dwell on past achievements, longing for their glory days, and remain trapped in self-aggrandizing and self-congratulatory fantasies that lead to depression, illness, or dependence on substances," observes Huỳnh Thị Ngọc.

On the other hand, young people who arrived in Little Saigon as teenagers and have never left often succumb to the temptations and negative aspects of modern society. "They often feel alienated from their Vietnamese-cultured families, which expect them to be obedient to their elders," explains Huỳnh Thị Ngọc. "Today's parents have to deal with their children differently, not through strict commands as we did in Vietnam." Many young individuals aspire to escape from their parents' influence as soon as possible. Those who successfully break away are seen as fearless and accomplished. However, approximately 40% of young people fail to leave their family homes. "These children usually lack a sense of purpose, as they have been overprotected. When they are finally released, they struggle to endure challenges or settle into a career."

Living in a tightly knit enclave, with parents scattered throughout the town boasting about the success of their siblings who have become doctors, pharmacists, lawyers, engineers, and other high-paying professionals, these young individuals who may not measure up to those standards succumb to intense pressure and high expectations. Consequently, they fall into a void and lose a sense of purpose.

Pondering the future of her center, Huỳnh Thị Ngọc expresses her concern that it may eventually have to close its doors due to a lack of funding. She notes that nowadays, there is a proliferation of massive pagodas at every intersection in Little Saigon. However, her tone turns somber as she reflects on how the community has changed. "Affluent individuals tend to invest in their future lives through pagodas," says Huỳnh. She sees this phenomenon as a reflection of the absence of virtue, belief, or reason. Huỳnh finds it futile to build more pagodas and donate money to them in the hope of redeeming fortune after death. She remarks, "Buddha attained enlightenment under the Bodhi Tree, not in a colossal pagoda. How is it that our monks cannot think beyond expanding their temples?"

Ironically, Huỳnh notices that if one visits pagodas in the morning, the monks are often unavailable for chanting sutras or counting rosary beads as they are at the gym. She attributes this to corruption, describing how the monks have commercialized the pagodas by renting them out for rowdy events and clubs. Huỳnh recalls a time when she visited a pagoda and heard loud music coming from one of the rooms. When she inquired about it, she learned that there would be dancing activities taking place that day. She questions how monks can meditate and recite prayers in such a chaotic environment, wondering how such a place can still be called a pagoda without any sense of serenity.

Youngsters do not perceive the practice of Buddhism in the same way as their parents do. They view it as a source of turmoil, distraction, and debauchery. Many of them neither visit pagodas nor believe in life after death. Huỳnh Thị Ngọc speculates that this could be attributed to the excessive religious fervor within the community. In recent years, there has been a proliferation of pagodas as people seek outlets for their spiritual yearnings. Huỳnh reflects critically, "I suppose people either prioritize their material wealth over their beliefs, or they lack a sense of transcendent meaning."

Huỳnh Thị Ngọc believes that if they can steer people towards more meaningful community activities, such as building schools or cultural centers, and make them aware of the futility of their religious endeavors, they may gradually drift away from pagodas. By emphasizing the importance of social engagement, they hope to rekindle people's drive to contribute to the community.

The younger generations, known as 1.5 and 2.0, silently disapprove of their parents' religious beliefs. In fact, the more they receive education, the more they tend to become secular. Meanwhile, their parents continue to be immersed in a sense of disempowering despair. However, Huỳnh Thị Ngọc remarks that attempts to regain past glory through extravagant acts of charity or excessive donations to pagodas for a better afterlife only tarnish the cultural image of Little Saigon.

Unlike those disengaged pessimists who feel frustrated or desolate as life speeds by, Huỳnh Thị Ngọc, a diligent full-time paramedic during the week and an unwavering school president on the weekends, does not lament the passing of her generation. She celebrates it.

"After spending most of my life in Little Saigon," Huỳnh reflects, "the community has shown unity in fighting against communism and in constructing pagodas, restaurants, and statues, but not in establishing a cultural center." She wonders if there will be no Vietnamese language or culture left among Vietnamese Americans. Without them, the community would be impoverished, as nothing else can sustain them. As the tireless volunteer asserts, "If we do not preserve our language and culture, eventually all the statues, restaurants, and pagodas will be demolished." With a barely perceptible smile, Huỳnh Thị Ngọc whispers, "What will become of the Vietnamese identity?"

MASTER QUẢNG THANH | MASTER OF EVERYTHING

Note: I have known the late Master Quảng Thanh for over 30 years. My mother was part of a group of Buddhist practitioners who supported his mission to establish a temple to aid in healing the souls of suffering refugees. We crossed paths a few times during public events, but it wasn't until the interview I conducted with him that I gained an intimate understanding of his life as an exile monk. I consider myself fortunate to have had this opportunity to speak with him, as it turned out to be our final encounter before he unexpectedly passed away from natural causes, just soon after.

Beneath the glossy facade of Little Saigon, there exists an underlying sense of unease. This feeling seeps into the deepest recesses of troubled souls yearning for solace. Vietnamese Americans, particularly the first generation of refugees, continue to grapple with their visceral turmoil. Painful memories of the Vietnam War and a profound emotional attachment to their lost homeland render forgetting an impossible feat.

"Maladies, despairs, agonies . . . will never dissipate," Master Quảng Thanh alluded to the proliferation of temples and churches that emerge daily in the enclave, as he guided us through every nook and cranny of Bảo Quang Pagoda—a sanctuary frequented by both residents of Little Saigon and visitors from other places.

Quảng Thanh was destined to be a healer. Before crossing the ocean to save lost souls in Little Saigon, he journeyed through the tumultuous war years in Vietnam, providing acupuncture treatments to underprivileged patients in remote provinces where access to medication was scarce. He saved numerous lives from tragic deaths and, even after the war ended, continued to revive broken souls by translating Buddha's philosophy and enlightening them through the practice of Buddhism.

Meditation, mantras, and rosaries are the essence of Quảng Thanh's life, yet he struggled to find peace in Vietnam. In 1984, he crossed the ocean and found himself stranded in Indonesia for several months. Alongside other South Vietnamese veterans, he established a temple named Kim Quang on the exotic island, providing solace to nine thousand stateless individuals grappling with nostalgia and an uncertain future. When the head of The Office of the United Nations High Commissioner for Refugees asked him to join his American sponsor, Quảng Thanh chose to stay, driven by his sense of duty as a Bodhisattva to rescue his Vietnamese compatriots from their dark abyss. Drawing upon his strong foundation in teaching methodology and pedagogy acquired from the Teachers' Training College in Vietnam, he successfully managed two temples, Garland 1 and 2, for 14 months in Indonesia before eventually departing for America. Through his Buddhist chants, he helped revive the spirits of those with traumatic hearts.

His temple-goers often sense a hint of bitterness behind his words, but it is accompanied by a genuinely compassionate optimism. His life, despite its unsettling nature, maintains a delicate balance between moments of chaos and serene bliss. After serving as an abbot in various temples across Little Saigon during his initial years in America, he harbored a dream of establishing his own temple. With his wisdom and the experiences of a tumultuous life, he worked tirelessly to bring this vision to fruition. In addition to his innate gifts, he poured his heart and soul into the endeavor. For him, the Bao Quang Buddhist Temple represents a tapestry of memories that envelop the entire community, including himself.

Life was once unkind to Quảng Thanh's dreams during the early days of his exile. He faced numerous challenges that couldn't be resolved through therapeutic and enlightening mantras alone. As he practiced Buddhism at home, people gathered to join his Buddhist chants for inner peace. However, he encountered a conflict with his Christian neighbor, whose resentment towards him was unfounded and irrational. Despite recognizing the fault in her attitude, Quảng Thanh hesitated to confront her directly.

The situation escalated when his neighbor filed a lawsuit against him, accusing him of allowing "guests" (Buddhists) to park their cars in the public space, which she believed was designated for her church's congregation. As the case went to court, Quảng Thanh, guided by principles of justice, questioned the arbitrator, "Are those who come to see me at my place any different from churchgoers or anyone visiting the church?" His implication that religious discrimination was dividing the community and undermining collective harmony left the jury feeling uncomfortable. Consequently, the Mayor intervened and decided to resolve the case through a compromise. This incident took place in 1990, highlighting the importance of fostering understanding and respect among different religious communities.

Among the Buddhist monks in Little Saigon, Quảng Thanh stands alone with his notable contributions. Not only did he establish the monumental Bao Quang Buddhist Temple, but he also possesses a genius that extends beyond religious matters. His encounters with various conflicting forces, which at times hindered his religious pursuits, have both limited and enriched him over time. Like vehicles requiring lubrication to function smoothly, connections between people also need nurturing. Quảng Thanh has a natural talent for this.

He embarked on a mission to knock on every door in his neighborhood, surprising the residents with thoughtful gifts on holidays. He carefully chose the perfect occasions to please others without being misunderstood as attempting to manipulate them. Quảng Thanh recounted an incident involving the white old lady next door, who had previously declined their gift. Undeterred, he took a different approach. He sent one of his disciples to the church and presented flowers and gifts to the pastor, explaining the situation. Through this gesture, the conflict between him and the church woman was swiftly resolved. Quảng Thanh proudly reflected on the incident, noting that she never stood in his way again.

In this way, Quảng Thanh skillfully navigates social interactions, finding ways to mend relationships and foster harmony. His ability to connect with others and resolve conflicts demonstrates his remarkable character and unwavering commitment to his beliefs.

He prioritized the preservation of cultural heritage for Vietnamese communities above all else. Even before leaving Vietnam, Quảng Thanh pondered the absence of Buddhist museums in a country with a thousand-year history of Vietnamese Buddhism. His vision became a reality when he constructed Bao Quang Temple, complete with an integrated museum. With significant contributions from devoted Buddhists, Quảng Thanh made the decision to invest in a temple that could accommodate the expanding community of believers.

In 2002, he acquired a complex consisting of a school and church, spanning 12,000 square feet, at a cost of $1.6 million. Remarkably, he managed to complete the project without incurring any debt. Quảng Thanh took charge of the construction process, ensuring that no Buddhists or sponsors interfered with his vision. Quietly and diligently, he transformed the old complex into a sacred hub for the Vietnamese diaspora communities. Each statue, pillar, and artifact within the temple was donated by Buddhists, and their names are displayed on placards attached to the respective gifts.

Utilizing his influence within the community, the master encouraged generous contributions for the construction of a parking structure and an auditorium, aimed at attracting more Buddhists. His ability to rally support and inspire generosity further highlights his leadership and dedication to the growth and development of the temple and its community.

As he oversaw the construction of the museum, Quảng Thanh emphasized that the collection of antiques, art pieces, and cultural artifacts within it were all contributed by devoted Buddhists. He humbly acknowledged that his role was limited to providing the ideas for the museum, while the Buddhists generously donated the items. This realization stemmed from his years of reaching out and inspiring Buddhist beliefs among vulnerable communities.

Since Quảng Thanh arrived in Orange County with his audacious dream of establishing the largest cultural center for Vietnamese refugees in Little Saigon, it took him a mere 30 years to turn his vision into reality. Bao Quang Buddhist Temple now stands as the prominent cultural symbol of Little Saigon, complete with a historical museum boasting the largest collection of cultural antiques in the United States. As Quảng Thanh enthusiastically guided visitors through the dazzling museum, he shared captivating stories about each article and their generous Buddhist donors. He proudly proclaimed, "For such a treasure trove, it would take generations of other ethnic groups to amass."

Quảng Thanh's diverse range of roles, including being a Buddhist monk, politician, artist, businessman, and shaman, reflects the complexity of his inner world. While he should ideally have detached himself from the secular world and dedicated his entire being to Buddha and the Buddhist community, his karma forces him to employ strategies as part of his existence in this transient and tumultuous life.

One of Quảng Thanh's strategies, as he shared with us, is to befriend bureaucrats in order to navigate through various challenges. He recounted how his proposals and paperwork would have languished indefinitely in the City office if the mayor happened to be out of town or unaware that the case involved Master Quảng Thanh. However, once the staff became aware of his close relationship with the mayor, their attitudes quickly changed. This was particularly evident during the construction of Bao Quang Buddhist Temple. When City staff inspected the blueprint and the old house that Quảng Thanh planned to renovate, they raised numerous complaints, one of which was the placement of toilets near the sanctuary, which was deemed offensive in their culture. Quảng Thanh explained to them the importance of separating toilets from sacred spaces, as they are receptacles of human excretions. However, once the mayor reviewed the project, his staff implored Quảng Thanh to disregard their previous complaints. In the end, Quảng Thanh compromised by adjusting his blueprint to include separate handicap toilets and other facilities within the compound. Through such experiences, akin to the beads of his rosary, he learned when to fight, when to withdraw from conflicts, when to seek reconciliation, and when to adapt with necessary twists.

These anecdotes illustrate Quảng Thanh's ability to navigate bureaucratic challenges and find effective solutions. Despite the complexity and inherent conflicts in his multifaceted role, he has learned to utilize his relationships and experiences to make progress while upholding the sanctity and cultural values associated with his religious endeavors.

Displacement, calamities, and hostility could never shatter his hope. Challenges have honed his resilience and shaped the significance of Bao Quang Temple. Once just an ordinary house tucked away in a quiet corner, it lacked a parking structure to accommodate the large crowds of devout pilgrims who gathered for collective rituals. Now, it stands as the most populous site, a landmark sanctuary radiating grandeur and sacredness. Unlike other Buddhist masters, Quảng Thanh managed everything by himself, without requiring the intervention of fellow Buddhists in his projects. He skillfully negotiated with builders to secure the best deals when constructing Bao Quang Temple, investing his attention in every detail, from the stupa building to the pavilion, which embodies Vietnamese Buddhism in perfect harmony between art and culture. Quảng Thanh confidently claimed, "True to its name, any international visitors would be awe-struck the moment they enter this temple."

Since its inauguration in 2012, Bảo Quang Temple has welcomed thousands of visitors, including government officials and ordinary civilians, during every festival. They arrive in delegations and groups, kneeling and praying in the sanctuary, then wandering around in awe, contemplating the cultural artifacts. Quảng Thanh revealed that they all donated generously, and since the temple is a nonprofit institution, any donation made is tax-deductible, which encourages even more charitable contributions. Through their donations, Buddhists can experience both tranquility and redemption. Quảng Thanh expressed his pride, stating, "I'm proud because visitors will come to realize that Vietnamese culture extends beyond Bolsa Avenue, with its businesses and restaurants. We proudly present this temple as a prominent cultural landmark." While many Buddhists in Little Saigon acknowledge and admire Quảng Thanh's various endeavors, his impact on the community is multifaceted. Some question his political stance, labeling him a communist sympathizer disguised as a Buddhist master. He vehemently denied such allegations, stating, "How can I earn the collective trust of this community while being disloyal to the anti-communism spirit?" Quảng Thanh used to confront extremists from the Cần Lao political party who fiercely attacked him on local TV and other public channels, particularly regarding the statue of Thích Quảng Đức, the Buddhist monk who self-immolated in Saigon during the Vietnam War to protest against President Ngô Đình Diệm's oppressive and discriminatory policies towards Buddhism. Quảng Thanh criticized the dysfunctional governance system under Ngô Đình Diệm, which he considered totalitarian. He questioned, "If he wasn't a dictator, why did we have to shout 'Viva President Ngô Đình Diệm!' whenever he appeared?" Quảng Thanh expressed deep disappointment with Ngô, who seemed to prioritize his own glorification. He also challenged his attackers, stating, "Look at what I have been doing for the community."

Overall, Quảng Thanh's journey and his interactions within the community are complex, with admirers recognizing his various contributions in cultivating Buddhism, healing broken souls, and maintaining simplicity and decency. However, others raise questions about his political stance, although he vehemently denies any disloyalty to the anti-communism spirit and highlights his commitment to the well-being of the community through his actions.

Nationalism, when taken to an extreme, can become tiresome, excessive, and foolish. Quảng Thanh has undoubtedly been deeply affected and scarred by violent national frameworks. Nevertheless, he continues to fight for a progressive community in Little Saigon by actively engaging as a senior advisor in political organizations. Through his beliefs and teachings, he has successfully transformed mindsets on various issues such as patriarchy, inter-religious marriages, domestic violence, and more. Recently, he was invited to be the most influential public figure, standing in a flower-decorated car as it paraded through Little Saigon during the national holiday of Black April, which commemorates the fall of Saigon in 1975. Quảng Thanh humbly questioned, "What could a monk like me do beyond Buddhist chanting? I've had to break social vices and heal broken hearts."

Master Quảng Thanh holds an optimistic outlook for the future of Bảo Quang Temple, as well as for all religions in Little Saigon. He believes that "Buddhism has trickled into the Vietnamese mentality and become an invisible yearning." Ultimately, he sees Buddhism as a means for the community to overcome trauma, sickness, and melancholy, allowing it to thrive in happiness and peace. Master Quảng Thanh is credited with performing miracles, surpassing those of doctors or shamans. He has revitalized dying patients and reconciled miserable spirits inhabiting living bodies. However, his loyal Buddhists worry that opponents may try to harm him due to his political impact and other privileges within the communities. Quảng Thanh, with a peaceful demeanor, simply responds, "Let them. Even Jesus was crucified without mercy. I am nothing. Why should I be terrified?"

Chapter 13

Safeguarding the Soulful Exile

Nurturing Art and Culture

NHÃ CA & TRẦN DẠ TỪ, FIERY SOULS

Note: I met Nhã Ca at her quaint office in Việt Báo Daily News located in Westminster. The serenity of her Zen-inspired office, adorned with a large photo of herself taken with the Dalai Lama, provided a stark contrast to the expected bustling atmosphere of a newspaper headquarters. As I sat on a Japanese-style bench next to a stack of the writer's books, Nhã Ca kindly requested me to send her greetings to my sister, Bùi Phong Thu. Thu, who serves as the principal of Hồng Bàng Cultural Center, had the distinction of her students winning Nhã Ca's "Vietnamese Children Write Vietnamese Essays" competition two years in a row. The interviews were conducted in Vietnamese.

A prolific and award-winning writer, Nhã Ca (the pen name for Trần Thị Thu Vân) has authored over 20 novels and continues to add to her impressive body of work. However, she does not shy away from acknowledging her role in the administrative aspects of running the newspaper and its related activities, including workshops, musical events, and book readings. Nevertheless, she openly admits her disdain for accounting and finance, recognizing that her true passion lies in writing. Alongside her husband, Trần Dạ Từ, Nhã Ca is dedicated to a shared mission, and you will have the opportunity to discuss with him how Việt Báo (Vietnamese Daily Newspaper) has become an integral part of life in Little Saigon.

For Vietnamese people who lived through the wartime, as well as younger generations growing up in times of peace, the powerful poems of Nhã Ca (pen name of Trần Thị Thu Vân) and Trần Dạ Từ (pen name of Lê Hạ Vĩnh) hold a special place in their hearts. These literary titans have mesmerized, tormented, wounded, and inspired anyone who has had the privilege of reading their works.

Trần Dạ Từ's prodigious poetry earned him remarkable acclaim in the canon of Vietnamese literature before 1975. He writes with lyrical, amorous, political, and always powerful language. His poems can be jubilant, somber, passionate, desperate, or hopeful, often within the same piece. His writing beautifully captures the essence of love in war-torn Vietnam. It was during this time that he met Nhã Ca, a charming and dreamy lady from Huế, Vietnam's former imperial city renowned for its literary residents. Despite fierce opposition from Nhã Ca's parents, who could not fathom entrusting their beloved daughter to a destitute poet, the two eloped when Nhã Ca was only 19. Throughout the tumultuous years of the 1960s, they wrote prolifically and passionately about war, love, disillusionment, and hope. Their enduring love for art and for each other remains unparalleled.

Yet, there were moments in their lives when the harsh reality overshadowed the romanticism of poetry. After the communists invaded Saigon and reunified the country in 1975, both Trần Dạ Từ and Nhã Ca found themselves blacklisted as "cultural guerrillas" and were imprisoned in the Gia Trung reeducation camp for a grueling 12 years (1977–1989). The fact that Trần Dạ Từ had been previously jailed in 1963 during the tumultuous period of South Vietnam's President Nguyễn Văn Thiệu was inconsequential.

During their traumatic imprisonment in that hellish facility, Trần Dạ Từ conceived his powerful poem, "Throwing children into thunderstorm (Ném con vào giông tố)," which he later transformed into song lyrics. This poignant poem and heart-rending song not only resonated with those who sent their children on perilous journeys across the ocean, but also served as a painful reminder of a history filled with unimaginable sorrow.

My vulnerable, young children
rejected by their homeland
shrouded in the darkness of vendetta
I clenched my teeth
throwing them into a thunderstorm.
Thunderstorm, thunderstorm
offshore, in the ocean
I'm sending you my beloved children
My flesh, my bone, my soul
My hope . . . (1979)

Those searing verses continue to resonate. Unfortunately, they had to seek political asylum in Sweden in 1989. The hospitality they received in Sweden was unparalleled, but Trần Dạ Từ and Nhã Ca felt uprooted in the chilling Nordic winter. Since their relocation to Little Saigon in 1992, they have tried to leave their past behind, perhaps choosing to forget the painful memories.

Through their commitment to love and hope, they embarked on another unexpected and enduring journey: journalism and cultural activism. They founded Việt Báo Daily with a simple mission—to connect their fellow countrymen through reliable news.

One magnificent gift they offer the Vietnamese diaspora in Little Saigon is the annual "Writing on America" contest. Launched on April 30th, 2000, with an award budget of $35,000, the contest has become the pulse of the refugee community. Thousands of writers across the nation share their life experiences of being away from home. "People find solace in writing. They find comfort in reading the writings of others. They use their written stories to communicate with their loved ones. Tears of sorrow and joy are shed," says Nhã Ca. "It's challenging work, but it's a labor of love. We have been fortunate to receive support from the community."

In 2020, Việt Báo presented its 21st compendium of "Writing on America," with each volume spanning 640 pages. Thousands of articles from these editions have been printed and reprinted in Vietnamese and foreign books and newspapers. Việt Báo's online platform has attracted an impressive 800 million readers to date, with some authors garnering over a million readers individually. Despite its popularity, the program has consistently faced financial stress. "We do have a few generous donors, but their numbers are limited," Nhã Ca acknowledges gratefully. She goes on to share a heartwarming anecdote, saying, "One sponsor contributed a couple of thousand dollars to cover the cost of organizing the annual award ceremony. I was deeply moved, and I told him, 'I don't know how to thank you. Please take a look at the decorative pieces or souvenir items I have in my office and choose whatever you like . . . it's just a token of my appreciation.'"

At the age of 80, Trần Dạ Từ captivates me with his agile and vibrant demeanor. He appears ageless, especially when engaged in conversation, exchanging witty remarks: "You must be wondering how this old codger can shamelessly be such a nuisance," he quipped, playfully pointing at his hearing aid as he observed my bemusement. Leaning closer, with his wide eyes fixed on my face, he added, "But forgive me, my hearing has been failing lately. So I have to read your lips and guess what you're saying." We both burst into laughter. As I witnessed him transform an inconvenience into humor and a senile limitation into a youthful prank, I couldn't help but feel that there was a kind of miracle in the way he embraced aging. People like him possess a spirit's wonder that surpasses the ravages of time with immeasurable might.

Whenever I anticipated posing my preconceived questions, Trần Dạ Từ amazed me with his astute observations that lingered profoundly in my mind for days after our meeting. Our conversation unfolded with one surprise after another. The queries I posed were unconventional, leaning more towards philosophical musings rather than typical inquiries one would expect in interviews with other public figures. Trần Dạ Từ appeared to have a knack for deciphering my incomplete thoughts and effortlessly filled the gaps in our communication with enlightening ideas. He left me in awe, utterly flabbergasted by his shrewd insights.

What sets Trần Dạ Từ apart and renders him unforgettable, perhaps, are his unwavering aspirations and boundless optimism. Having endured the heartbreak of surviving war years, and subsequently finding himself confined in a reeducation camp for over a decade, Trần Dạ Từ has witnessed the atrocities of war, experienced famine, endured the monstrous genocide, faced communist tyranny, braved brutal camps, and embarked on a harrowing flight for freedom. Through it all, he has savored and delved deep into every facet of an exilic existence with the profound sensitivity of a refined writer.

Since his family settled in Orange County, Trần Dạ Từ has never ceased his furious writing. With unwavering dedication, he has toiled tirelessly for eight days a week, 52 weeks a year, spanning an impressive 28 years. Only adverse weather conditions have managed to convince him to take a break.

During our conversation, I inquired about the preservation of the Vietnamese language, culture, and art for future generations in the Vietnamese diaspora. Trần Dạ Từ, with expressive passion, responded, "The flow of art and literature has been disrupted, troubled, and lost due to the tumultuous events of history, including wars and forced displacement." He paused, allowing his words to resonate, and then eloquently recounted the profound loss suffered by Vietnam. He reflected on the fact that much of Vietnam's invaluable literary treasure, written in Chữ-nôm (Southern Script), has been lost over time. Since the 10th century, when the Vietnamese adapted the Chinese script to create their own language, thereby ending over a thousand years of Chinese colonialism from 111 BC to 938 AD, Vietnam's official written language had been Classical Chinese, or Chữ-Hán.

Trần Dạ Từ shared his deep admiration for literary figures such as Nguyễn Công Trứ and Hồ Xuân Hương, renowned poets and scholars from the 19th century who wrote in the Southern Script (chữ nôm). However, he lamented that much of their monumental work remains untouched by local scholars, as access to the national libraries where these ancient texts are kept is restricted.

"Those libraries welcome American and international scholars only, not Vietnamese academics," Trần Dạ Từ remarked with a wry smile.

"Western civilization is both a blessing and a curse," Trần Dạ Từ reflected, his eyes turning somber. He recounted how the introduction of the Roman alphabet to Vietnam in the early 17th century by Alexandre de Rhodes, an Avignonese Jesuit and lexicographer missionary, swiftly replaced and overshadowed the literature and poetry written in the Southern script. Influential scholars such as Đặng Thái Mai, Nguyễn Văn Tô, Phạm Quỳnh . . . translated celebrated works from the Southern script to chữ Quốc Ngữ (the Western alphabetical national language). "But they missed out on much of the essence in that literary trove," Trần Dạ Từ shared, recalling a conversation with one of his friends. While the Roman alphabet offered a more charming and accessible writing system for the Vietnamese people, who sought liberation from Chinese influence, it disrupted the continuity of Vietnam's history, culture, and traditions. Trần Dạ Từ sharply remembered, "Our cultural house has changed its keys with each ebb and flow of history, causing substantial loss of our past." As we delved deeper into the disjunctures of history and culture, Trần Dạ Từ's thoughts drifted back to the revolution of 1945, when the dislocation of people and culture further exacerbated the ruptures in Vietnamese society.

"This is our karma," Trần Dạ Từ surmised, "because we have repeatedly lost our exuberant, revelatory, and engrossing literature and art." He recognized that all poets and writers possess a distinctive sensitivity to the vicissitudes of life, and they wouldn't miss documenting the fluidity of their era in any language, be it Southern calligraphy or Western script. Wars and historical disruptions not only massacre human beings but also ravage literature and culture. At his age, Trần Dạ Từ recalled the plight of his literary predecessors like Thế Lữ, Huy Cận, Xuân Diệu, and Tự Lực Văn Đoàn, who were mercilessly tormented during the revolution of 1945 for their "impure" writing and portrayal of human foibles and follies. Their pre-1945 works were subsequently sanitized by revolutionaries who believed in nothing but violent ideologies. "This ruthless cultural genocide has impoverished our literary capital," Trần Dạ Từ wistfully expressed. However, he found solace in the revival and widespread readership of most quintessential literature before the revolution on websites such as thivien.net, its Facebook page, and other social media platforms. It was a historical journey through the tumultuous landscape of Vietnamese literature. He had reason not to be too pessimistic about the future of Vietnamese culture in Little Saigon. Since its establishment in 1992, the couple had been frequent hosts of cultural events. The most recent one I attended was a musical performance titled "The Road to Love (Con đường tình ta đi)," which paid tribute to the late legendary musical composer Phạm Duy, just before the outbreak of the pandemic in 2020.

Trần Dạ Từ is skeptical about the demise of Vietnamese literature and culture, and he is right to be. Their literary works continue to thrive, as the younger generation, propelled by the forces of globalization, carries libraries on the "Cloud." With his historical perspective on the unique evolution of Vietnamese literature, TDT reassured us by saying, "Now living in America, we have a growing number of notable writers like Việt Thanh Nguyễn, Ocean Vuong, and others." He smiles and adds, "Nhã Ca and I will continue to write. When we retire, we will write even more." I wonder when they will retire. In the meantime, they persist in examining Vietnamese literary works in school curricula. Trần Dạ Từ beams with delight as he looks at his wife seated beside him, and we discuss her historical memoir, *Giải Khăn Sô Cho Huế* or *Mourning Headband for Hue* (translated into English by Olga Dror, Indiana University Press), which is extensively taught in American schools. They believe that her book is the first immigrant work to be included in the American education curriculum.

TÔ VĂN LAI | THE ART FOR BROKEN SOULS

Note: Most fans of the "Paris by Night" show, which is claimed to be the world's most popular Vietnamese musical variety show, would be familiar with the late Tô Văn Lai, the founder of Thúy Nga Productions in 1983 in Paris, France. Although it started as a labor of love, the enterprise was not commercially successful until Tô Văn Lai and his family relocated to Little Saigon. My brother, Dương Bùi, is acquainted with Tô Văn Lai and many of the recurring performers. He arranged for me to interview Tô Văn Lai at his retail shop on Bolsa Ave. The interview was conducted in Vietnamese.

There are three things that most Vietnamese families, whether in Little Saigon or elsewhere in the Vietnamese diaspora, hold dear in their homes: fish sauce (nước mắm), morning glories or water spinach, and Paris By Night DVDs. While fish sauce and morning glories satisfy the taste buds with familiar flavors, Paris By Night provides solace to nostalgic hearts. Peter Tô Văn Lai, the father of Paris By Night and the iconic vaudeville show for Vietnamese refugees, is not just a stellar divo, a prominent music composer, or a phenomenal artist. He embodies all of these qualities and more, transcending boundaries as a cosmopolitan and sophisticated avant-garde figure.

Before leaving Saigon, Tô Văn Lai taught math and philosophy at Nguyễn Đình Chiểu High School in Mỹ Tho. He lived a noble life in the heart of the metropolis, mingling with the intelligentsia, and enjoying the singles of Thái Thanh, one of the first iconic singers of the "New Vietnamese Western-style music" whose unique and warbling voice mesmerized him.

While Thái Thanh captured the nation with her diverse repertoire of Northern Vietnamese folk songs, French hits, and Western opera, Tô Văn Lai's foray into music production was initially a failure. He reminisces, "I lost. Saigonese highbrows were stingy," referring mostly to doctors and pharmacists who were focused on money and teetered between financial concerns and artistic pursuits. "They craved the CDs, yet barely bought them." As a fervent aesthete, Tô Văn Lai feared mediocrity. However, he realized that unlike math and sciences, which have concrete solutions, arts evoke a plethora of emotions. His distinct and sharp taste seemed offbeat to popular ears. What he considered kitschy, maudlin, and sentimental turned out to be an irresistible lure to others.

The second CD he launched in Saigon featured the songs of Thanh Tuyền, another diva from the same "New music era" known for her Southern folk songs. These songs resonated in every coach taking people from the city to their hometowns in the countryside, floating through the streets.

Migrating to Paris in 1976, Tô carried with him a collection of cassettes—songs by Vietnamese southern divas. These melodies served as solace for the displaced. During the daytime, Tô Văn Lai worked as a car repairer, changing oil, nuts, and bolts for cars. Then, every night under the starry Parisian sky, Tô Văn Lai and other refugees would sing, relieving their alienation and sadness. It was during this time that Paris By Night was born.

However, when Tô Văn Lai attempted to sell the first videotape of Paris By Night, some acquaintances expressed doubt, questioning the viability of bringing Vietnamese music to the Western market. They argued that the Vietnamese immigrant audience, having lived in the West for most of their lives, had fragmented Vietnamese language skills, and thus the product would not have a lasting impact. Undeterred, Tô Văn Lai pressed on with his project, fueled by his unwavering belief in the emotional attachment and nostalgic yearning among the Vietnamese diaspora.

Tô Văn Lai firmly believed that people only truly value and connect with their cultural heritage when they interact with others in their work and daily lives. As immigrants settled and sponsored their families, the Vietnamese community grew, and so did their longing for romantic melodies that would soothe their nostalgia, melancholy, and despair.

"Intellectuals always find a silver lining in every cloud. They never shy away from facing adversity," Tô Văn Lai enthusiastically recounted, reflecting on his memorable visit to Anh Bằng, a prominent musician at the ASIA Center, during his business trip to Little Saigon in 1983. It was late in the evening as they chatted over dinner when the telephone rang. Tô listened intently as Anh Bằng cheerfully conversed with someone on the other end of the line, revealing that the Alpha company had ordered 500 cassettes from his music production center. "What an enormous market!" Tô and his wife exclaimed in awe. In Germany or Switzerland, where the Vietnamese community was relatively small, they would only sell a few cassettes occasionally. Inspired and driven by the desire to captivate a larger and more promising audience, Tô and his family made the decision to leave France and move to the United States.

What makes Paris By Night an enduring marvel is not only its enchanting programs but also its remarkable masters of ceremonies. From the inception of the show in the City of Light, Tô Văn Lai sought to have the best MCs, so he approached the former owner of the most famous music parlor in Saigon, which had popularized Lệ Thu and Khánh Ly, immortalizing their voices. "He disappointed us in his first appearance," Tô recalled, "as he used Vietnamese imprecisely, and I was concerned that people in Vietnam would look down on us here for losing our language." Subsequently, Tô changed MCs one after another, but none possessed the charisma, allure, and wit he sought. Determined to find a gem, Tô Văn Lai discovered one in a bookstore. He approached the owner of Tú Quỳnh bookstore in Paris, Phan Hoàng Yến, and asked, "What is your best-selling book?" She recommended titles by writer Nguyễn Ngọc Ngạn, explaining, "His family escaped Vietnam by boat, but his wife and children perished at sea. He captured those poignant moments that touch everyone's heart." Without hesitation, Tô Văn Lai reached out to the author, Nguyễn Ngọc Ngạn, who at the time was going door-to-door selling insurance, and invited him to lead Paris By Night. Nguyễn Ngọc Ngạn swiftly became a legendary MC with his extraordinary elocution.

In Tô Văn Lai's recollections, living in exile was a deeply painful experience, particularly during the initial years away from their homeland. As night fell in Paris or amidst the harshness of winters, a saying from his friend, author Dương Anh, echoed in his mind: "We never truly appreciated Southern chants in Vietnam, as they seemed sentimental, ordinary, and outdated. It is only when we are displaced from our homeland that these familiar melodies stir our souls so passionately." These chants gradually seeped into their lives, providing solace for their exilic agony and sustaining their hope. "This is how Paris By Night came to be: it was created for the Vietnamese in exile." The early videos of Paris By Night wholeheartedly embraced the nostalgia that most refugees experienced. The primary genre at that time was Vietnamese opera, which firmly anchored itself in the hearts of its audience.

One time, during a visit to Los Angeles for a medical exam, Tô Văn Lai found himself feeling overwhelmed with pressure. When a female doctor noticed his demeanor and inquired about it, he coolly responded, "If you don't know me, I am running Paris By Night." His succinct introduction astounded the doctor, who couldn't hide her admiration and reverence. She exclaimed, "Other communities have established their own townships here: the Japanese have Japan town, the Chinese have Chinatown, but the Vietnamese community not only has Little Saigon but also Paris By Night, which I believe is the emblematic hallmark of Vietnamese culture that no one else could have created. You are truly incredible."

As it turned out, the doctor herself was one of the millions of loyal viewers who found Paris By Night to be an emotional therapy that healed their wounded souls—souls that often wandered adrift.

The Vietnamese refugees, even after achieving success in America, find it difficult to lead a peaceful life without embracing their past, no matter how painful it may have been. In 1986, the 10th edition of Paris By Night was released with a fateful theme: "Giã từ Saigon" (Farewell to Saigon). Tô Văn Lai and his cast etched the title deep into the hearts of the audience. The show commenced with the anthem of South Vietnam, a rousing melody that urged people to rise up and march to the warfront to save their country. The moment the melody resonated, it surged vigorously into the souls of the audience, enveloping their hearts with passionate emotions: the shattered villages, a child crying beside the lifeless body of their mother, blood and flowers and flags, an ocean of people, and a war-torn Vietnam. The audience mourned, and tears streamed down their faces, creating a profound silence.

That poignant performance incorporated images from the documentaries carried by former Lieutenant General of the Republic of Vietnam, Trần Văn Trung, when he escaped Saigon. "He entrusted them to me, capturing Saigon during and after the war, and I projected many of them as a backdrop to the performance," Tô vividly described the artistry of Thúy Nga's "Farewell to Saigon," which elicited a cathartic response from the audience, who had become emotionally reliant on his productions. Thuy Nga thrived on this emotional connection. "Giã Biệt Saigon (Farewell to Saigon) created a miracle," Tô's face instantly brightened with triumphant joy and genuine emotion, as he recounted how this powerful program diverted the Vietnamese refugee community from their addiction to Hong Kong television series that had torn their families apart in the 1980s. "Everyone was mesmerized by New Heavenly Sword and Dragon Sabre, The Legend of the Condor Heroes, Demi-Gods and Semi-Devils . . . People were so engrossed in these captivating series that they neglected their chores, abandoned their responsibilities, and even divorced their spouses . . . Without Paris By Night, they might not have escaped the irresistible allure of these Hong Kong dramas, as there were few Vietnamese alternatives to watch."

Paris By Night is not a mystery; it is a masterpiece of collective passion and grandeur. Tô Văn Lai and his daughter have skillfully embraced the romantic notions of nostalgia, hope, and loss in every program, interweaving them with recorded images from both Vietnamese and foreigners who have come and gone from Vietnam. The production crew of Paris By Night consists of Hollywood professionals whose cutting-edge staging technology has made the show exceptionally splendid and immensely popular. However, what continues to enchant the audience for many years, beyond the magnificent staging, are the two charismatic MCs, Nguyễn Ngọc Ngạn and Nguyễn Cao Kỳ Duyên, whose captivating narratives and entertaining conversations have become the heart and soul of every program.

Paris By Night is a poignant journey, offering a glimpse into the profound melancholy experienced by Vietnamese refugees who, even after many years, continue to mourn the loss of Saigon. It captures the powerful moments of departure and return, where promises were exchanged and hopes cherished.

Through its performances titled "The homeland we always carry," "The Banyan tree and the River bank," "Tears for Vietnam," and "Which Spring we will return?," Paris By Night evokes a sense of longing and nostalgia. The familiar melodies composed by prominent artists such as Trịnh Công Sơn, Vũ Thành An, Ngô Thụy Miên, and sung by legendary voices like Khánh Ly, Thái Thanh, and Thanh Tuyền, transcend sorrows, give voice to dreams, and provide solace to the displaced Vietnamese community. It is a concert that speaks to the souls that have been broken.

Paris By Night has experienced its heyday, with the production continuously improving its program content and elevating its level of sophistication. It has embarked on multiple tours across different countries, including Europe and Australia, and has been celebrated by Vietnamese audiences worldwide. To sustain its rising production costs, Tô Văn Lai and his family have had to rely on business sponsors both in the US and Vietnam. However, Tô Văn Lai foresees a grim future for the show, as he witnessed the widespread sale of counterfeit Paris By Night DVDs, both old and new, during his trip to Vietnam. He recounted an encounter with a DVD store owner who proudly showed him around Saigon in her glossy BMW and boasted about selling 5,000 pirated copies of Paris By Night per day. Tô Văn Lai's optimism for the future of Paris By Night can only be sustained if the audience becomes more conscientious and resists the temptation to purchase pirated DVDs. Unfortunately, people often measure art not by its aesthetic value, but by their own financial considerations, even when that art touches their broken hearts.

TRÚC HỒ | A HAVEN BETWEEN THE SHORES

Note: My brother, Dương Bùi, introduced me to Trúc Hồ, a Vietnamese American musician, songwriter, and now producer. I had the opportunity to meet Trúc Hồ at his Broadcasting Television Network (SBTN) located in Garden Grove. Dương, who is the President of the Association of Vietnamese American Physicians in Southern California, frequently appears on SBTN programs and shares a close friendship with Trúc Hồ. During our meeting, the interview was conducted in Vietnamese.

On a crisp and bright late summer morning, we find ourselves standing outside the office of Trúc Hồ, the CEO of Saigon Broadcasting Television Network (SBTN). Behind the closed door, he appears engrossed in his computer screen, furrowing his brow and seemingly unaware of the world around him. His serious and contemplative expression challenges our preconceived notion of a romantic musician whose melancholic and passionate ballads captivate sentimental hearts. With a gentle knock, we anticipate encountering a prickly and irritable individual, bothered by unexpected visitors. However, contrary to our imagination, Trúc Hồ greets us with a shy smile. "I was not born for these challenges," he jokes, gesturing towards the unfinished task on his computer and the stack of papers, which appear overwhelming to an artist like him. Just as he settles into the conversation, his assistant knocks on the door and hands him a post-it note, reminding him of an upcoming meeting. Struggling with conflicting ambitions and responsibilities, he appears to have lost his balance, his inner peace, even in the midst of his beloved community, Little Saigon, a haven for the Vietnamese diaspora.

Disillusioned with the communist regime, Trúc Hồ fled Vietnam in 1981, carrying with him a precious hair clip belonging to his sweetheart. Crossing the border into Cambodia in March 1981, the 16-year-old felt a wave of relief, liberated from the oppressive confines of his homeland, eagerly anticipating a fresh start. However, his journey took a turn when he was arrested in Thailand for illegally entering their territory. Feeling desolate, uncertain, and desperate, Trúc Hồ was released after spending a week tasting the hardships of prison life. "Food was scarce, and water was never sufficient for drinking, let alone bathing, so I was constantly dirty, thirsty, and famished," he recalls. During his stay at one of the International Red Cross camps, NW9, located on the Thailand-Cambodia border, he found himself unable to sleep. Night after night, the deafening sounds of bullets and grenades filled the sky as communist forces ruthlessly attacked Cambodia. Eventually, the United Nations closed the camp, and Trúc Hồ, an orphaned teenager, was given priority to leave two months later, ahead of other asylum seekers who often had to wait an average of one to two years. From being stateless, Trúc Hồ acquired a new identity: that of a refugee.

Arriving in Huntington Beach, California, in August 1981, Trúc Hồ was sponsored by a Vietnamese family who quickly dampened his dreams as soon as he expressed his desire to pursue a career in music in the land of freedom. They shook their heads disapprovingly, asking him sarcastically, "Who can survive here with such a lousy job?" Instead, they advised him to pursue engineering or a science-related field. Taking their advice to heart, Trúc Hồ embarked on a journey of exploring various possibilities for his future career, starting with English, then computer science, and finally mathematics. However, after a semester or two, he realized that he was lost and felt that this was not the life he truly desired. "My lifelong dream was to immerse myself in music. It was the reason I left Vietnam, where artistic freedom was an elusive luxury. Everything was controlled by the communists," Trúc Hồ recalls. He remembers that the only music he could play in Vietnam after the reunification was revolutionary songs. "My musical creativity had to be unleashed in America." Driven by his passion for music, Trúc Hồ made the bold decision to drop out of high school and leave the sponsor's house. He moved in with his friend, now a lawyer named Đỗ Phú, and wholeheartedly pursued his musical aspirations.

Having majored in classical piano, composition, and commercial music, Trúc Hồ fearlessly delved into the world of music. He joined Anh Tài's band, a Vietnamese American music band that had been playing in Saigon before 1975. Trúc Hồ also collaborated with Trần Ngọc Sơn, the son of a celebrated musician in the community named Anh Bằng, and together they recorded their songs at Dạ Lan, the familial center. They sold their CDs in the market and performed around the world, fueling Trúc Hồ's growing passion for Vietnamese music. His love for Vietnamese music began with the first Vietnamese song he ever heard, "Trúc đào" ("Oleander"). Trúc Hồ then took on the role of acoustician and keyboardist for Anh Tài, and later became the musical director for the Asia Center, albeit briefly, as he departed shortly after the release of their first music video, "Đêm Saigon 1" ("Saigon Night 1"), in 2001.

Alongside Việt Dzũng, a popular MC in local events and radio stations known for his staunch anti-communist stance, Trúc Hồ embarked on a journey to various refugee camps in Southeast Asia to develop their political project titled "The Journey to Freedom." During the production of the documentary, Trúc Hồ crossed paths with Đinh Xuân Thái, the program director for Little Saigon Television (LSTV) and Radio, who provided valuable documents for the project. This encounter led to a collaboration between them in establishing SBTN, a television network, in 2001. Their ultimate objective was to create a platform for Vietnamese Americans to connect and engage with their community, fostering a sense of collective voice and visibility. Trúc Hồ believed that through SBTN, they could make a collective impact and have their own representation in elections. Concurrently, Trúc Hồ continued his work for Asia, driven by their mission to preserve and cultivate the musical legacy of the pre-1975 era, often referred to as the "golden music." Within the soul of every Little Saigon resident, old and young alike, flows a river of memories. It is a river that runs calmly, meandering through lush greenery and verdant fields, reflecting the shadow of the home they once belonged to. This river runs deep and never fades away in the nostalgic, wistful, and melancholic melodies composed by Trúc Hồ, a musician from a bygone era. He understands, with great fervor, the power of music as the elixir of life for a displaced community.

To combat the potential amnesia and erasure of the history of the Republic of Vietnam, the Asia concerts, directed by Trúc Hồ and Việt Dzũng, transcend mere entertainment value by interweaving historical narratives into their art. When viewers, spanning across generations, witness the performances of Asia, they are transported instantaneously to the heroic past of South Vietnam, which has seemingly faded in the wake of other transformative arts within the community. Through Trúc Hồ's skilled direction, Asia brings its audience back to their roots, rekindling their diminishing history and reawakening their forgotten values. Deceased musicians are resurrected on stage as Asia's indelible storytelling unveils the untold inspirations behind their timeless creations. In essence, Asia not only revives history and preserves the music legacy for future generations, but they also serve as fervent custodians of the vanishing Vietnamese traditions, values, and beliefs. Trúc Hồ has wholeheartedly dedicated 25 years of his life to this commitment, resulting in the creation of 78 magnificent episodes under the banner of Asia Entertainment.

It was due to his deteriorating health, following five surgeries of varying degrees, that Trúc Hồ decided to step away from Asia and focus solely on SBTN. "It continues to be a challenging struggle," he admits. "As a premium TV channel, we had to work tirelessly in the early years before gaining popularity within the community and attracting more households willing to pay to watch it, around 2005–2006." However, not long after this accomplishment, in 2011, SBTN had to face the emergence of free local TVs, which proliferated on the Internet and other platforms. Local Vietnamese American TV stations began to spring up wherever Vietnamese Americans resided. "SBTN has been grappling with these free TVs for seven years," Trúc Hồ reveals. Consequently, his current reality is far from the sanctuary he envisions for his creation. Instead, it feels like a claustrophobic space where survival takes precedence over the arts.

Embracing the ever-changing lifestyles within the community, Trúc Hồ and SBTN have embarked on a path of divergence, transforming their channel into an application that can be accessed on any digital device for an affordable price of $8.00 per month. "This is a monumental effort on our part, and if it doesn't succeed, we won't be able to survive," he admits. The truth is that SBTN can only sustain itself if 50 thousand households subscribe to their channel. However, an even more pressing concern is their unwavering commitment to preserving Vietnamese culture and arts for future generations amidst the relentless pace of the world. Trúc Hồ's palpable and timeless anguish reflects the reality that nothing should be taken for granted, especially when it comes to arts, culture, and history, which require collective nurturing. In a world where everything can be commodified, one cannot truly appreciate anything without making an effort to protect it. "Our culture and history will perish," he warns, "if the community becomes complacent in neglecting them."

Why Asia and SBTN? It would be an indifferent dismissal to perceive their survival as anything less than the preservation of a community, the Vietnamese diaspora, and the historical legacy of Vietnam's South in the global consciousness. "Asia has been a part of the lives of many generations, both within Vietnam and abroad," Trúc Hồ explains, "and through our work, they have come to understand our historical narrative." Asia and SBTN allow Vietnamese diaspora to connect with their mother tongue and sing Vietnamese songs. Even those living in Vietnam gain insights into the brief yet glorious journey of the Republic of Vietnam, experiencing perspectives that differ from what they are exposed to by the totalitarian regime at home. "The paramount contribution of Asia and SBTN," Trúc Hồ asserts, "lies in their ability to provide authentic voices as living witnesses of history." The resurgence of Bolero in Vietnam is also attributed to Asia's unwavering efforts to preserve the country's musical heritage. "No singer in Vietnam can achieve stardom without at least performing a Bolero song," he concludes.

"Our identity, the refugee identity, must be safeguarded and passed down from one generation to the next," Trúc Hồ suggests. As part of SBTN's recent agenda, he has created and developed SBTN Voice, a show that attracts young talents of Vietnamese origin who were born and raised overseas. "You can witness our efforts on YouTube," he adds with a touch of humor. Trúc Hồ fears that without such a talent show, young Vietnamese American talents may lose touch with their culture and identity. While his passion and determination to preserve the history and culture of the Vietnamese diaspora remain unwavering, Trúc Hồ is ready for a transition. "I'm actively seeking and keeping my fingers crossed for the younger generation who are not indifferent to our history and traditions." Only if the youth create their own network and reconnect with their roots, guided by the experiences of their preceding generations, can they uphold a collective voice and preserve the Vietnamese diasporic legacy.

"But they are leaving," his eyes turn somber, "those young talents chase after fame and fortune; they quickly assimilate into the mainstream economy and turn away from the community. Our company is not an ideal destination for those who are solely driven by their dreams." Unlike national television stations in Vietnam, where the state budget generously subsidizes their programs, or big companies like Pepsi and Coca-Cola that sponsor their work, television channels overseas must be financially independent. Consequently, the scarcity of human resources becomes an inevitable challenge. "Why doesn't your company attract more advertisements from businesses in Vietnam?" we ask him. "Because it goes against our ideology," he frankly responds.

What clearly distinguishes Asia and SBTN from other entertainment centers is their commitment to preserving the "refugee identity, freedom, and anti-communism" that they have steadfastly pursued for many decades. While this ideological embodiment in every program may resonate with some unsung veterans or the first generation, it could potentially alienate younger audiences who have no personal connection to the past conflicts. How much longer will this political tension persist, one may wonder. Needless to say, as long as the older generation maintains their power and resistance to change behind the scenes, their descendants may choose to distance themselves from this biased narrative and embrace the diversity that global culture offers. As for Trúc Hồ, he simply has a humble dream: to see SBTN continue its mission so that he can leisurely sit at his piano once again and compose music.

YSA LÊ | IN QUEST OF ECSTASY

Note: Since its inception, the Vietnamese American Arts and Letters Association (VAALA) has piqued my interest. Unfortunately, I have consistently missed all of its events due to scheduling conflicts. However, during my visit to UCI to meet Thủy Võ Đặng for her work on VIET-Stories, Đặng introduced me to Ysa Lê and her fellow colleagues at VAALA. We had an initial introduction and gathering at the Brodard Chateau in Garden Grove. Subsequently, on another trip to Orange County, I had the opportunity to engage in a conversation with Le at the VAALA office in Santa Ana. She kindly provided me with a brief tour of the center, which brought to mind the many classrooms I am familiar with at the university, complete with desks, chairs, billboards, pens, brochures, and promotional items for events. I felt a sense of belonging and comfort in that environment. The interview was conducted in English, although we exchanged a few words in Vietnamese.

"No man ever steps in the same river twice," Heraclitus once said. If art is likened to a river, for the old-timers of Little Saigon, that river seems to have stopped flowing. It carries the weight of their nostalgic attachment to their homeland, becoming a stagnant river of memories that provides solace to their exiled and troubled souls. Why do these individuals persistently romanticize their past?

"I witnessed enraged individuals storming around us, vandalizing and expressing their fury towards an art piece by Brian Đoàn," recalls Ysa Lê, Executive Director of the Vietnamese American Arts and Letters Association (VAALA). She vividly remembers the moment of terror when a furious crowd of protesters attacked her and threatened violence against visitors just days after VAALA launched their FOB II: Art Speaks exhibition in Little Saigon. They demanded the removal of a photograph taken by Brian Doan, a renowned artist and photographer based in Los Angeles, known for his exploration of Vietnamese identity during the postwar era through his photography. "They were angry at Brian Doan's diptych in which one of the photos depicted a girl wearing a red tank top and a yellow star (which is the Vietnamese flag) and a small bust of Ho Chi Minh on the coffee table," says

Lê, her voice still shaky as we sit together at the Santa Ana headquarters of VAALA, the sanctuary of arts, on a bright autumn morning.

Ysa Lê's involvement with VAALA was not a random occurrence. She grew up surrounded by the arts. One of her cherished childhood memories was accompanying her father, the esteemed journalist and writer Lê Đình Điểu, to book launches, art performances, and exhibitions when he co-founded VAALA with a group of close friends, including the renowned music conductor Lê Văn Khoa. VAALA was their shared passion. Even at a young age, Ysa Lê became acquainted with literary giants such as Mai Thảo, Nguyễn Xuân Hoàng, Nguyễn Mộng Giác, Võ Phiến, and others, as their book signings and events were hosted by VAALA. These literary heroes shaped her enduring love for the arts.

When Ysa Lê's father passed away in 1999, she felt a deep sense of loss and despair, and VAALA fell into a state of quietude. Overcoming the agony took more than a year, but it was during this time that a senior member of the association encouraged her to reignite the flame her father had ignited and revive VAALA. In 2000, Ysa Lê expressed her desire to her mother to volunteer for VAALA for a couple of years as a way to honor her father's memory. For over 20 years now, she has been dedicated to this journey, navigating through both successes and challenges, determined to carry on the legacy of VAALA.

Ysa Lê was not alone in this endeavor; all VAALA members joined her in resuming the organization with great enthusiasm. In 2001, they held their first event, an exhibition featuring two artists: Huỳnh Thượng Chí, known for his artistic work on pearls, and Suzie Vuong, a visual artist inspired by nature's beauty, emotions, music, and poems. Both artists have since flourished in their professions and continue to support VAALA. Despite having a modest budget, they managed to organize a landmark concert featuring Đặng Thái Sơn, an internationally celebrated pianist who flew from Canada to Little Saigon for a grand performance that attracted over 1,000 spectators. The success of the concert motivated Ysa Lê and the VAALA officers to host several more engaging events, including recitals, exhibitions, and book signings, to fund their community services.

The turning point that propelled VAALA to national and international visibility came in 2003 when Ysa Lê decided to include cinema in their agenda. They collaborated with many Vietnamese American filmmakers such as Tony Bùi, Charlie Nguyễn, Timothy Linh Bùi, Nguyễn-Võ Nghiêm-Minh, and Victor Vũ, further raising VAALA's profile.

Ysa Lê's devotion to art is fueled by her unwavering passion. Together with Trâm Lê, another VAALA's board member, they strive to cultivate art as a therapeutic force within the Vietnamese American community in Little Saigon. Their initiative, the FOB: A Multi-Art Show, aims to bridge the gap of silence and foster intergenerational harmony through art. FOB is an identity often imposed on the Vietnamese diaspora, akin to a melancholic song. However, Ysa Lê and her VAALA comrades seek to redefine this label and create something distinct. With determination in her eyes, Ysa Lê states, "We want to claim something different, not as 'Fresh of the Boat.' We should reclaim our identity. It could be 'Friend of Bolsa,' it could be anything."

With unwavering tenacity, Ysa Lê and her VAALA colleagues rallied for voices within the community. Ysa Lê approached Đỗ Việt Anh, then CEO of the Nguoi Viet Daily, to request a space for the first FOB exhibition. To their delight, VAALA secured an entire floor to showcase artworks by artists under 40 years old. Vietnamese American film directors, Charlie Nguyễn, Tuấn Andrew Nguyễn, and Victor Vũ screened their films, while other artists displayed their art pieces. Concerts were held day and night, celebrating nothing but the arts. For two weeks, the event was filled with praise, gratitude, and a resounding sense of connection.

If nostalgia serves as a healing remedy for shattered souls in the new land, art emerges as a bridge spanning troubled waters. VAALA has transformed chaos, trauma, and identity into works of art. Ysa Lê, along with the young members of Vietnamese Language and Culture (VNLC), a student-based group at UCLA, embarked on creating the first Viet Film Fest. Despite their modest budget, their ambition knew no bounds. They first approached Ann Frank, director of UCI South East Asian Archive, who shared a deep love for Vietnam and connected them with the Chair of Humanities. Without hesitation, the Chair generously provided financial support, enabling Ysa Lê's group to realize their VFF dream in no time.

Looking back, Ysa Lê cherishes the memories of the inaugural Viet Film Fest. She enthusiastically mentions the remarkable short film "Anniversary" by Hàm Trần and the captivating documentary "Better Than Friends" by Tuấn Andrew Nguyễn. She proudly exclaims, "They have all emerged as prolific artists and thrived in the film and art fields." Is there anything sweeter than witnessing the fruits of your labor of love recognized and appreciated? Ysa Lê modestly omits mentioning some of her well-deserved accolades: the New California Media Arts and Culture Award in 2003, the University of Southern California Asia Pacific Alumni Association Service Award in 2012, and the VIMO Luminary Champion Award.

Ysa Lê's passion for VAALA has not waned but rather intensified over time, as her vision aligns with that of like-minded individuals, and she finds herself invigorated by the community's enthusiastic involvement. One notable project she spearheaded in collaboration with fellow art enthusiasts is the influential Fôtô Project, a free youth workshop hosted by VAALA. The inaugural project received support from various sponsors, including Garden

Grove City, Macy's, Union Bank, and others, who pledged funds ranging from $1,000 to $5,000 each.

Ysa Lê and her co-partners invited renowned guest speakers, including scholars and artists, to engage with the young participants on topics such as immigration, family, and feminism. The workshop specifically targeted young women between the ages of 16 and 23. "We provided them with artistic tools to express their emotions and concerns through art," Ysa Lê enthusiastically recalls. She fondly remembers managing the first 10-week photo project, which involved 20 students from diverse backgrounds who were able to cultivate artistic gems through the workshop. The students learned various skills, including film production, photography, and printmaking. Ysa Lê's eyes light up with joy as she recounts taking all the students to a San Pedro artist's studio, where they had the opportunity to experiment with different art forms.

"I believe artists possess a unique charisma or power to engage people in conversation," Ysa Lê asserts confidently. However, she appears momentarily puzzled when asked about VAALA's impactful outreach to the Vietnamese American community. "It's challenging," she confesses, as many people are not as curious or passionate about art compared to other temptations such as family gatherings, food, and entertainment.

Ysa Lê holds a more optimistic view of the Viet Film Fest, which attracts a larger audience, both young and old, who come to admire their idols such as Tran Anh Hung (The Scent of Green Papaya), Charlie Nguyễn (The Rebel), Tony Bùi (Three Seasons), Hàm Trần (Journey from the Fall), and others. For the younger generation, who were born and raised in America, the Vietnamese language becomes a barrier. They don't read Vietnamese newspapers, so they feel disconnected from Vietnam. Ysa Lê hopes that the Viet Film Fest will bring these youngsters closer to Vietnamese culture and foster a collective effort to preserve it.

The Viet Film Festival in 2019 saw a great pool of volunteers, approximately seventy of them, who assisted in various tasks during the event. Ysa Lê states, "Only through films will different generations be stitched together and find a common voice." However, due to COVID-19, the annual event was interrupted, and Ysa Lê is excited about experimenting with a digital platform for the 2021 edition of the Viet Film Festival. She expresses her enthusiasm for Tony Nguyễn and Eric Nong, who have joined their dedicated team as the Digital Director and Artistic Director, respectively. Ysa Lê hopes that the digital platform will reach a much larger audience than before.

"We are currently in our twilight moment," Le shares, "and we need to rejuvenate VAALA." Le desires to step back and train a new generation to take on leadership roles within the association. They have started by creating an operational procedure document for the Viet Film Festival, ensuring that future successors of VAALA will know how to efficiently run the event and maintain the association. The struggle to sustain this organization is intense; they face quandaries, challenges, and everyday pressures, with community backlash lurking just beneath the surface.

VAALA is essentially Lê's passion, as she works full-time as a pharmacist. This requires her to juggle her responsibilities with resilience and stamina. The main challenge lies in navigating the manpower and network necessary for the association, so that artists can contribute their gifts and talents without struggling financially. "I require expertise in running a non-profit organization like VAALA," Lê declares.

The sardonic contradiction within the community is that people often invest more in their "afterlife" than in something equally enigmatic to them, such as arts during their lifetime. While churches and temples are able to raise substantial donations for their religious rituals, VAALA struggles to survive on modest funding from the shrinking art-loving communities. Needless to say, the efforts of Lê and other members of VAALA are tremendously indispensable. What surpasses their determination is their empathy, endurance, thoroughness, integrity, and unwavering hope. FOB II: Art Speaks was a testament to their fierce fight for the arts.

FOB II Art Speaks showcased history through art, delving into the literary masterpieces of the "Nhân Văn Giai Phẩm Affair," a liberal movement of cultural-political dissidents in North Vietnam from 1954 to 1958, advocating for freedom of speech, creativity, and human rights. The event also featured artists from Vietnam who displayed their art pieces at the gallery. Stories of unconventional protestors like Ngô Kỷ, an outspoken and controversial political activist, and Đoàn Trọng, a journalist from Little Saigon TV, were also highlighted. LA Times published an article on a photo by Brian Doan, which immediately stirred the community of hardcore anti-communists. They vehemently objected to the artwork due to the presence of a Vietnamese flag. "They demanded that we take it down. We refused, and they protested," Lê vividly recalls the incident. That particular art piece encompassed the essence of what they aimed to convey in the exhibition: the freedom of art and its role as a fearless voice for the community. "All those protesters could perceive was a flag, while the exhibition was trying to explore different layers of issues between arts and politics in Vietnam as well as within the Vietnamese American community. The exhibition was not seen in its entirety" Lê expresses her disappointment.

Art can be both captivating and bewildering to people. For some, anything that stirs their wounds and reopens old wounds is seen as devoid of artistry, regardless of the intended message behind the artwork. One of the protestors managed to discover that the exhibition was taking place in an area not permitted for such activities, leading the city manager to shut it down.

Later, one of the elders told the organizers that they had gone too far, as those antagonistic agitators viewed the art with animosity, resentment, and ignorance rather than appreciating its sublime and boundless nature. The exhibition was deemed a failure in reaching out to the masses, according to a prominent artist from VAALA, due to the ignorance of the crowd. It was as if casting pearls before swine was always a futile endeavor. However, quitting was never an option in Lê's mind. The silver lining for VAALA was that after Lê applied for the rezoning of the street where the VAALA office was located, a city resident who was also an art lover connected her with the city officials. As a result, not only was VAALA granted the necessary zoning, but the entire avenue was transformed into zoning for public galleries. Trâm Lê, who co-curated the FOB II: Art Speaks exhibition, became the arts and culture specialist for the city of Santa Ana.

Those who adamantly dismiss every artistic aspiration as futile embody everything that is out of touch with contemporary Little Saigon: a regressive yearning for the past, animosity, intellectual narrow-mindedness, and bitterness. It falls upon the younger generation to rescue Little Saigon from this collective philistinism—a mindset that disdains and devalues art and beauty. The enduring artistic spirit of VAALA serves as a reminder of Andrew Lam's reflection in his book "Birds of Paradise Lost," where he asserts that "the only way back is therefore in going forward. One cannot go home again, not to relive the long-lost world or capture the past, but one can take up the mantle in that familiar, yet entirely new country."

"How do you find balance in your hectic life as a full-time clinical pharmacist, a passionate supporter of the arts, and a wife?" we inquired. Lê diverts her gaze, attempting to conceal a modest smile behind her delicate fingers, before responding, "My husband, who is also my partner, has a heart as vast as the ocean." However, we sense that although Lê doesn't vocalize it, she must also be thinking of her father. Engaging with VAALA has seemingly allowed her to maintain an everlasting bond with her father through the preservation of Vietnamese arts and culture.

ANN PHONG | ART THAT OUTLIVES US

Note: I met Ann Phong while she was volunteering at the Vietnamese American Arts and Letters Association (VAALA) and the VietFilm Festival. Our initial discussion centered around how VAALA could sustain its mission of connecting and enriching communities through Vietnamese art and culture. However, what truly captivated me was Ann Phong's life as an exiled visual artist who uses her brush strokes to depict her journey as an immigrant and to raise awareness about environmental issues. Her paintings have received praise from art critics and have been showcased in over 150 solo and group exhibitions in galleries and museums around the world. In 2018, Ann Phong was honored as one of the recipients of the City of Santa Ana Grant for individual artists. I had the opportunity to meet her again at the former VAALA office in Santa Ana on a Wednesday. Since most VAALA activities take place on weekends, the place was deserted and had a cold atmosphere. However, Ann Phong's warm yet determined personality illuminated the entire space. Our interview was conducted in both Vietnamese and English.

There are two things that trouble the old-timers of Little Saigon: fusion food and arts, which evoke a sense of unfamiliarity. This unfamiliarity is perceived as intolerable by some. These nostalgic individuals reside in the past, where each memory can bring them both tears and joy, causing them to dream as if time has stood still. Traditional Vietnamese food, for instance, with its simplicity of rice, fish sauce, and water spinach, can bring them immense happiness. However, anything labeled as fusion is seen as a loss. The same sentiment applies to the arts.

Ann Phong never wants to be seen as an outsider, but she often feels like one in Little Saigon. According to her, Vietnamese Americans, across many generations, mostly have remained unchanged. The first generation tends to stick within the confines of Vietnamese culture and does not appreciate innovative arts. If it weren't for her teaching position at the California State Polytechnic University at Pomona Department of Art, Ann Phong may have struggled to make a living. She teaches both to support herself and to pursue her passion for art. In a community where art is still regarded as trivial and artists are viewed as wanderers, Ann Phong finds herself somewhat isolated. However, she doesn't mind. She channels her pains into her paintings. Her journey as an immigrant was filled with pain, and even a car accident brought her great suffering. It seems that the word "pain" is inherently intertwined with Ann Phong's art and her life, as both have flourished from her experiences of pain.

For refugees who have crossed the ocean, the darkness of moonless nights evokes haunting horrors. It was during these dark moments of their journey when even the presence of lights could lead to death. Ann Phong's paintings disturb us with their stark and poignant images that are filled with emotional resonance. She portrays the violent ocean, sinking boats, and people struggling in vain. Who would willingly want to relive those traumatic moments? Her artwork, anchored to this theme, rarely finds new homes in collectors' galleries, as few can bear such an obsession with the perilous journey across the Pacific Sea.

Her daring brushstrokes mourn the ocean's blue, now tainted with trash. Oil spills, dead fish, bottles, and blood-stained waves . . . the pain of the ocean. Ann Phong's artwork resembles a condemnation, questioning, "Who is killing the ocean?" Through her art, she denounces human brutality and negligence towards the environment. "I depict human abundance, apathy, and ignorance that harm our nature," she passionately explains. Using the carcasses of deceased creatures as materials, Ann Phong creates a hallucinatory clarity in her paintings that grips the minds of viewers long after they turn away.

Her unique blend of colors and natural materials adds layers of charm and meaning to her artwork. This is not a gimmick; however, it has been met with hostility by a group of old-fashioned individuals who find nothing endearing about her creations, devoid of familiar images such as lotus ponds, ladies surrounded by lilies, or buffalo boys. "Why don't you paint those nostalgic images of Vietnam? It's an easy way to make money," an old guest once urged her with a disdainful smile before departing. Undeterred, Ann Phong quietly hangs up her paintings, one after another, like beacons of hope.

"The younger generation is more drawn to the arts," remarks Ann Phong, who served as the former Board President of VAALA (2009–2013). "VAALA is attracting an increasing number of young volunteers who cannot speak Vietnamese and expect me to present my work in English." And she does. Her exhibitions captivate a growing audience of young visitors. Ann Phong aligns herself with progressive artists who are open to embracing new ideas, who understand the popular culture of Vietnamese American communities, and who authentically infuse their artwork with their own experiences. Another group of artists includes those who obtained their degrees in Vietnam and are deeply influenced by Vietnamese culture, which they bring with them to America. As observed by Ann Phong, these artists tend to isolate themselves from Anglophone Vietnamese American artists. Their artwork remains firmly rooted in the past, in their homeland, preserved in the haunting shadow of its own history for ages.

Retrospectively, Ann Phong's migration to the U.S. seemed predestined. While she didn't flee Saigon on the day it fell, she persevered in pursuit of her dream to pursue art. Graduating from high school in 1977, she eagerly attempted to pass the entrance test for the College of Arts, but unfortunately failed twice. Under the communist government, her family's history of serving in the American army deprived her of educational opportunities. Ann Phong vividly recalled cycling through the streets of her native Saigon, witnessing the widespread hunger and desperation that plagued the population between 1977 and 1978. The newly established government of Vietnam, after taking control of Saigon, initiated a campaign to purge those deemed bourgeois. Determined to pursue her artistic aspirations, she ultimately passed the entrance exam for the University of Education, where there was a demand for art teachers to replace those who had been detained in reeducation camps following the liberation. Upon graduating from the art pedagogy program, Ann Phong secured a teaching position. However, a life-altering event occurred when one of her students, whose family had purchased a boat, persuaded Ann Phong to leave Vietnam behind.

Ann Phong's early days in the U.S. mirrored the complexity of her paintings—a convergence of paths, overlapping and diverging. In 1981, she experienced her first chilly winter when she stayed at her sister's house in Connecticut. Coming from a tropical region where the sun never ceased to shine, Ann Phong found the cold in Connecticut unbearable. Before long, her boyfriend persuaded her to join him in California, prompting her to leave Connecticut behind. Balancing ESL classes, pre-dental classes, and a part-time job at an orthodontist's office drained her energy. "I consumed copious amounts of coffee every day to stay composed and agile," she confesses, reflecting on those exhausting days.

Her artistic talent became evident when the orthodontist, observing how skillfully she bent wires for patients, encouraged her to pursue a career in dentistry and even promised to share his clinic with her upon graduation. However, during a particularly tumultuous period, Ann Phong was involved in a car accident that landed her in the hospital for a significant amount of time. It was during this period of reflection that she contemplated her life in America and her true aspirations. "What is my dream?" Ann Phong reveals. "Ultimately, I made the decision to abandon everything and pursue my passion for becoming an artist." She transitioned to a life of artistic fulfillment after graduating as valedictorian from an art school. "I have had extensive exhibitions in various European countries," she says, beaming with satisfaction.

If Ann Phong were to compromise and pursue a life of extravagance, she could easily churn out mass-produced, kitschy paintings for commercial gain. "But that's not why I paint," she admits. "My true vocation is teaching art at California Polytechnic in Pomona." Whenever she finds free time, she immerses herself in painting. Her artwork captures the intense metamorphosis of identities, encapsulated within powerful blocks of colors that push against the boundaries of tumultuous lines and circles. It's art that reflects chaotic emotions. "I see the ocean within me," she explains, "and I depict my community struggling to emerge from the dark depths of the sea."

Ann Phong points to a painting dominated by dark hues—a moonless sea with a black hole piercing through the vastness, an abyss. Within this depiction, bodies float, and fish swim towards the sun. Her brushes guide the painting towards a burst of energy. She portrays Vietnamese women as pawns in a chess game played by men who seem to have lost their male power in exile. These vulnerable and voiceless women, however, become more assertive in America. Ann Phong's art also expresses her indignation at the exploitation of natural resources in Vietnam by transnational corporations. She employs dry humor in artwork like the bronze drum of Vietnam, cleverly alluding to the older generation of Little Saigon. "These individuals resist change and therefore disconnect themselves from the youth," she elaborates on her recurring themes.

Colors can be deceiving, and Ann Phong knows how to use them to her advantage. She adorns her paintings with vibrant, captivating colors, not to convey superficial, carefree, or showy messages about life, but rather to entice more viewers into engaging with her art. "I incorporate found objects and trash to illustrate how nature suffers," she explains while showcasing her artwork. "If we fail to appreciate our environment today, we will face toxic consequences tomorrow. If humans triumph, nature loses." These paintings, when observed more attentively beyond the dazzling colors, reveal a disquieting darkness. Why do we expect the most cheerful art from an artist who has every reason to feel joyless? Nevertheless, Ann Phong perseveres in her relentless pursuit of finding a glimmer of hope in life and art.

Her journey has been challenging, but her passion knows no bounds. Ann Phong dedicates herself each day to sharing her love for art through her lectures with students and showcasing her artwork to the community. She encourages her students to embrace their true selves in their art, but she also imparts knowledge about all aspects of Vietnamese American arts. Wherever she goes, she carries her artwork with her, reaching out to anyone who shares her artistic philosophy. She even persuaded the official pageant of the Vietnamese American community to purchase one of her paintings as a gift for the University of California, Riverside. "My name is in there, and my piece is exhibited in the gallery," she jests. Ann Phong has come to appreciate the community where her art can have an impact and be influenced, particularly through community media and newspapers that recognize her passion for art. Her paintings are intentionally disconcerting in every sense. She boldly asserts that "stillness" numbs true art. Like lava, the artist must seethe within every work.

Competition in the art world is intense, especially with the rapid advancement of technology. Every artist must navigate this challenging landscape, and Ann Phong is no exception. She embraces technology with the help of Huỳnh Thương Chi, who assists her in installing a sound chip behind each art piece, allowing viewers to listen to her stories behind them. Like a social media user, she promotes her paintings on platforms like Facebook, sharing each new creation with her audience. While she may sometimes feel uncomfortable with technology, Ann Phong, at her best, recognizes its potential to explore innovative creations that may not be possible through other art forms. When we introduce her to the idea of blending technology, such as virtual reality and augmented reality, with art, her face lights up with excitement, exclaiming, "wow!"

For the future of the arts in Little Saigon, Ann Phong envisions a vibrant and trendy cultural center where people of all ages can come together to appreciate and engage with various art forms. Reflecting on the "Viet Stories: Recollections & Regenerations" event held by Professor Linda Vo at the Nixon Presidential Library in Yorba Linda in 2018, which showcased the work of several Vietnamese American artists, including herself, Ann Phong advocates for exhibitions, talks, and performances that can educate and inspire people, bridging the gap between them and different artistic expressions. Through these initiatives, she believes that the notion of the artist as an outcast will gradually fade away, as everyone, with the passage of time, seeks something beyond material abundance. In this ethereal realm, the arts can fill the void and provide a sense of fulfillment. Ultimately, Ann Phong's unique artwork adds a bold and distinctive touch to the tapestry of Vietnamese American art, making it an ideal pursuit for the arts in Little Saigon, perhaps.

THUY VO DANG | AGAINST OBLIVION

Note: Frank Jao accompanied me to the Orange County & Southeast Asian Archive Center at the University of California, Irvine Library, where I had the opportunity to meet Thuy Vo Dang, the curator and research librarian. I was particularly interested in her projects that curated exhibits and conducted oral history interviews to preserve the memories of the Southeast Asian diaspora. I needed someone who could provide me with a broader perspective on the history of Little Saigon. Thuy Vo Dang's work, generously supported by the Jao Foundation, was exactly what I was seeking. Her analysis and insights proved invaluable, helping me connect many of the puzzle pieces. Later, I met Thuy Vo Dang for a conversation at Coq-au-Vin in Fountain Valley. We both ordered Vietnamese chicken vermicelli noodle soup for breakfast, a popular dish from the North. However, we hardly touched our bowls, as our discussion about Little Saigon became the main and delightful focus of our meeting. The conversation took place in English.

Before delving deep into the Vietnamese community in San Diego and Orange Counties, Thuy Vo Dang had distanced herself from them, for fear of being censored, disciplined, or rejected. She sensed their pain and resentment towards communism, but their confrontational protests filled her with anxiety.

"My thesis was more of an armchair analysis. I simply examined Paris By Night, the popular musical, to conduct a cultural analysis. I didn't dare to approach the community because I was so afraid of them," Thuy Vo Dang confessed. In 1999, when the Hi-Tek incident occurred, she was still in college and witnessed the community's strong reaction against Trần Trường, who had displayed images of Hồ Chí Minh and the communist flag in his video store. "How does this change anything? How can we move forward and reconcile a past that still haunts all of us?" Thuy Vo Dang questioned, filled with concern.

She began exchanging emails with other young people in the community, hoping to understand their perspectives on the protest. "I received a hateful email from an unknown student from Occidental College. She accused me of being a communist and used offensive language to insult me. I was horrified," Thuy Vo Dang recalled.

The first generation of Vietnamese Americans, concerned about the erasure of their struggles and experiences in mainstream American history, express their gratitude towards America or protest against communism whenever they perceive their political power being threatened. They continue to fight against the deliberate omission of their history in dominant narratives. "Their anger stems not only from losing their homeland but also from having their political power and agency stripped away," discovered Thuy Vo Dang, an archivist and curator of Southeast Asian diaspora history at UCI. After spending several years immersing herself in the Vietnamese refugee communities, conducting interviews, and observing their reactions and behaviors, Thuy Vo Dang has embraced this sense of "representational belonging" among her fellow community members.

Fleeing Vietnam eight years after the fall of Saigon, Thuy Vo Dang's family arrived in upstate New York in the summer of 1984. Initially placed in a large two-story house, they ended up sleeping together in one room. Their sponsors, all members of a Lutheran church, were welcoming and supportive. In fact, two or three sponsors took care of each person in Thuy Vo Dang's family. Thuy's sponsor was a young single woman who would pick her up and bring her to various social gatherings. The first English word that Thuy spoke to this sponsor was "McDonald's." The family lived in that predominantly white community for six months until her father realized they couldn't sustain themselves there. Through an "informal network," they discovered where other Vietnamese refugees were congregating and where public assistance was more suitable for a large family like theirs. As a result, they decided to move to Orange County, California.

"We had a tough time living in a new community where Vietnamese refugees were not welcomed," Thuy Vo Dang recalled. She remembered her neighbors using derogatory words when referring to Vietnamese refugees like herself. "They called us gooks and treated us with hostility," Thuy recalled, noting that she didn't fully grasp the hurtful nature of those offensive words as she was still unfamiliar with American popular culture at the time.

Thuy Vo Dang and the other kids in the neighborhood would often gather together after school since there were no specialized daycare facilities available, and their parents were occupied with work. They would then go to a Thầy (a Vietnamese word for "teacher") who had previously taught in Vietnam but was unable to find a teaching job in the US. Instead, he taught them Vietnamese. Thuy Vo Dang remembered this man as someone who tutored and disciplined his students with a ruler. "He would sometimes use physical discipline. He was very strict. However, my father trusted him because he had been a teacher in Vietnam."

In the early 1990s, home invasion crimes were rampant in Orange County. The perpetrators were primarily teenagers, either newly-arrived refugees from Southeast Asia or those whose parents were often occupied with work and unable to closely supervise them. When Thuy Vo Dang's family relocated to Stanton, a neighboring city to Garden Grove, they found themselves grappling with the same challenges. Thuy's father took on various jobs, from furniture delivery to gardening and landscaping, in order to support the family. Thuy Vo Dang enrolled in a public elementary school in the third grade, facing the difficulties of adapting to a new language, which took her a considerable amount of time to overcome.

Her older siblings became caught up with the "wrong crowd." On one occasion, Thuy Vo Dang woke up to discover bullet holes in their garage. "My father decided that we had to move away from those they considered 'Bụi đời' (street kids)," she recalled. As a result, they relocated to San Bernardino and Riverside, where her father started his own landscaping and gardening business, employing her brothers to assist him. With her fluency in English, Thuy Vo Dang played a role in negotiating with clients. Eventually, they were able to purchase a house, bringing immense joy to the family. Their American dream had been partially realized. Unlike many other Vietnamese parents who strongly influenced their children's career choices, Thuy Vo Dang's parents allowed her to pursue her own dreams.

Thuy made her own choice, albeit in a state of turmoil. Her high school counselor advised her to opt for a community college. In her innocent naiveté, Thuy Vo Dang questioned, "What about UC? What about a private college?" Lacking any further guidance or support, Thuy Vo Dang ultimately decided to attend Scripps College in Claremont, a women's college with an enticing image that fueled her aspirations of becoming a dreamy poet or an ambitious journalist in that idyllic campus. This choice would shape her destiny.

While studying English and Asian American Studies majors at this private liberal arts college, where only four Vietnamese American students were enrolled, Thuy began working for the Asian American Student Union for her work study program. She created a newsletter, immersing herself further in this creative world that captivated her. Thuy Vo Dang delved into cultural studies and discovered a myriad of intricate historical perspectives. The course that shook her out of her tranquility was "Museum Vietnam," which was part of the humanities curriculum.

"Rick Berg, an American veteran who fought in the Vietnam War, taught the course," Thuy recalled vividly how his lessons opened her eyes. "He showed a series of Vietnam War movies that I had never seen before. I remember halfway through each screening, I couldn't bear it any longer and had to stand up and leave the auditorium. It was so painful, and I lacked the vocabulary to express my feelings, the critical thinking to analyze it."

Thuy Vo Dang approached the professor and questioned why he only screened films that portrayed refugees and people like her as one-dimensional victims, while focusing on scenes of explosions and enemies shooting at Americans. She asked why there were no films that showcased the multidimensional humanity of refugees. This encounter led to many more productive conversations between Thuy and her professor.

"The professor ended up becoming my thesis advisor, and I wrote my thesis on Vietnamese American Literature," Thuy Vo Dang recounted. She could never forget the moment when another professor, while looking at her thesis, asked, "What's that? Is there such a thing?" This thought-provoking question compelled Thuy Vo Dang to dive deeper into literature and ethnic studies during her doctoral studies. It became her personal journey to explore and understand her own identity, which remained enigmatic to a young Vietnamese refugee living in a foreign land where she experienced both acceptance and isolation. She found herself entangled in the complex history that still weighs heavily on the Vietnamese community.

On one occasion, when Thuy Vo Dang and her friend visited a museum in 1999 during a Coca-Cola exhibition featuring modern art from Vietnam, an elderly Vietnamese woman stopped them at the entrance and asked, "Do you know that inside this exhibition there is art related to communism?"

"No, we didn't know," Thuy responded, feeling conflicted. Despite the woman's intimidating demeanor, Thuy Vo Dang and her friend proceeded through the entrance and viewed the artwork. Afterwards, Thuy Vo Dang contemplated the wounds, anxieties, and fears that compelled the elderly woman to stand in front of the museum every day to deter visitors. The war had deeply scarred her soul, leaving her inconsolable. "It made me pause and reflect on the community work I was doing. This community is so volatile, filled with unresolved emotions," Thuy Vo Dang shared. She didn't want to be labeled a communist, nor did she want to be despised by the people she identified with. By creating some distance, Thuy Vo Dang believed she could keep herself safe.

But Thuy Vo Dang never stopped observing the community, immersing herself in their stories through reading, viewing art and other media, and attempting to understand their hearts. In 2003, she volunteered as an assistant to the general secretary of the Vietnamese Federation, an organization led by first-generation Vietnamese refugees in San Diego. All the members were men over 50 years old. Thuy Vo Dang worked closely with an elder she called "Chú Sơn," (uncle Son), whose Huế accent posed a challenge for her understanding, as she could only grasp about 75% of their conversations. However, they built a strong relationship, and Thuy Vo Dang became well acquainted with his family.

During her time at the federation, Thuy Vo Dang's fiancé was also recruited to help with bookkeeping, and they both volunteered there for five years. "I learned so much from them, observing how they navigated the public sphere and led their private lives," Thuy Vo Dang remarked. She engaged with these first generation community leaders, conducting interviews and creating newsletters for the organization. This work enriched her dissertation, which focused on the cultural politics of anti-communism among the first generation and how these cultural norms were passed on to subsequent generations.

Thuy Vo Dang reflected on collective memory and history, recognizing that the public hostility towards communism served as a tool for shaping their historical narrative, often driven by a political agenda. Transforming such an assertive community was undoubtedly a challenging and demanding process.

"We lost our history" was a recurring statement that Thuy Vo Dang encountered in the oral history interviews she conducted. The history of South Vietnam seemed to have vanished, leaving no trace in Vietnamese archives, libraries, or public institutions. For the generation born after the war, including Thuy Vo Dang, their memories of the war and the displacement it caused were hazy. They only realized the absence of their stories in history, where refugees were omitted, and the difficult choice they made to leave their homeland went unmentioned.

The first generation of Vietnamese refugees imparted a lesson to Thuy Vo Dang: no matter what knowledge she gained through her American education, there would always be a gap. Despite Thuy Vo Dang's efforts to assure them that she had access to the best library resources and conducted extensive literature reviews on Vietnamese American immigrants and refugees, there was still a sense of disconnection and a feeling that their experiences were not fully represented.

Plagued by internal divisions and conflicts, the Vietnamese community struggles to envision its future. Thuy Vo Dang vividly recalled an incident in 2004 when the older generation raised $25,000 to create a newspaper ad that simply read "Thank you America!" This gesture troubled her as it reflected a community's public articulation of a "refugee debt" narrative at the expense of investing in critical needs in social services, cultural preservation, and the arts. Thuy Vo Dang firmly believed that with the arts, they could preserve their history and bring about transformation.

Thuy Vo Dang expressed her conviction in the power of organizations like VAALA (Vietnamese American Arts & Literature Association), which was established in 1991. VAALA has organized art exhibitions and film festivals that have attracted thousands of viewers. However, Thuy Vo Dang lamented the difficulties in securing private donations for the arts, as some people underestimate its importance. Nevertheless, she remained optimistic about the future, placing her priorities on arts, culture, and historical preservation. She also believed in the collective compassion and dedication of the community, as these qualities would help keep their history alive and thriving.

In her role as the curator of the Southeast Asian Archive at UCI, Thuy Vo Dang regularly organizes programs and exhibits for the community. On one occasion, she taught a class of 30 students, aged 15–16. One of the students discovered a book that contained a picture of her grandmother, Kim Hà, holding her mother. The student was filled with excitement and deep emotions upon seeing the image. Thuy Vo Dang explained to the students that these pictures would be studied by researchers from around the world who would come to visit and learn about how Vietnamese people lived and integrated into the history of America. This experience was truly gratifying for Thuy Vo Dang.

Despite recognizing the community's shortcomings and imperfections, Thuy Vo Dang has learned to love it. She envisions a future for Little Saigon that is fluid and transformative, where subsequent generations of Vietnamese from different cities around the world converge. This convergence will create a cosmopolitan Little Saigon with a rich diversity of delicacies, cuisines, and identities. It will give rise to a new composition of nostalgia and fantasies, harmoniously sustaining and energizing the community. As Thuy Vo Dang passionately stated, "As long as you can create your own history, it will never be erased or fabricated." The next chapter of Thuy's journey takes place at UCLA where she has joined the faculty of Information Studies to train future generations of cultural heritage and memory keepers—librarians, archivists, and curators.

Chapter 14

Ethnic Tapestry

Vietnamese Politics in Harmony

KATHY BUCHOZ, UNDER HER WING

Note: Like many individuals interested in the early years of Little Saigon, I had heard about Kathy Buchoz. She was renowned for being an unwavering advocate for the resettlement of Vietnamese refugees. Serving two terms as the mayor of the City of Westminster and being a prominent figure in the local business community, Buchoz played a crucial role in the economic growth and development of Little Saigon. Her bold and unconventional support for the initial wave of ethnic businesses endeared her to the Vietnamese refugee community. I had the opportunity to meet her in Frank Jao's conference room, where our conversations took place in English.

If Kathy Buchoz were to write a book about her life, she would begin with the first time she encountered Vietnamese people. It was in 1976 when Kathy, working in the real estate business, had her office located across the street from the first Vietnamese family who opened their restaurant. Kathy's father, who owned an insurance company and served as the director of the Westminster Chamber of Commerce at that time, encouraged her to visit the new Vietnamese business and see what they were selling. "It was late morning when I entered, and the owners were setting up before opening," recalls Buchoz. "The man introduced himself as Hảo Trần, and their restaurant served Vietnamese food." As she speaks, Buchoz struggles to contain her overwhelming emotions. "Just before I left, Hảo asked me to wait a moment while he nudged his wife back into the kitchen. Shortly, she returned with their three little children. After explaining to them in Vietnamese that I was their neighbor across the street, he told them to show me what they could do." Buchoz pauses, then vividly describes a powerful scene that remains etched in her memory: the three Vietnamese children, standing before her, reciting the Pledge of Allegiance. "Never before in my life had I encountered someone who recited the Pledge of Allegiance with such profound meaning," admits Buchoz, still in awe.

"I do believe that, at one time, perhaps three thousand years ago, I was Vietnamese," quips Kathy Buchoz, as we both feel a warm camaraderie, a sense of kinship when discussing Vietnamese Americans in Little Saigon. Whether they are in Little Saigon or elsewhere, if they spot Kathy among other white Americans in bustling places, they would instinctively reach out to her. There seems to be a unique empathy in Kathy that these lost souls can hardly find in any other strangers in this adopted homeland. And her profound compassion for the displaced community has never waned over the years. "Their resilience, unwavering resilience, impresses me," Kathy says, referring to the refugees. She has wholeheartedly supported and celebrated that resilience, indeed.

Everything about Vietnamese refugees has never ceased to captivate Kathy Buchoz. "They are phenomenal," she says, referring to their unwavering resilience in the face of countless challenges. Balancing between Vietnamese and American cultures is akin to fighting another war. The first wave of Vietnamese refugees, arriving in Orange County after the war, carried with them nothing but despair, trauma, and loss. "They were a legion of miserable exiles," Kathy recalls. "They were deeply sorrowful. Their losses were immense, their terrors overwhelming." The first generation quietly grappled with their painful memories, which they hoped to shield their descendants from, fearing the unimaginable pain that could haunt them or tear them apart. Through her interactions with newcomers, Buchoz has encountered many veterans who shared this burden, attempting to bury their experiences in amnesia. However, the community's desire to preserve their history led to the development of the first history program at UCI focused on the Republic of Vietnam, no matter how painful it may be.

"For the first generation, their war melancholy never fades," Buchoz recounts the early days of Vietnamese refugees in Orange County, where they experienced profound sadness and confusion. "American sponsors provided them shelter, helped them secure viable jobs, and supported their settlement in the most dignified manner possible." Despite this assistance, these displaced individuals faced yet another battle on the new shores: assimilation. Having never left Vietnam before, they struggled to adapt to a culture that wasn't always accepting of their differences. "They immediately stood out," Kathy recalls. "Their clothing, their cuisine, their limited English proficiency—everything about them was different." Kathy's friends, who worked as principals and teachers in schools where the children of Vietnamese refugees attended, expressed frustration at the challenges their Vietnamese students faced due to their limited English skills. Some teachers questioned why they had to spend so much time teaching them, suggesting that if they couldn't speak English, they shouldn't have come to the country in the first place.

Years later, those once incensed teachers told Buchoz that Vietnamese students turned out to be their best students ever. "They exhibited unwavering commitment to their studies and held deep respect for their teachers," Buchoz recalls the praise bestowed upon Vietnamese families. "Even their parents were incredibly courageous. They wanted their children to receive a good education, so they did everything in their power to support them." If Buchoz were to describe the Vietnamese people she has encountered, she would say, "They never give up. If you tell them they can't do something, they will prove you wrong."

Looking back, Buchoz admires their tenacity, despite the flaws, failures, and regrets that come along the way. Many individuals succumbed to violence, particularly teenagers who were young, wild, and rebellious. Interacting with local kids influenced their lifestyles, and Vietnamese children couldn't tolerate their parents' strictness and manipulation, leading to rebellion. They challenged their parents' values and beliefs, and when this resistance backfired, they formed groups and wreaked havoc in the neighborhood.

Buchoz recalls that the city had to establish task forces to address Vietnamese and Cambodian gang activities during that time. The community turmoil resulted in stigmatization, prejudice, and assault. "The police would often pull them over, just like they did with Black individuals, assuming that anyone who appeared Vietnamese must be up to something wrong," Kathy recounts tragically comical incidents where the police misinterpreted Vietnamese gestures and arrested them out of fear and hatred.

During her tenure as mayor, Buchoz made it mandatory for the police to undergo courses on Vietnamese culture so that they could better understand and engage with Vietnamese communities.

Before the chaotic times, only a small number of Vietnamese families resided in the area, and the first shopping center, "Bolsa Mini Mall," was owned by Americans, the Parsons family. Today, it remains the only property on Bolsa still owned by Americans. Around 1979, when Buchoz was volunteering for the United Way, she visited businesses to collect money. "The mall was huge and vacant, and the owner was desperate," Buchoz recalls. However, before long, an influx of Vietnamese refugees flocked to the area. The owner offered six months of free rent for newcomers to start their businesses in the mall. One Vietnamese family moved in and spread the word to their brothers, sisters, and relatives, resulting in a swarm of Vietnamese families occupying most of the mall space.

Dreading the idea of living alongside Vietnamese refugees, many white American residents quickly sold their properties and moved away from Westminster. Buchoz was working in real estate at the time, and one of her colleagues would go around the area, advising neighbors to sell their houses as soon as possible or risk losing their investment. The narrative was that the arrival of Vietnamese refugees would decrease property values. In response, everyone followed suit. "It was a terrible situation, truly terrible," Buchoz recollects. Realtors made immense fortunes during this time of anxiety. In hindsight, Buchoz sees it as somewhat of a fortunate turn for the Vietnamese who were desperately seeking new homes for their families. Nevertheless, it was a challenging resettlement marked by harsh rejection and bitter resentment. This took place in 1981 when Buchoz served as the Mayor of the City of Westminster.

Right in the midst of the second meeting during her initial term as mayor, in a crowded hall, a person stood up and approached the microphone. He said, "Madame Mayor, I have a petition here that I want you to read and take action on." As he scanned the room filled with people observing their conversation and eagerly awaiting her response, his intensity grew, demanding her to harbor the same animosity towards the subject of the petition. The petition stated that they opposed the city granting business licenses to individuals from Indochina, encompassing Vietnamese, Cambodians, and Laotians. Buchoz was taken aback, but she managed to suppress her anger and turned to a colleague who was equally stunned beside her. "I will read it," she calmly stated, but the agitated speaker pounded the desk forcefully, exclaiming, "Madame Mayor, I want to know your answer. What are you going to do about this?" It was more than a mere dispute. Buchoz held nothing but disdain for the unruly crowd, whom she regarded as "corrupted un-American" individuals tarnishing the reputation of the town, reveling in their ignorance of justice. "Do you know what I'm going to do with this? I'm going to throw your petition in the trash!" Those grumbling dissenters stormed out of the hall in anger. The incident turned into a heated controversy, making headlines in local newspapers the following day.

Buchoz struggled to find an appropriate term for that resentment, recognizing that it did not originate from genuine patriotism or nationalism. Instead, it seemed to stem from meanness, bigotry, prejudice, or something of a similar nature. During Buchoz's tenure as the president of her Homeowners Association, when Vietnamese refugees were settling in the county, she called a meeting where the association publicly was given a notice urging residents to be vigilant and keep their children indoors at night. "It was as if they believed the Vietnamese would harm their children or something," Buchoz remarks, reflecting on the hostility that prevailed. This antagonism, according to Buchoz, was rooted in a lack of empathy and biased perceptions. She, too, acknowledged her own biases, confessing, "I couldn't help it." The Vietnamese community occasionally reinforced her biases. "Their intense drive for assimilation plays a role," Buchoz admitted. Affluent families spoiled their children and sent them to private schools, solely focused on their financial success regardless of the cost. This relentless pursuit turned privileged children into spoiled brats devoid of compassion and a broader understanding of humanity. They were unable to see beyond their own worlds.

Shrugging her shoulders, Buchoz expresses her despair regarding the Vietnamese communities in Little Saigon. "They quarrel, betray, and even destroy one another," her eyes darken, "which clearly indicates a profound lack of trust." However, she still maintains a sense of optimism. "We must hold onto hope," Buchoz asserts, "we need to focus on the positive: they are thriving. Most Vietnamese. They are building and expanding their own community. They are educated and business-minded." She then passionately discusses the history of Little Saigon, which she has witnessed since its inception. "You know, I know this place like the back of my hand." After stepping out of the political arena in 1984, Buchoz decided to organize tours in Little Saigon. Over the course of 20 years, she has encountered numerous Vietnamese visitors, mostly young professionals who were unaware of the origins of Little Saigon until they joined her tours and heard her stories. Despite its flaws and imperfections, Little Saigon has always held a captivating allure for Buchoz. In 1984, she chose not to seek re-election for the Westminster city council. She finds even more reasons to believe in its brighter future when Frank Jao, the owner of the Asian Garden Mall (or Phúc Lộc Thọ), one of the first landmarks of Little Saigon, whom she describes as an "unmatched expert in political savviness," texts her almost daily with an inspiring message: "Never lose faith!"

TONY QUANG LÂM | THE MAN WHO DARES

Note: I met Tony Lâm at his home, where the spacious living room exuded a tranquil atmosphere overlooking a beautifully manicured oriental garden. His wife, Mậu Hợp, graciously offered me a cup of tea. During our conversation, Lâm fondly recounted how, when his family escaped from Vietnam, he had also brought along two teenage daughters of a close friend. Coincidentally, one of those girls later married one of my brothers, reminding us of the smallness of the world. Our discussion revolved around our respective families and continued for over an hour, until his children's family arrived for dinner. Throughout our interaction, we conversed in Vietnamese, occasionally switching to English and French to exchange a few words.

In 1992, Tony Lâm made history by becoming the first Vietnamese American elected official in the United States. He secured a seat as the councilman of the City of Westminster, undertaking a campaign that followed the traditional path of mainstream American suburban politics. His platform centered on issues such as public safety and fiscal accountability, without any groundbreaking or revolutionary agenda. Nevertheless, his victory brought immense pride and served as a powerful source of inspiration for the wave of refugees who had recently settled in their new homeland just 17 years prior.

While the Vietnamese American community's votes accounted for only a third of the support he needed to win, the complex and nuanced relationship Tony Lâm had with his constituents propelled him on a decade-long roller-coaster ride. This journey had its highs and lows, impacting his health and fortune, but never dampening his indomitable spirit. Ultimately, he will be remembered in the history of Little Saigon as a courageous and caring individual who fearlessly dared to make a difference.

Throughout his lifetime, Tony Lâm has consistently proven himself to be a dynamic force with boundless energy. Born in Haiphong, a city in northern Vietnam, he endured a tumultuous childhood by any measure. Under the yoke of French colonialism, Lâm and his family were repeatedly uprooted during evacuations. At the age of 10, Tony Lâm embarked on a journey of escape alongside others from Haiphong, evading the French forces, armed with just a single jacket, a shirt, and a solitary pair of shorts.

Life was exceedingly challenging, and at a tender age, Tony Lâm had to work hard to earn a living. He undertook a variety of jobs, from rolling tobacco to participating in propaganda campaigns, all while maintaining a determined focus on his education. It wasn't until 1954 that his brother, an artillery officer, took him to South Vietnam. However, shortly after his arrival, their father, a family-oriented man, decided to return home and bring all his loved ones with him. This left Tony Lâm's father unemployed in Hanoi, and as a result, Lâm had to join the Navy, where he received a significant portion of his English education. After three years, taking advantage of a new policy allowing military discharge, he left the Navy in search of new challenges.

Trapped in the turmoil of the Vietnam War from its turbulent beginnings to its tragic end, Lâm displayed unwavering determination in every job he undertook. As a diligent and hardworking man who never took anything for granted, he proudly shared his impressive resume: serving as a representative assistant to Robert Burns, an American official responsible for supporting President Ngô Đình Diệm's Strategic Hamlet Program aimed at combating the communist insurgency; working for the Rand Corporation on studies related to Việt Cộng motivation; and managing his own companies, Lâm Brothers Corp., running Cam Ranh Bay depot and piers for 50,000 US troops stationed on this peninsula, and Fideco, which exported high-quality frozen shrimp and produced fish meal for poultry farming using state-of-the-art machinery imported from the United States. It goes without saying that one could easily imagine him boasting about his exceptional skills and diverse expertise all day long.

In early 1975, foreseeing the imminent fall of Saigon, Tony Lâm made preparations to escape Vietnam. On April 21, he and his brother hurriedly made their way to the Defense Attaché Offices (DAO) at the US Embassy in Saigon, only to be greeted by long lines of desperate people awaiting evacuation. The scene was chaotic. Tony Lâm had to call upon Burns, who worked for USAID and after his retirement, worked for Tony Lâm, for sponsorship and relationship support. On that fateful day, his extended family—his wife, six children, and his brother's children—were rescued, along with many of his closest friends and business partners. However, true to his daring nature, Tony Lâm chose to remain behind voluntarily to help evacuate people. He dedicated himself to serving at the airport around the clock, assisting with the massive evacuation efforts. It wasn't until the morning of April 24th, when Burns insisted that he leave before being arrested, that he finally packed his belongings and departed on a C-130 to Clark Airfield to be united with his family and then on to Guam on the 24th of April, 1975.

Tony Lâm has never been one to seek leisure. As a refugee for the third time in his life, he thrives on audacity and the challenges of resettlement. Upon reaching the refugee camp Asan in Guam, where over ten thousand people were crammed into 20 garrisons originally built for B52 bomber crews, Lâm wasted no time in volunteering to take charge as camp manager for the next three months. The camp housed refugees of various nationalities, including Australians, Germans, French, Filipinos, but predominantly Vietnamese. The conditions were cramped and chaotic.

At the age of 38, Tony Lâm set about revolutionizing life at the camp. Not content with the poorly cooked meals provided by the quartermaster unit working at the mess halls, Lâm took charge. As the troop leader, he assigned two Vietnamese women, one on each floor, to prepare meals that the entire camp could appreciate.

However, Lâm's dedication went far beyond providing food. Serving as the camp's source of inspiration, he galvanized the radio broadcasters and orchestrated daily news broadcasts for the refugees who grappled with nostalgia, despair, and melancholy. Confronted with the intention of over 2,000 individuals yearning to return to Vietnam, Lâm engaged them in heartfelt conversations, providing solace and earnestly urging them to reconsider their departure. As a result of his efforts, approximately 200 people opted to remain at the camp. Regrettably, the remaining 1,800 chose to return and tragically most found themselves imprisoned upon reaching their homeland.

For all refugees at the camp, Lâm arranged for priests and monks to provide solace and alleviate their pain. He even brought in Korean bands to entertain them, offering respite from the hardships and displacement they endured. Apart from facilitating radio communication for the refugees and addressing various logistical challenges, he played a key role in arranging a beauty contest aimed at bolstering morale. Just moments before the announcement of the winner, Tony Lâm suggested that all the contestants be declared Queens, a gesture that earned him an unexpected comment. In front of a crowd of 10,000, the Governor of Guam quipped, "Tony Lâm, you truly have the makings of a politician!"

However, the costs associated with Tony Lâm's initiatives often proved to be overwhelming. At times, his well-intentioned efforts were misconstrued and subjected to criticism by a handful of detractors. One incident stands out: when some individuals in the camp became agitated about Lâm's supervision of the clothes barrack, he decided to unlock it for everyone. This decision backfired, resulting in a chaotic scene where people wrestled and ended up tearing the garments to shreds.

Tony Lâm and his family made the decision to leave after three months, relocating to US Marine Base Camp Pendleton in southern California. They stayed there for another month before Lâm was selected to oversee the camp once again, this time with the sponsorship of Mr. Shidler, a former U.S. Colonel in charge of transportation logistics he had met in Cam Ranh. Lâm then moved to Sarasota, Florida to manage the colonel's self-storage business.

Just a month after, feeling isolated and disconnected, and struggling to meet living standards with his trivial income, Lâm decided to relocate to Huntington Beach, California to be united with his parents and his brother's family. In September 1975, they took up residence in Orange County and have remained there ever since, never wavering in their commitment to the community.

It feels like déjà-vu. Life was incredibly challenging for Lâm as a newcomer in a foreign land. He navigated through hardships, barely making ends meet, juggling jobs such as pumping gas, vending his mother's dried food, and overseeing the shipping and receiving of Navy bombs. Eventually, he found stability in selling insurance for Equitable Life Insurance, an eight-year-long job that provided him with enough to support his family.

Nevertheless, Tony Lâm's journey within the Little Saigon community was anything but straightforward. Despite his genuine intentions, he found himself entangled in one complication after another. As he managed his initial modest venture, Tony Lâm Service, which primarily focused on insurance sales, Lâm also aspired to uplift the community. Every dawn, he would depart his home at 5 a.m. to queue up at the Immigration Service Office in Santa Ana. Here, he aided his clients in applying for green cards, charging a nominal fee of $10 each.

It didn't take long for his compatriots to draw him back into various community organizations. He was a co-founder of the Vietnamese Lion's Club and played a pivotal role in organizing the first Tết New Year celebration, which closed off Bolsa Avenue between Bushard and Magnolia, with Phước Lộc Thọ in between. His efforts continued steadfastly for the subsequent four Tết Festivals. Lâm also worked closely with Republic of Vietnam Armed Forces veterans and members to inaugurate the Republic of Vietnam Armed Forces Day.

As the first vice-president of the Vietnamese American Chamber of Commerce of Orange County in 1980, he effectively served as the organization's Chief Operating Officer, witnessing the development of the first businesses owned by his fellow refugees. Undoubtedly, Lâm left his mark on many of these projects, including the installation of the Little Saigon signage on the freeways. Lâm recalled his involvement, stating, "It wasn't my idea. It was Du Miên's, but I helped make it a reality." He even drove all the members of the lobbying committee, along with Assemblywoman Doris Allen, in his station wagon to meet with state agencies and interested parties. Assemblywoman Doris Allen subsequently wrote the petition to Governor Deukmejian, with the co-sponsorship from 28 elected officials across the state, to advocate for the Little Saigon "Next Exit" signages.

Amidst the formidable challenges and intricate complexities that often confront a newly elected official, Tony Lâm's determination and unwavering commitment to his community have remained resolute. He constantly had to navigate through cultural disparities and manage demanding expectations.

At the age of 82, having nicely recovered from knee surgery, Lâm smiled as he vividly described every corner of the town from those early days. He remembered every name, as they represented indelible moments in his life.

In 1984, Tony Lâm arrived at a crossroads and opted to shift his attention from political activism to concentrate on his own restaurant, Viễn Đông (Extreme Orient). Concurrently, he took up the mantle of an Air France representative, facilitating the transportation of goods to Vietnam. During this period, Lâm reflected on his contributions to elevating the lives of "tout le monde" (everyone), highlighting the notable presence of individuals like Quách Nhứt Danh and "Thanh Air France," who emerged as the first nouveaux riches within the community. He employed Trần Đình Thục as a PR representative for his shipping service, and Nam Tran to handle freights. The success of his lucrative business allowed Lâm to establish an extravagant office on the second floor of the Song Long (Double Dragons) Restaurant in Westminster.

With this move, Lâm yearned for a tranquil existence, undisturbed by community life's tumultuous currents. Yet, adversity persisted in finding him. Lâm recalled Trần Trường's incident. In 1999, Trần Trường hung a picture of Ho Chi Minh inside his Westminster video store and unfurled sensitive emotions among Vietnamese refugees in Little Saigon. During this juncture, Tony Lâm, mindful of his role as an elected public figure, was reluctant to express his political opinions openly due to the potential civil liability and trouble it could cause him and the City of Westminster. His actions and words were guided by the counsel of a City Attorney, citing the nuances of the Constitutional governance structure, including the sanctity of free speech.

"For 73 days, protesters camped outside my restaurant, Viễn Đông, because I, as a city councilman, did not show up at the protest line," Lâm bitterly recounted. It was a series of unfortunate events. The angry protesters engaged in destructive behavior such as puncturing tires and exposing themselves in front of customers. They even sent girls to order coffee and intentionally smashed the cups. The assault took a toll on Lâm, leading to his hospitalization for open heart surgery. Lâm also suffered significant financial losses: $200,000 due to missed transfer opportunities and an additional $450,000 in legal fees. "That tragedy ruined me," Lâm shared, trying to suppress his pain.

When resentment is mild, it may eventually fade away. However, when it becomes intense, it has the power to deeply damage souls. Vengeance can trigger a cycle of escalating revenge, perpetuating an endless cycle of negativity. In 2002, he withdrew from the political arena, but chose to support Andy Quach, who took over his position on the City of Westminster council.

Still bearing the emotional scars, Tony Lâm joined forces with Đông Phương (East Orient) to establish an upscale soymilk and tofu plant called Đông Phương Đậu Hũ (East Orient Tofu). He dedicated four years to the venture but eventually had to leave because his wife was unhappy with the monotonous life of wandering alone in their garden every day. Tony Lâm then took up a franchise of Lee's Sandwiches in Westminster. Soon afterwards, he decided to retire.

If Tony Lâm were to showcase all his contributions to Little Saigon, it would require a vast gallery. When Lâm ran for election as a city councilman in Westminster, he made promises to be a "tax fighter" and a "crime fighter." However, he quickly realized that the fight would be challenging, as he had anticipated, especially due to the entrenched culture of Vietnamese traders who were accustomed to the cash system and evaded taxes. Lâm observed that the entire Little Saigon community paid only $700,000 in sales taxes annually, while Westminster Mall alone paid a million dollars. Crime rates remained high, with incidents of theft, money laundering, and fraud occurring frequently. During his service, Lâm even took it upon himself to apprehend thieves, referring to himself as the "old cowboy." A significant portion of the offenders consisted of individuals on probation or gang members struggling to establish a sense of stability in their lives. Lâm's efforts led to a notable decline in home invasion cases, reducing the percentage from 60% to 47% in 1992. Lâm successfully achieved this objective by advocating among his fellow council members for the allocation of funds towards Police Target Teams, aimed at addressing the prevailing crime issues. Nevertheless, his path towards nurturing a more favorable community was not without obstacles. Lâm firmly believed that fostering unity among his Vietnamese compatriots held paramount importance in shaping a brighter future for Little Saigon.

"I had a dream of transforming the district into a French quarter, complete with a beautiful promenade adorned with Western-style retro lamp posts, inviting sidewalk cafes, and ample perpendicular parking. I envisioned a vibrant quarter with underground electricity and high-end establishments like McDonald's, Subway, and other food stores," Tony Lâm recounted.

Driven by this aspiration, Tony Lâm extended invitations to a collective of Vietnamese Americans and American architects to collaborate closely with the city planning team. The goal was to conjure a fresh blueprint for both Bolsa Avenue and Little Saigon. One of his creative proposals to the city council was to relocate the sub fire station situated on Moran Street, thereby freeing up more parking spaces to entice a larger influx of visitors. This strategic move, he believed, would not only enhance foot traffic but also augment the city's revenues. Lâm orchestrated an immersive expedition to Santa Monica, where the delegation examined the essence of its main street. This fact-finding mission aimed to resurrect the ambiance of the Catinat shopping precinct in Saigon, Vietnam, encompassing underground cable infrastructure, aluminum lamp posts, and bus stops adorned with distinctive Vietnamese design elements.

"I wanted to attract more tourists traveling from Knott's Berry Farm and Disneyland, and even proposed setting up meters to generate additional income for the city," Tony Lâm passionately shared his vision he had for the city he served. Unfortunately, he was disappointed to see that the city only made half-hearted efforts to realize his dream. "They were afraid of a backlash from the white American community, and they were unwilling to take a stand when Vietnamese residents in my district paid lower taxes," Lâm concluded, understanding the city's hesitancy.

An audacious leader at heart, Tony Lâm sees bureaucracy as a poor vision and a hindrance. In 2015, when the Department of Defense planned to commemorate the 50th anniversary of American involvement since March 1965 when the US Army landed in Da Nang, Tony Lâm took action. He invited DoD officials to visit the memorial and enlisted master sculptor Tuấn Nguyễn to create a miniature bronze statue from the Westminster War Memorial to be displayed at the Pentagon. The cost of the sculpture was estimated at $9,000.

Tony Lâm wasted no time and called upon Vietnamese veterans to request an official letter from the Department of Defense within a tight two-month timeframe. Frustrated with the process, Tony Lâm took it upon himself to raise the necessary funds. Eventually, the miniature statue was shipped directly to the Pentagon, where it is now permanently displayed. "It is a symbol of our community," Tony Lâm remarked.

When asked about his perceptions, hopes, and expectations for the next generation, Tony Lâm admitted that he still had some disappointments with certain young individuals. He observed tendencies of groupism and cronyism among them. He also noted that wealthy individuals tend to avoid involvement in complex and intricate communities, often choosing to reside in areas like Huntington Beach or Irvine. Nevertheless, Tony Lâm maintained optimism and envisioned that the younger generation would come to understand the power of solidarity and the importance of actively participating in the American mainstream. He hoped they would create remarkable accomplishments and seamlessly integrate into society. Tony Lâm held onto the belief that the community would thrive, and he crossed his fingers in anticipation of that outcome.

If one were to explore Little Saigon today, it would be difficult to imagine that this vibrant Vietnamese enclave was once a desolate area with only a few makeshift dwellings. Remarkably, every corner of this beautiful space bears the name of Tony Lâm, a testament to his immense influence and contributions. Despite his detractors, Tony Lâm is also fortunate to have a loyal support base that recognizes him as a historic community organizer, offering unwavering backing for his audacious endeavors.

In acknowledgment of Tony Lâm's lifelong dedication to public service, the City of Westminster Council orchestrated a ceremony on May 3, 2022, to rename West Park as Tony Lâm Park. Speakers included Republican US Representative Michelle Steele, former Democrat US Representative Alan Lowenthal, California Senator Janet Nguyen and other City and County dignitaries and friends. This distinction marks it as the sole park named after a living Vietnamese American in the United States, with no counterpart elsewhere in the world. "I am profoundly proud of this recognition," Lâm reflects with a sigh. "On a side note, I am approaching my 87th birthday soon [2023]. Gratefully, I have navigated through life's challenges, persevering through its highs and lows. The time has come for me to relish my well-deserved retirement, enveloped by the warmth of my family, and savor leisurely games of mahjong."

Tony Lâm's residence in Little Saigon exudes serenity, adorned with lush fruit trees and blossoms, all meticulously tended by his devoted wife, Hợp. Throughout their journey, Tony and Hợp have been blessed with six children and a legacy of 15 grandchildren. During their engagement, Hợp aptly deemed Tony a "lucky boy." This sentiment holds true, for without Hợp's companionship, Tony Lâm's journey wouldn't have been the same. His identity today is profoundly shaped by her presence. However, the impact of Tony Lâm extends far beyond the confines of his home. Little Saigon and its myriad inhabitants stand as beneficiaries of his enduring friendship and caring leadership.

Above all, the enduring legacy of Tony Lâm's service imparts a crucial lesson: the vision for an illustrious future for Little Saigon transcends the individual Tony Lâm and belongs to every Vietnamese American within Orange County. This truth remains unwavering.

VĂN TRẦN | TOUGH ON SILENCE

Note: My friend Tiến Nguyễn, who is a co-author of mine and an adjunct faculty member at California State University Fullerton, introduced me to Văn Trần (or Trần Thái Văn in full Vietnamese). I was intrigued to meet the man who gained fame through a picture in which he, a 23-year-old young man at the time, stood next to Gov. Deukmejian during the unveiling of the "Little Saigon—Next Exit" sign in 1988. I arranged to have lunch with Văn Trần at the Brodard Chateau, and our conversation was conducted in English.

Among the prominent "transformers" who have contributed to the growth of Little Saigon in Orange County, the capital of Vietnamese refugees in the heart of the US, Trần Thái Văn, also known as Văn Trần, holds a less conspicuous role but possesses a powerful voice in the community.

Many politicians, driven by their own avarice and narcissism, often prioritize personal gain over the needs of the people. They may break their campaign promises or even betray the trust of those who vote for them, limiting economic benefits and social progress to themselves alone. In contrast, Văn Trần, a passionate Vietnamese American politician and attorney, has consistently fought for liberal democracy and inclusiveness within the Vietnamese community in Orange County. Born in Saigon, Vietnam, in 1964 and immigrating to the US just one week before the fall of Saigon, Văn Trần represents the spirit and aspirations of many within the 1.5 generation. As a lawyer, he has taken the people along with him in every political stride, amplifying their voices, shedding light on their dilemmas, seeking consensus, and bringing about remarkable transformations in local politics.

"The most perilous thing of all is your absence at a political banquet," Văn Trần recalled a congressman advising him during one of the assembly meetings, "you must secure a seat, otherwise, you will be on the menu." This belief has profoundly influenced Văn Trần's political consciousness. He has successfully won seats, notably on the Garden Grove City Council, receiving the highest number of votes in the city's history. He was also elected to the California State Assembly, representing a portion of Orange County that includes Little Saigon, serving for a decade from 2000 to 2010. A true politician at heart, Trần never takes justice for granted and recognizes the need to fight for it passionately. However, the path of a fighter can sometimes be a lonely one.

Văn Trần refers to himself as the "black sheep" in his family since "all my siblings and relatives are doctors, pharmacists, and dentists; my mother is a dentist, my father is a teacher . . . " Tran's pursuit of a career in politics deviated from the conventional path chosen by his family. When he discussed his choice with his parents, he somehow disappointed them. His mother may have wondered how she had strived fiercely in this foreign land to pursue her beloved profession, supporting the entire family with her single income, and sending all five children to college and graduate school, only to have one of them pursue such an unconventional job. "Why do you want to become a politician?" she asked Văn Trần, shaking her head. As a mother in the first generation of Vietnamese refugees, like many others, she expected her son to become a doctor, dentist like her, or at least an engineer. Why choose a job that did not fit into the traditional categories? Only his father, a lifelong educator, stood by him in his unconventional ambition. Tran obtained his Bachelor's degree in political science, a Master's in Public Administration, and a J.D. from Hamline University School of Law. It is no wonder that, within the traditional mindset of Vietnamese society at that time, he was seen as an outlier.

But Văn Trần was admired by many community organizers in Little Saigon, who remembered him as a fearless political warrior. "I was the media darling back then," Văn Trần revealed with pride.

Thanks to his internships with two Republicans, Congressman Bob Dorman and State Senator Ed Royce, while studying at UCI, he was articulate and well-connected. He frequently appeared in local media, covering his social activism, protests, propaganda, and other political activities during the anxious 1980s when the first and second waves of Vietnamese refugees fleeing communist Vietnam flocked to Orange County in search of a new home. These Vietnamese newcomers faced bigotry, oppression, and numerous stereotypes in a land dominated by white supremacy. "We are the newest pilgrims who conquered America by U-Haul," Văn Trần enthused, recalling the legions of Vietnamese people moving to California from all corners of the US at the turn of the twentieth century. Văn Trần's family, including his parents and all five children, were car-pooled by a friend of his father from Grand Rapids, Michigan, to California, a journey that took four days and five nights to reach Santa Ana in 1980. Within a year and a half, his mother completed all the necessary supplementary courses at UCLA, enabling her to open a dental clinic on Bolsa Avenue. Meanwhile, his father found work as a teacher in social sciences in their school district. They realized their American dreams, while many other Vietnamese asylum seekers, intellectuals, and manual laborers still lived with nightmares of suspicion, apprehension, and unjust incarceration.

"Do you remember the Medi-Cal scandals in the Vietnamese community in 1982 and 1983?" Văn Trần recounted, his voice still agitated. "I watched those news reports on TV and couldn't believe my eyes: many Vietnamese doctors and pharmacists were handcuffed and put on the street, and nobody defended them." Văn Trần was a high school senior at the time, still uncertain about his future, wavering between majors and colleges. The scandal awakened him. "They were all part of the elite class, intellectuals, but they were treated like criminals, like trash. What did that mean for the rest of us?" Văn Trần recited from his tenacious memory. "Hundreds of millions of dollars were alleged to have been lost and defrauded, yet nothing had been proven. The news insinuated guilt without direct evidence." He was incensed by rumors that the Ku Klux Klan was marching on Bolsa and the stigmas imposed on the vulnerable community. "Even as a naive high school senior, democracy and human rights were elusive concepts to me, but instinctively and intuitively, I felt the urge to fight for our collective voice, to reclaim justice for the people."

It wasn't a hasty or reckless decision for Văn Trần to pursue his political path. He remembered how, as a precocious child of only 6 or 7 years old during the Vietnam War in Saigon, he started becoming "socially conscious." Although his memory of the war before his family was evacuated by the American army five days before Saigon fell was vague and fragmented, he couldn't forget how deeply immersed he was in all the newspapers of that chaotic time, such as "Chính Luận (Righteous Voice)" and "Trắng Đen (Black and White)." He "naively" bought into every news analysis he read. Since then, he has tried to make sense of the historical complexities and has developed a sophisticated vision as a discerning political commentator.

Looking back, his political passion stemmed from the intolerance of social injustice during the political turmoil of the early 1980s, which cast the Vietnamese people as culprits and a threat to predominantly white neighborhoods. "We were a vulnerable community. Nobody defended us, except for one guy that I know, Ed Royce, who was the State Senator at the time. He said not every Vietnamese person was bad, and their children were doing well in school and in the community," Văn Trần recalled how Vietnamese people were marginalized in their own struggle, with only one white man speaking up for them in a "nice and positive way." Văn Trần believed it was his destiny to have the opportunity to work for Ed Royce after he became a US congressman in 1993.

"Encroachment of the government on virtually every aspect of American life has inspired me to run for Congress," Văn Trần declared during his campaign for the United States Congress in 2010. He didn't exaggerate.

As a political science student at UCI in 1985, he began working as an LBJ Congressional Intern for the congress in Washington for three months. Văn Trần became the first Vietnamese person to be a Congressional staff member at the age of 20 when he went to work for US Representative Bob Dornan for two years before joining the team of California Senator and US Representative Ed Royce. "I gained valuable experience," Văn Trần reminisced about his early years in the political arena. Even before attending graduate school and law school, he dedicated all his time to the fight for erecting freeway signs for Little Saigon.

The first challenge Văn Trần encountered as a public servant was perhaps his own limited agenda. He was not a fantasist but a realist. What he envisioned for a thriving community did not align with everyone's dreams. He believed that his conservative liberal approach, aimed at revitalizing the community's economic benefits, had its limitations. He attributed the harsh realities to "the community" and their "unrealistic expectations." Văn Trần recalled a conversation with some Vietnamese residents early in his term as a state assemblyman, "They asked me if I could help alleviate poverty in their area. OMG, I'm just a state legislator from the minority party." While he didn't disregard their plight, he didn't feel equipped to tackle it directly.

Suffice to say, Văn Trần possesses political prowess gained from his privileged experiences serving other legislative figures. However, he still grapples with deciphering every nuance of politics, as its complex realities often defy his intellectual analysis. His political theories do not perfectly capture the intricate dynamics of the community. "The antagonism is still very intense," Tran referred to the anti-communist politics within the community. While on the surface, people may appear politically unified, they are increasingly divided, harboring a distorted perception of internal and external enemies. This paranoia, frustration, and extremism cannot be reconciled if the community leader is also an extremist. Văn Trần openly acknowledges his conservative views. "Politically, I would not want to go back [to Vietnam]. I don't think it's safe," Văn Trần asserted, expressing his reservations about the country he fled. In 2007, he vehemently protested the visits of Vietnam's president to the United States and, using his political influence, opposed any visits by Vietnamese communist officials to Orange County.

During his tenure as the California assemblyman, Văn Trần assumed the role of chairman of the Select Committee on International Trade. While seeking to promote global business for the largest state in the US, Văn Trần is less sanguine about prospects of trade collaborations between Vietnamese businessmen in Little Saigon and those in Vietnam. "There are many political undercurrents that may impede these possibilities," he hesitated. He is politically prudent, perhaps. For he trusts, with his sensitivity, he could fathom well the Vietnamese diaspora's nostalgia and sentiment, which he deems "pathological" and inescapable facts of life. So he fiercely protects them by bolstering a solid boundary against Vietnamese "outsiders." If one could approach Văn Trần once, he would proudly narrate his family epic of pilgrimage from Vietnam, to Grand Rapids, Michigan, and finally California that he claims the heroic journey to conquer "the land of freedom" and "diversity" But he would never relate, certainly, his bitter loss to Rep. Loretta Sanchez (D-Calif.) in the 47th Congressional District in 2010, which temporarily set back his political career. For more than anyone else, he understands the flaws of his conservatism and extremism, which ruined his political script, but may offer didacticism to the next Vietnamese leaders in Orange County. "If you wanted to, I would offer my service speaking to your students about a career in politics." For the future of a cosmopolitan Little Saigon, an extremist model seems awry, indeed.

ANDREW ĐỖ | THE UNCOMPROMISING PUBLIC SERVANT

Note: A former prosecutor, Andrew Đỗ, won election for county supervisor representing District 1 in 2015 and was reelected in 2016 and 2020. He was previously elected as a city councilmember for the City of Garden Grove in 2008. I had the opportunity to meet Andrew Đỗ a couple of times during the Tết events in Little Saigon. However, the man I met for the interview was different from the one I had seen in official settings. Andrew Đỗ greeted me in the lobby of the Hilton Convention Hotel in Anaheim, dressed casually and appearing relaxed—a departure from the image of a typical fierce politician. The conversation took place in English and lasted for almost two hours. The interview occurred on May 26, 2019, at 4:00 P.M. at Starbucks, Hilton Anaheim.

Andrew first lived in Alabama before moving to Garden Grove, California. After high school, he attended college at the University of California at Davis and later earned a Juris Doctor degree from the University of California Law, San Francisco. Andrew considered himself assimilated, which he described as being "whitified" in order to fit in at a time when Vietnamese still faced much hostility from the Vietnam War. As a result of going to college and law school and later practicing law away from Little Saigon, he did not develop a deep connection with the Vietnamese community earlier in his career, which he perceives as somewhat close-knit and insular. According to Andrew Đỗ, these traits stem from a culture built primarily on entrenched personal relationships within the community. For instance, he notes that a majority of older Vietnamese Americans are not comfortable outside Little Saigon, which is their comfort zone. The lack of English proficiency leads to a feeling of insecurity, which hinders their progress.

As one of five supervisors overseeing Orange County, which is the sixth largest county in the U.S. with over 3.2 million residents, Andrew Đỗ has worked tirelessly to help Little Saigon grow, which he still sees as akin to a teenager physically bigger but not yet fully aware of its potential. Andrew sees the strength of Little Saigon lies in it having a political voice, and he sees himself, just like other people in his age group, as being particularly well positioned to help the community traverse the language and cultural divide.

Andrew believes that a better future is built by being open-minded and forward-looking. Andrew saw his long history as a county employee as an asset, which allowed him to work well within the wheels of government to identify needs and find resources to help many Vietnamese Americans who often suffer in silence. His idealism can sometimes collide with others' self-interest, however, which he believes is a big challenge in Little Saigon. According to Andrew Đỗ, Vietnamese politics in Orange County are in disarray, with many elected officials prioritizing their personal interests over the community's. He criticizes many Vietnamese office holders, including Janet Nguyễn, Tài Đỗ, Phát Bùi, Tyler Điệp, and others, accusing them of being more concerned about petty, take-down politics than uniting and building a strong voice for the community. Andrew Đỗ expressed his frustration at the indifference shown by other Vietnamese elected officials towards real issues that impact the community, such as homelessness, mental health, lack of senior services, etc.

Since assuming office as county supervisor in 2015, Andrew Đỗ has been fighting for his beliefs, often going it alone because he found it difficult to maneuver through the maze of different factions and loyalties within the community. This deliberate strategy to remain above the frays, preferring to let his work speak for himself, led to Andrew being perceived in the past as not necessarily being in touch with his community. He asserted that being misunderstood in the beginning was a price he was willing to pay in the pursuit of change. He believed that the Vietnamese Community should judge elected officials through the work they do and being Vietnamese shouldn't be the only qualification voters look for.

Andrew Đỗ argued that the leaders of many community groups band together, whose loyalties ebb and flow based on personal whims, readily turning on people they no longer like. He believes this ever-shifting political landscape makes it very difficult and requires much "care and feeding" for younger people to effectively represent the community. Andrew Đỗ is candid, as his dedication stems from a sense of public servant. Andrew gave up his position as a trial attorney in an Irvine civil law firm to run for county supervisor. Both he and his wife previously served as deputy Public Defenders and later as deputy District Attorneys for Orange County. In fact, at the time of his interview Andrew's wife was serving as a Superior Court Judge and is now the first Vietnamese American Assistant Presiding Judge in America. Andrew Đỗ chose an unconventional career path by going into politics because he wants to use his knowledge and experience to give back to America and to help the Vietnamese Community.

"For me, the only measure of success," Andrew Đỗ smiled at me, "is whether we can achieve a level of unity like the Jewish American community or the Indian American Community, where they can stand together, be a political force, and function as a unified unit rather than countless individuals pursuing their own interests." His voice resonated with passion as he spoke. However, at the time of our interview he was not optimistic about the current state of politics in Little Saigon. Nevertheless, he believed strongly in the personal strength, ingenuity and success of Vietnamese Americans in America.

Andrew Đỗ envisioned a future where younger people can be empowered and encouraged to navigate their own paths yet retain their identity as Vietnamese, but he does not believe division and inner-fighting within the community will make that likely. He believes Little Saigon is more than the spiritual home for Vietnamese expatriates; it is also a historical legacy that we must preserve for future generations to remind them of the eternal human desire for freedom.

Citing the coarse language and base name-calling in Little Saigon politics, Andrew distanced himself from the "barbaric" activities that he believes weigh down the community. For his 1.5 generation peers who are part of Việt Tân, who hold themselves out as an anti-Communist party with the goal of reclaiming their lost country (the Republic of Vietnam), Andrew Đỗ is an outsider. He keeps the politics of anti-Communism at arm's length, seeing those organizations as tools of convenience for some rather than ones fighting for real achievements.

Andrew Đỗ has a relatively well-informed understanding of Việt Tân, from its early formative days to its absorption into the Democratic Party, but he sees his Viet Tan peers, who lack political depth, as becoming easily co-opted. In them, Andrew Đỗ also sees political operatives who are more opportunistic than philosophical. According to Andrew Đỗ, city council politics are bogged down with all of these dynamics. When asked what he can do in his position at the county level, Andrew Đỗ responded, "I can exert my political influence to ensure that no political machine gains control."

Andrew Đỗ expressed skepticism about the leadership of Little Saigon being under the control of any clique, whether it was the Văn Trần Team before or the Janet Nguyễn Team that has been trying to flex their muscle in recent years. Andrew is mercilessly fighting against such political control, not out of personal animosity, but because he believes such power will inevitably lead to abuse at the expense of the Vietnamese American Community. Andrew Đỗ unsparingly stated, "I have to disrupt any machine they are creating."

When asked about the difference between the Janet Nguyễn and Văn Trần Teams, Andrew Đỗ believed they approach politics in different ways. He sees Trần Thái Văn situation before as too much power consolidated in too few people, while Janet Nguyễn pursues a "divide and conquer" approach. Andrew Đỗ believes that Janet Nguyen's goal now is to use position in the California Legislature damage the reputation and limit the effectiveness of all Vietnamese elected officials so that no one can challenge her. He wishes that such "slavish" mentality should give way to a bigger thinking where we all stay in our own lanes and help build a stronger political voice for our community.

Andrew Đỗ believed that the Vietnamese American Community has grown such that it should view itself as an equal partner, no longer seeking approval but contributing, instead, with our innovative ideas. Andrew Đỗ cited his work as an example of this philosophy. Over the past 8 years, he started many initiatives which has reduced homelessness, created the first mental health system and built more housing in Orange County. He believes Vietnamese success in America is recognized and something people truly respect and admire.

Life continues to move forward, and within the political landscape, different individuals take center stage. In 2020, Janet Nguyễn was elected as a member of the California State Assembly, representing the 72nd district, taking over from Tyler Diệp. Previously, she served as a state senator for one term from 2014 to 2018, but lost the reelection to Tom Umberg. Prior to her role as a state senator, she was a member of the Orange County Board of Supervisors, representing the 1st District, from 2007 to 2014. During that time, Andrew Đỗ served as her chief of staff and later succeeded her as a board member. Văn Trần, on the other hand, was a member of the Garden Grove Council before becoming the State representative for the 68th District from 2004 to 2010. His council seat was succeeded by Janet Nguyễn in 2004.

On the surface, Little Saigon appears to thrive and hold promise for a prosperous future. However, Andrew Đỗ expressed that the community has not fully captured the essence of innovation in order to attract start-ups or big business. He highlighted the fact that the economy of Little Saigon still relies significantly on Foreign Direct Investment (FDI), such as funds from the EB-5 Immigrant Investor Visa Program from Vietnam and China, as well as investments from overseas in retail, entertainment, media, and other sectors. The growth of Little Saigon relies on good management, especially those approaching the centi-million mark in revenues, noted Andrew Đỗ. He believes that the community needs to move away from the philosophy of simply working harder, which is a hallmark of relying on a mom-and-pop business approach.

Andrew Đỗ can, perhaps, be viewed as an idiosyncratic leader. Confronting demagogues is important to him, especially those who use mainstream political establishments to limit opportunities to other Vietnamese.

Andrew Đỗ has given considerable thought to the future when he eventually steps away from politics. He does not want to leave his community in a state of "vacuum" or, worse yet, "turmoil." To ensure a smooth transition, he shared his succession plan with us, exuding some joy at the prospect of leaving politics. Part of his plan involves helping coach individuals to be credible candidates and value public service; his steadfast belief in being a servant-leader comes from his Catholic upbringing. Andrew Đỗ plans to establish a Cultural Center for Vietnamese Americans, where art and cultural artifacts will be exhibited, and an ancestor altar will be built to remind future generations of our history. He has also set aside thirty acres of the land in the newly dedicated county cemetery to serve as cemetery for veterans and public employees of Việt Nam Cộng Hòa (Republic of Vietnam). "What I want to do is create concrete, enduring memories of our country," expressed Andrew Đỗ.

Andrew Đỗ is passionate about everything he does, not afraid to take risks. He has played for many years in a music band, participated in sports throughout his life, and coached his children in soccer, volleyball and basketball. He enjoys a fulfilling life that is worlds apart from the draining nature of the political arena, which often depletes his energy. Andrew Đỗ firmly believes in his convictions and does not believe in looking back.

The sense of community and the desire to give back are values Andrew Đỗ learned when his family was welcomed in Alabama, with strangers donating money and household goods and teaching his family how to move forward with their lives and assimilate into mainstream culture. Andrew Đỗ reminisces about an American sponsor who taught his father how to drive and how his family relied on hand-me-down utensils, church support, and the embracing larger community.

In a democracy, the task of serving the public stands as one of the most intricate and challenging missions. It is an undeniable reality that pleasing every individual is an unattainable goal. Reflecting on the discourse with Andrew Đỗ, I hold immense admiration for those who opt for this journey and wholeheartedly dedicate themselves to upholding the peace, order, and effective governance that we, as recent immigrants, cherish.

Chapter 15

The Community in Transit

SUNNY NGUYỄN, ODE TO 7 LEAVES

Note: One thing leads to another. When I asked Tâm Nguyễn Sr., the founder of Advance Beauty College, about the future of his historic endeavor, he directed my attention to his son, Tâm Nguyễn Jr., with expectations of a successful succession. In turn, Tâm Nguyễn Jr. introduced me to Sunny Nguyễn, a friend of his who embodies the entrepreneurial spirit of the second generation. I arranged to meet Sunny at his tea shop in Fountain Valley at 9 A.M. We sat at a bar-height table adjacent to a reading corner, which was separated from the ordering area by a small bookshelf and a potted ficus tree. Our conversation was conducted in English.

Strolling around Little Saigon in Orange County, one can blissfully forget the feeling of exile or living in an exotic place oceans away from Vietnam. The air is saturated with the pungent aroma of phở, an exquisite soup that satisfies the palate of every nostalgic soul, along with the melodic Vietnamese accents and tunes of reminiscence. This romantic whirlwind awakens a sense of intimacy and a sentimental attachment to bygone memories that grips anyone who feels a connection, both near and far, to their Vietnamese heritage. Within this comforting space lies 7-Leaves Cafe, a sanctuary that not only quenches one's thirst for Vietnamese flavors but also ignites something greater.

It is not merely about offering an "authentic taste from Vietnam." Sunny Nguyễn, along with his three brothers and three family friends, had a visionary and transformative perspective. They curate the best beverages and fast food from various cultures, utilizing top-notch ingredients and adapting recipes to cater to the evolving tastes of millennials. Alongside the traditional Vietnamese iced coffee they grew up with, you'll find Japanese matcha soy tea, Thai tea, taro milk tea, strawberry hibiscus tea, and more. They even offer creative variations of popular herbal teas and oolong tea, ensuring a diverse and delightful menu.

The lead co-founder of 7-Leaves Cafe, Sunny Nguyễn, was not destined to own these chain cafes that have garnered praise since the launch of the first store in Little Saigon. "I ventured into this business out of a sense of emptiness," he reflects. After earning a BA in economics and an MBA from USC, Sunny Nguyễn found himself at a crossroads. What he had learned in school seemed elusive upon graduation. Ready for a gap year, Sunny Nguyễn impulsively applied for a branch manager position at an American Bank. Surprisingly, the employer, after interviewing Sunny, who had nothing but ambition, decided to give him a chance. "He hoped I would excel like the former manager, the only Vietnamese guy, Nick Nguyễn, who had established excellent rapport with the Vietnamese community," Sunny Nguyễn recalled.

Initially lacking experience in finance or real estate, Nguyễn faced significant challenges. However, he immersed himself in a couple of "best-selling" business books that served as his mentors, instantly inspiring him in every step he took.

Living in a community where the prevailing expectation is for children to become doctors, lawyers, or engineers, choosing to sell drinks may seem odd, unconventional, and imbalanced. When asked why he chose to stay in the community of Little Saigon instead of seeking new opportunities elsewhere, Sunny Nguyễn responded, "This place is our home. My family left Vietnam when I was only 3 years old, and my memories of the country are somewhat blurred. I grew up here, among this community, so I consider it my home."

Sunny Nguyễn recounted how his family initially squeezed into the confined garage of their sponsor when they first arrived in El Monte in 1983. His father, Chánh Nguyễn, who didn't speak English, worked as a landscaper for the host family. Shortly after, the family moved to Garden Grove, where they have been settled ever since. "We lived on welfare, but we never saw it as a problem as long as we were together. My brothers and I had ambitious dreams," Sunny recalled. However, when they achieved their dreams, they realized that success did not necessarily equate to happiness. "We still felt a void in our lives," Sunny Nguyễn reflected on that tumultuous time.

That void, as Sunny Nguyễn observes, represents the absence of human consideration when people forge ahead without contemplating the impact of their actions. It signifies an unethical change, a cruel optimism devoid of empathy. Sunny Nguyễn then ponders on how to cultivate growth while preserving the human aspect. "How can you conduct business and still be good?" he wonders, and he passionately discusses his philosophy of serving and connecting with the community as an exemplary model. He believes in ethical management, a style that embraces uniqueness and values.

The four brothers, Vinh, Quang, Sơn, and Hà, along with Mai Lý (Quang's future wife), Denny Lý (Mai's younger brother), and Triết Hồ (a childhood friend of the Nguyễn family), formed a group of seven. In 2012, they embarked on their journey with a small 1,100 square foot store in the heart of Little Saigon. Quang, the software designer, conceived the concept of 7 Leaves (representing the seven founding members) and designed the logo. "Quang is my yin and yang. He pays meticulous attention to every detail, while I take a more macro perspective," Sunny Nguyễn explains.

They started with a simple yet original menu, incorporating unique drink ideas inspired by their travels to other countries. "We serve beverages that don't exist in Little Saigon, and our expanded and original menu caters to every palate, not just Vietnamese Americans. We want everyone to feel at home here," Sunny Nguyễn's eyes sparkle with delight.

Authenticity is another key factor that sets 7 Leaves apart. "We draw inspiration from the companies we admire, but we also bring our own unique touch. We're the only ones that have a kitchen. We meticulously prepare our drinks like herbal tea, mung bean milk tea, and matcha. We use fresh, juicy fruits instead of artificial flavors. By incorporating these qualities and values, we aim to foster a healthy community," Nguyen passionately asserts. And he means it.

The community is discerning and perceptive. Each of the 35 stores in California, Nevada, and Texas is consistently filled with a diverse crowd. With nearly a thousand employees, Sunny often receives requests from acquaintances, primarily from the first generation of Vietnamese refugees, asking if he would consider hiring their family members or friends as cashiers, or if the company has management offices at the stores. "We don't have individual offices, and we believe that's the right approach to eliminate unnecessary distractions. Moreover, we don't endorse nepotism," Sunny Nguyễn reveals.

7-Leaves Cafe exclusively hires newcomers to the industry. "Newbies bring enthusiasm and a strong desire to serve," Sunny Nguyễn believes. The company receives thousands of applicants who aspire to work for this growing business, but they specifically seek out individuals who can be trained and molded into a unified and passionate team. "We have an amazing team," Sunny Nguyễn proudly states. Currently, 7-Leaves targets the Asian demographic, which accounts for around 50% of the market in cities such as Houston, Texas, San Jose, and Dallas. Their ultimate goal is to establish a Vietnamese American brand on a national scale and eventually expand internationally. Sunny Nguyễn recalls a time when he was eager to grow rapidly, but his brothers advised him to consider slowing down their vision. Together, the founders actively search for suitable locations for their chain stores. While 7-Leaves Cafe shares some similarities with Starbucks, it offers a distinctive experience focused on the enduring harmony between values and connection, providing a unique richness in every aspect.

"We grew up in America but were raised in traditional Vietnamese culture. I have a deep affinity for Vietnamese cuisine and the bonds of family. My dream is to create a communal house where multiple generations of my family can live together," Nguyễn passionately expresses. Young Vietnamese Americans may see them as elders whose past, paradoxically, never truly existed. "We are forever caught in between, embracing both Vietnamese and American cultures. Therefore, we aim to be the bridge that connects the old and new generations of the Vietnamese community, both here and abroad." This philosophy is skillfully woven into every drink recipe and the warm ambiance that encourages continuous education through reading at 7-Leaves Cafe.

Values serve as inspiration, yet Sunny Nguyễn, his brothers, and their friends choose to deviate from their father's values, which revolve around anti-communist activism and tend to divide rather than unite the community. "I want to do something different from my father. I want to transform the Vietnamese community through our business," Sunny Nguyễn shares his aspirations, aiming to break free from the "stigma" that has plagued the community. "We refuse to sacrifice our integrity for wealth." Nguyễn reflects on how recklessness, greed, and self-centeredness can jeopardize the future of the community. Nguyễn and his "band" strive to create a familial community where Vietnamese traditions, values, and culture can thrive and be passed down to their children. "My brothers and I live together. Our children grow and learn within Vietnamese culture. Having our parents live with us is a beautiful thing!"

Happiness, according to the 7-Leaves brothers, lies in cultivating "authentic" relationships. They have embarked on a journey together, navigating the highs and lows of life, from humble beginnings in a garage to achieving success. "I consider this place my home," Sunny Nguyễn emphasizes, expressing his sentimental attachment to Little Saigon. However, the impact of 7-Leaves extends far beyond, blooming in various locations. Sunny Nguyễn remarks, "The traditional Vietnamese business model is often stagnant, with the same store existing indefinitely at the same location, offering the same services." The presence of 7-Leaves in Little Saigon and elsewhere challenges this outdated mindset, ushering in the potential for a cosmopolitan space.

Business and aspirations have granted the owners of 7-Leaves a nomadic lifestyle, yet their hearts and souls remain rooted in the in-between, the liminal space that embraces both stillness and evolution. Transformation is their driving force. "We started from nothing, but flourished through our hard work. Only in America can we achieve so much through our labor," Sunny's face radiates with pride as he reflects on the experience of his 1.5-generation, which quickly adapts to mainstream culture compared to ethnicities like Chinese and Koreans who have been settled in America for many generations. "That is our significant advantage. We can learn more rapidly. I see it as our strength. We progress swiftly and create our own uniqueness," he affirms.

"What is your vision for the future of Little Saigon?" we asked Sunny as we prepared to leave 7-Leaves Cafe at twilight, when the delicate sunlight still lingered on the window blinds, casting striped shadows on the floor near our table. "Bright!" he exclaimed. "The community stands at the precipice of change. They truly need a role model. They need a compass. So we aspire to be pioneers in a community where grim politics still resist change, and limited freedom in career choices often leaves many individuals unfulfilled, unable to reach their fullest potentials due to rejected dreams."

An audacious dream is not a flaw and should never be corrected. Sunny Nguyễn and his remarkable partners dared to leave behind stable jobs, predictable lives, and a sense of emptiness to pursue such a risky dream: not just achieving success without pleasure, but infusing pleasure into their success. 7-Leaves Cafe serves as an inspiration to all: embodying audacity, opulence, and happiness. It is an ideal model for the future cosmopolitan Little Saigon, where aspirations do not perpetuate a tyrannical culture but instead foster transformative divergence, encapsulated by the bold slogan adorning the walls of every 7-Leaves Cafe: "Be the change you wish to see in the world." Why not?

What truly unsettled Sunny Nguyễn at the peak of his professional career was the overwhelming emptiness. "Advancing in one's career is like clearing a path. You have to cut through the bushes on the sides. But what remains is a profound loneliness," Nguyễn reveals, shedding light on why he decided to call it quits. Leaving behind prestige, financial gain, and perhaps even moments of happiness, Sunny embarked on a journey around the world. Upon his return, he shared his profound sense of emptiness with his three brothers: Vinh, Quang, and Ha, who were, at the time, a hospital manager, software designer, and lawyer respectively. Their feelings resonated with one another. Without any hesitation, they all chose to abandon their safe and secure jobs, taking a risk to pursue a new opportunity and fill the void.

The brothers, whose names hold great significance in Vietnamese culture, representing the nation's glory, came together to establish a cafe with a unique drink brand. When Sunny Nguyễn shared their plan with their parents, they were devastated. After all the sacrifices they had made for their sons, they never anticipated such a "corruption"—what they perceived as a curse for the family.

VIVIAN CAO | THE MANIFEST OF ENCHANTMENT

Note: My very first interview for this book project was with Vivian Cao's parents, Tony Tai Cao and his wife. Tony was one of the first refugees who graduated with an engineering degree and was able to open his own machine shop in Santa Ana and employ Vietnamese settlers. Cao's wife, a chiropractor, founded the first Sunday school teaching Vietnamese. As the parents narrated the challenges of their pioneering community work in Little Saigon, Vivian's name popped up multiple times as their savior. I met Vivian twice in her father's machine shop. The discussion was conducted in English and Vietnamese.

Until when will Little Saigonese stop being described as "nostalgic," "lost," "forgotten," "invisible"? Numerous facile beliefs have surrounded the perceived "silence" between the older generation and the younger one. "The generation gap is troubling," the elderly would complain endlessly if asked about their relationship with their offspring. They would continue to lament how their children unapologetically neglect their parents' traumatic past or how those rebellious youth disavow their forefathers' history, which has virtually fallen into oblivion. Many second-generation individuals would say, "Come on, let's move forward. We should celebrate our American dream here. Why do we have to agonize over a past we did not experience?" This may sound callous, but it rings true, as the generational divide appears insurmountable if neither generation makes an effort to understand the other.

The future is not as bleak as many people may imagine, as not everyone chooses to distance themselves from their parents and traditional values. Our in-depth conversation with Vivian Cao, a second-generation pharmacist who has thrived in both her business and her relationship with the older generation, presents a far more optimistic outlook for Little Saigonese. Striking a balance between the old and the new, the past and the present, she epitomizes the beautiful harmony between two generations. "I embrace the in-between," she says, exuding charm and confidence. By immersing oneself in the world of the 2.0 generation of Vietnamese Americans, who were born and raised in this Vietnamese enclave in Orange County, optimism shines through their stories.

Vivian has had a privileged life. She grew up deeply immersed in both generations and learned to appreciate the blending of cultures from a very young age. Raised by disciplined and ambitious parents who toiled away in America for the future of their children, Cao understands their dreams, and she tirelessly strives to be a source of pride for them. "My grandparents also lived with us, so I had to learn and speak Vietnamese with them," Vivian Cao recalls, her eyes sparkling with pride. While she speaks flawless English when conversing with us, she seamlessly switches to Vietnamese, equally fluent, to accommodate her staff who insist on communicating in Vietnamese. "If you know my generation, I'm one of the most fluent in English," Vivian says, then offers me a cup of water in Vietnamese, saying, "con mời chú uống nước." Having acquired all these mannerisms, Vivian can comfortably navigate between American and Vietnamese cultures in her daily conversations with people from all walks of life.

Unlike her less fortunate peers whose families struggled to make ends meet for their survival, Vivian is destined for abundance and happiness. Having spent her peaceful childhood in Costa Mesa and Huntington Beach, receiving her education in private schools and pursuing an MBA at Pepperdine University, Vivian never had to experience the hardships of life in America. However, she does occasionally face her own internal battles. "Sometimes, my father appears distant, austere, and bitter. While he may be generous in his philanthropic activities and work with city and government officials to support future generations, I am unsure of his true feelings regarding his culture," Vivian says. It is a remarkable idea—her indifference towards her strict parents, whose traumatic escape from Vietnam continues to haunt them, becomes her tenacious driving force for success in America. She witnesses their animosity towards the home country that devastated their lives and forced them to a foreign land. Suddenly, they became isolated and guarded, struggling with language barriers, marginalization, and cultural loss. Her parents' generation, all refugees, share these haunting pains that create a divide between them and their Americanized children. If there is one thing that brings both generations together, Vivian emphasizes, it is audacity. They are all warriors. Like her Vietnamese peers in the community, Vivian strives academically and in life for her parents, knowing that their fierce aspirations for her are a path to a bright future.

"You cannot go far without your family," Vivian reminisces about the time she quit her job as the assistant director for a biomedical company located just three miles away from home when her mother fell ill during a trip. "I was at a point in my life where everything seemed promising and rosy." However, she left behind all those opportunities and returned home to care for her mother. Her realization was simple: "No matter how far one may go, there is only one mother." This philosophy permeates her life, strengthening her emotional bond with her family and fostering deep gratitude towards them. Vivian acknowledges that her education at the largest Catholic school west of the Mississippi, known for its culture of charity and outreach, has played a role in shaping her beliefs and attitudes. Every year, the school would ask students about their future plans and group them together to share their aspirations. Vivian vividly remembers the profound insight that resonated with her at the time—students should not disappoint parents who sacrifice a great deal to provide them with education. This transformative experience has shaped her with renewed determination.

"Independence doesn't mean completely detaching from your family," Vivian reflects on her active involvement in social activities, her close friendships with black feminists, and her immersion in American culture. However, she admits, "99.9% of every decision I've ever made has been influenced, if not entirely, then at least 99%, by my family." While Vivian acknowledges that she can afford to live on her own if she chooses, the allure of independence doesn't tempt her. Growing up in an extended family where everyone has had a profound impact on her, she values their presence deeply. Her grandparents, parents, three aunts, and other relatives have all played significant roles in shaping her life. Since she was only three years old, Vivian has witnessed their struggles, and she recognizes the weight of their sacrifices. "You can't live without a heavy conscience if you're going to betray their sacrifices," she compares their challenging lives to high-stakes gambling. "Every waking moment of my parents' lives is devoted to us, their children." She understands that the legacy her parents want to pass on to her also carries the weight of their unhealed wounds. A sense of shapelessness.

When it comes to the disparity between wealth and poverty, Vivian Cao believes that everyone has their own karma. She is surrounded by many individuals who have endured difficult lives for decades since their escape from Vietnam in search of freedom and prosperity. "Not everyone has been able to secure a roof over their heads, and not everyone has had the opportunity to seize lucrative prospects like my parents did. The competition is intense," she acknowledges. Vivian recognizes her own fortune, as her family is financially stable, and she has never had to struggle in a cutthroat world. In their family business, her parents "ask, but never force" her to get involved or share responsibilities. Love flows naturally within their interactions. Vivian genuinely enjoys being a part of her family's business and dedicates herself to it with passion. She effortlessly embraces Vietnamese traditions and values as well. She accompanies her mother to elderly clubs where they engage in conversations with 80–90-year-old ladies and celebrate the beauty of their community. As her father begins to age, he seeks a peaceful retreat and entrusts his daughter with the family business, which she manages with ease.

Aimlessness is not Vivian's choice. She envisions her future through the influence of the heroes in her life. Her love for family and community was nurtured during her time in the Hung Dao girls' scouts, where she dedicated 40 hours to community service before high school graduation. Her deep understanding of filial piety and other values was cultivated through her experiences with the Buddhist scouts. Beyond her family heroes, if there is someone Vivian idolizes, it must be her Godfather and Buddhist master, Hang Truong, whose religious lectures captivate her with great fervor. "A milestone in my life occurred in 2009 when I met my Godfather," Vivian Cao reminisces. She was chosen to host a show with him on YouTube, aiming to popularize "modern" Buddhism in the community. This new form of Buddhism was redefined with more flexibility, allowing believers to pray, chant the Bible, and worship wherever they are, not solely at the temple as traditional rituals require. His wisdom and compassion profoundly impacted her life. "I admire his ability to transform elusive and complex teachings into relatable, approachable, and understandable lessons." Through her conversations with such a religious pillar, which people rarely engage in due to their preconceived notions that conventional monks are stern, reserved, and unapproachable, she is awakened by his compassionate service to society, known as "Hội từ bi phụng sự" in Vietnamese. To Vivian Cao, charity is beautiful in all its forms, and she believes that humans are inherently benevolent.

Vivian's capacity for community work is as vast as her empathy and endurance. Articulate, nimble, and graceful, she is often entrusted with tasks that cultivate community relations or facilitate political campaigns. She has an extensive knowledge of the demographics, history, and traditions of Vietnamese American communities in every county. She understands the dynamics of allies and adversaries, as well as the strengths and weaknesses of her people.

One of her notable roles was assisting Andrew Do, one of the few Vietnamese American DAs in Orange County, in his successful campaign to become the supervisor of the 1st District. Vivian continues to work alongside him, helping shape his strategic agenda. They embarked on a project to provide free shuttle services for the elderly in Westminster, which faced significant opposition from various individuals and even neighboring communities.

"We didn't compromise because it was a crucial project to support the elderly in our community who couldn't drive. However, the route was eventually canceled due to its short distance and low ridership," Vivian explains. She then expresses her enthusiasm for the establishment of County Community Services Centers (or Trung tâm Phục vụ Cộng đồng) in Orange County, Santa Ana, and Anaheim. These centers serve as one-stop shops where representatives are always available to assist people, primarily the elderly, in filling out forms. Additionally, they offer free presentations and distribute groceries every three weeks.

With Vivian's considerable assistance, Andrew Do also transformed an abandoned bus terminal into a 400-bed shelter for the homeless, providing them with three warm meals a day, access to showers, laundry facilities, and even coffee. All of these endeavors, aimed at creating a more sustainable, welcoming, and productive community, are what Vivian considers a "manifestation." These initiatives may be unfamiliar to the traditional mindset of the older generation in the community.

Conventional Vietnamese Americans often seek solace in charitable acts, believing that their generous donations will bring them good karma or ensure prosperity and happiness for their descendants. Vivian Cao questions how they can be certain that their contributions truly reach those in need. She maintains a sense of skepticism towards this form of philanthropy that lacks tangible evidence of its practical impact. "Charity is not a form of therapy or a redeemable coupon for the afterlife," she candidly states.

According to Vivian, cultivating an enchanting community requires more than simply making donations. It necessitates ensuring that everyone within the community has a viable and, ideally, content life. This involves improving infrastructure, empowering the elderly, and providing shelter for the homeless. She envisions genuine acts of benevolence that are practical and organic in nature. Over time, all shadows and uncertainties must dissipate, allowing the light to manifest itself fully. Ultimately, the happiness of a community cannot be achieved through vanity or by evading the challenges that need to be addressed.

Vivian Cao's perspective on the Vietnamese community in Little Saigon has undergone a significant transformation since the onset of COVID. "I hope I'm not misrepresenting who I was just a few years ago," Vivian wrote me an email from her Bakersfield office in California in November 2023. Since 2020, she has served as the District Director for Senator Shannon Grove, overseeing the Central Valley and High Desert communities. Amid the pandemic chaos, Vivian observed a remarkable unity among the Vietnamese people, honoring their roots and ancestors. Despite differences and divisiveness, community leaders rallied to provide, protect, and advocate for the most vulnerable, including the elderly, those with language barriers, and those with limited access to resources, including healthcare.

"Even though I've moved two hours away from Little Saigon, it remains close to my heart. From a bird's eye view, I'm thrilled to see my generation actively investing in preserving our Vietnamese community abroad," reflects Vivian Cao.

Her parents, first-generation Vietnamese migrants, couldn't be prouder of their daughter. Vivian's lifelong exposure to community work, inspired by her parents, and her experience as a policy advisor and community liaison at the Orange County Board of Supervisors, have positioned her well in her current role.

Vivian's accolades are stacking up, including the 2021 Volunteer of the Year from the Bakersfield Metro Community Emergency Response team and her appointment as a Community Volunteer Leader with the American Red Cross for her role as a congregate Shelter Manager during the Fall 2020 wildfires. Vivian Cao, along with four other second-generation Vietnamese Americans, earned a place on the "2022 NAAPPPA 40 under 40 List" by the National Association of Asian Pacifics in Politics and Public Affairs.

Vivian Cao, alongside Sunny Nguyễn, symbolizes a community in transition. A growing trend among successful young entrepreneurs is reshaping the image of divisiveness in Little Saigon and ushering it into the 21st Century, forging a distinct identity. This includes initiatives like bilingual shows on TV and YouTube, new fusion and upscale Vietnamese dining experiences, and increased dialogue beyond the political sphere, particularly concerning culture, health, and food.

Index

About the Authors

Tung X. Bui is Matson Navigation Co. Distinguished Professor of Global Business at the University of Hawaii at Manoa Shidler College of Business. He has published 12 books and more than 200 research papers. With thousands of Vietnamese refugees, his family were among the first settlers in Orange County. His story about Little Saigon is both an intimate family business and, a reflection on the history of a community that seeks to preserve its cultural identity and to secure a brighter future for their descendants.

Quynh H. Vo is a professorial lecturer of Asia, Pacific, and Diaspora Studies in the Department of Critical Race, Gender, and Cultural Studies at American University in Washington D.C. Her research projects engage particularly transnational Asian American politics and aesthetics; power and revolution; race, gender, and sexuality; US empire, migration, and neoliberalism. Her recent publications include: "'We Were Born from Beauty': Motherly Aesthetics and Poetics of Displacement in On Earth We're Briefly Gorgeous by Ocean Vuong" in *Reclaiming Migrant Motherhood: Identity, Belonging, and Displacement in a Global Context*, Maria D. Lombard, ed. (Lexington Books, 2022) and "Vietnamese Literature and Ecofeminism," in *The Routledge Handbook of Ecofeminism and Literature*, Douglas A. Vakoch, ed. (Routledge, 2022).